BROTHERS
IN ARMS

BROTHERS IN ARMS

*The Unique Collection of
Letters and Photographs
from Two Brothers at the Front
during the First World War*

Edited by

KAREN FARRINGTON

Pen & Sword
MILITARY

First published in Great Britain in 2015 by
PEN & SWORD MILITARY
An imprint of
Pen & Sword Books Ltd
47 Church Street
Barnsley
South Yorkshire
S70 2AS

Copyright © Karen Farrington, 2015

ISBN 978-1-47382-561-1

Typeset by Concept, Huddersfield, West Yorkshire, HD4 5JL.
Printed and bound in England by CPI Group (UK) Ltd, Croydon CR0 4YY.

Pen & Sword Books Ltd incorporates the imprints of Pen & Sword Archaeology,
Atlas, Aviation, Battleground, Discovery, Family History, History, Maritime,
Military, Naval, Politics, Railways, Select, Social History, Transport, True Crime,
and Claymore Press, Frontline Books, Leo Cooper, Praetorian Press,
Remember When, Seaforth Publishing and Wharncliffe.

For a complete list of Pen & Sword titles please contact
PEN & SWORD BOOKS LIMITED
47 Church Street, Barnsley, South Yorkshire, S70 2AS, England
E-mail: enquiries@pen-and-sword.co.uk
Website: www.pen-and-sword.co.uk

DEDICATION

This book is based on a handwritten biography by Lieutenant Colonel Robert D'Arblay Gybbon Monypenny (Robin), his letters from the front, and his compilation of diary entries and letters from his brother, Lieutenant Phillips Gybbon Monypenny MC (Phil) who was killed in action 28 June 1918.

It is dedicated to Phil's memory, but also to the millions of young men worldwide who perished in the First World War, including Robin's commanders, comrades and the men under his command who died in the trenches, men of whom he speaks so highly in his writings.

Robin's grandchildren, Joanna, Tim and Simon, grew up listening to the lighter tales of his past. This book captures the full story of those fateful years between 1914 and 1918.

Contents

List of Plates

Robin's daughter Sheila with his uniform and medals.

Thanks to his camera Sheila has had a greater insight into Robin's experiences at war.

An unnamed soldier brews up at the front.

Parapets and parados were sturdy with sandbags to protect against rifle fire. However, they were less effective against artillery barrages.

Before steel helmets were issued men favoured woolly hats against the cold.

To avoid sniper fire, sentries used periscopes to observe enemy activity.

Despite the hardships there was a great sense of camaraderie in the trenches.

Men soon grew used to the lack of comforts and apparent perils of trench life.

Phil was delighted when he won the Military Cross given to soldiers for 'exemplary gallantry'.

Phil's bronze commemorative plaque, also known as the Dead Man's Penny, issued to mark those who lost their lives in the conflict.

Acknowledgements

A special thanks go to Sheila Ford (née Gybbon Monypenny), Robin's daughter, for access to the original letters and photographs. Sheila, and Robin's other children, Joy (dec.) and Gerald (dec.), transcribed part of these writings into type or handwritten copies. Sheila's son, Tim, compiled all the writings and many of the images. The family would like to thank Karen Farrington for believing in Robin's story and bringing this book to life and Ian Hook, curator of the Essex Regimental Museum.

Introduction

Warfare had been a frequent feature of European life for centuries, but the tempest that erupted in 1914, after leaden clouds brewed for several decades on the continent's horizon, took human conflict to a grim new level.

There was wholesale destruction: to regiments, to historic towns, to the dreams and aspirations of a generation, to a way of life. Almost every family across Europe was affected, as loved ones either died or were forever and irretrievably changed. The number of those killed and wounded by the war's end was 37 million. More than a third of the men mobilised in Britain were casualties. The number for France and Russia was closer to three-quarters, while ninety per cent of the men who were enlisted to fight for the Austro-Hungarian Empire perished or were injured.

The Monypennys were just one family among millions to mourn the loss of a promising and vibrant life taken too soon for uncertain gains. With this and other deaths, a glorious future was denied to many, as nations were hobbled by their losses. Letters home from the front, cherished for years by a spinster aunt, give a partial picture of Phillips' melancholy war story.

But as one brother died so another came home, a witness to the carnage and the bungled orders, the courage of comrades and the heart-sickening duties shouldered by many and shirked by a few. And it was the legacy of the living, to tell their story to future generations and shine a light in the murky shadows of encounters that remained achingly distant from most people's daily lives.

Robin's letters, also lovingly preserved, were fleshed out by his memories written into numerous exercise books. Although he put pen to paper when he was much older, his recollections of these formative and gruelling years remained pin-sharp. Evidence from regimental diaries kept throughout the conflict chime perfectly with his accounts. Starkly unsentimental and unnervingly clear-eyed, his words are all the more affecting.

A century after the start of the First World War, the story of Phil and Robin Monypenny and their contrasting fates has been brought together, thanks to the letters, the memoir, some staccato entries in a short-lived diary and a few fascinating photos. Each chapter is put into context by an introduction, containing an overview of the war at the time and information hewn from the archives.

Together, these detail-rich literary avenues have made the Monypenny family outstanding for the timely insight now given to subsequent scholars of the war.

✳ ✳ ✳

Before the war there was nothing to distinguish the family from thousands of others who emerged from the Edwardian era in the comforting embrace of empire.

Conflict survivor Robert D'Arblay Gybbon-Monypenny – known to his family as Robin – was born on 10 October 1892 on the Jinglam Tea Estate in Sikkim, India, in the foothills of the Himalayas. He was the first of six boys.

Long before his arrival, the Monypenny family had been cushioned by considerable wealth. Robin's great-grandfather Thomas, who had fought at Waterloo in the West Kent Militia, was MP for Rye in Sussex. However, struggling to pay off debts incurred during an expensive lawsuit, he had to sell one significant family home, Hole House in Rolvenden, Kent. Thomas's son Robert (Robin's grandfather) was compelled to sell the other, nearby Great Maytham Hall, which would later become the inspiration for Frances Hodgson Burnett's *The Secret Garden*.

Consequently, with no English estate to call his own, Robin's father Herbert became a tea planter in India. Robin returned to England in 1904 and, with brother Rex, was deposited with a maiden aunt when his parents and younger brothers went back to India with their mother, who was known in the family as 'a daydreamer'. Aunt Ethel, aged 43 at the time, was his father's sister and was by his account a stern and outwardly unaffectionate woman. With her Robin felt deprived of a warm family life. Evidently, however, she was stoical, loyal and generous and it was these qualities that would later unexpectedly nurture Robin and his brothers as they fought in the trenches.

The boys were sent to Bedford School where Robin was resentful and quarrelsome, although he excelled at shooting and boxing. He nearly avoided the First World War altogether. In 1912 he applied for a post with the Indian Police, coming thirty-fifth out of 300 candidates. Unfortunately, the police employed only the top twenty-six. A year later he tried again after spending the year with a crammer in London. This time he was twenty-sixth when they were only accepting the first twenty.

Although he was keen for a role in the Indian Police, like many boys Robin had undertaken army officer training through his school – although he didn't go to Sandhurst, where career officers were instructed. Ironically he discovered that an application for the British North Borneo Chartered Company had been successful on the day he joined the British Army after the outbreak of war.

Rex began training for a career in the diplomatic service that would take him to Persia – present-day Iran – while Robin was at war. His third brother, Phillips Burnley Sterndale Gybbon-Monypenny, six years his junior, followed in his footsteps from Bedford School into the army. Three remaining brothers, Bertie, Richard and David, were too young to serve.

Now it was to Aunt Ethel that Robin and Phil turned during the bleakness of their wartime service. With their parents overseas, she provided the anchor point when they were being buffeted by waves of fighting. In turn, she evidently held them in great esteem treasuring their letters, which were kept by Robin after her death and later by his daughter, Sheila. Thanks to Ethel they were kept furnished with necessities in the trenches. And thanks to her key elements of Robin's story – and that of his brother Phil – can now be told.

✳   ✳   ✳

The Monypenny family are of very ancient Scottish lineage. The family seat was Pitmilly in the kingdom Fife for at least 700 years.

Their story begins when Duncan I was killed by Macbeth's men at Bothnagowen near Elgin in 1040. Macbeth took the throne but was defeated and killed seventeen years later at the Battle of Lumphanan in 1057.

According to legend and stories passed down through the family, Duncan's son Malcolm fled to England after his father's death and was befriended by a wealthy Frenchman named James Dauphin. When Malcolm asked him for some pennies to aid his cause against Macbeth, James replied: 'Sire, I will lend you monie (many) pennies'. He was true to his word, and Malcolm was later crowned Malcolm III of Scotland in 1058.

Malcolm then gifted the lands of Pitmilly, Kinkell and Earlshall to James Dauphin's eldest son, arranged his marriage to a kinswoman of Macduff, Thane of Fife, and bestowed the name of Monypenny. Hence the Mony-penny coat of arms includes a dolphin (Dauphin being French for dolphin).

The first historical record that we are aware of is in 1211, when Thomas, Prior of St Andrews, granted by charter the lands of Pitmulin to Ricardus de Moniepennie, 118 years after Malcolm's death.

Adapted from Parish, W.D. Letter from David Monypenny at Pitmilly (21st Laird), dated 3 March 1719, to his cousin Captain James Monypenny at Hole in Kent (Robin's great-grandfather). *Notes and Queries: A Medium of Intercommunication for Literary Men, General Readers, etc.*, 7th Series, Vol. 8, Jul-Dec 1889, p. 185 (John C. Francis, London).

CHAPTER ONE

'England had indeed been unprepared!'

For the majority, the First World War arrived without any element of surprise. Even the most politically unwitting could detect a measured lurch towards hostilities by the Europeans – and knew that Britain would inevitably be dragged into the fray.

It wasn't necessarily thought to be bad news either. The greatest fear among a sizeable bunch of keen recruits was that the conflict would have drawn to a close before they had a chance to bear arms. Honour, glory, patriotism and valour were watchwords of the day. If the causes of war were hazy in some people's perception, most were pretty certain that Britain was in the right and her defence was now essential. Few dwelt upon the concept of mutual destruction. But how did it come to this?

There's no trim and tidy explanation for its outbreak although the death of Archduke Franz Ferdinand of Austria in Sarajevo on 28 June 1914 is the acknowledged trigger point. At the time the Austro-Hungarian Empire that he was to inherit was on shaky legs, while Serbia, home of assassin Gavrilo Princip, was ambitious and expanding.

Ultimately, after some failed negotiations, the killing prompted the Austro-Hungarian Empire to declare war on Serbia. With that, Tsar Nicholas II of Russia mobilised troops to honour a previously signed Slavic alliance, designed to protect Serbia from just such a threat.

This in turn provoked Germany to come to the aid of its Austro-Hungarian neighbour, and to declare war on Russia. France, being already paired with Russia through diplomatic ties, was then inevitably at war with Germany.

Britain might have sat it out despite an existing three-way agreement with Russia and France. But when Germany invaded Belgium en route to France another treaty was contravened and Britain felt obliged to act, with Lloyd George calling it a war 'on behalf of little five-foot-five nations'. Thus two rival camps were created.

Initially, with the heads of state of some of the chief protagonists closely related, it looked like an overblown family squabble. Ultimately Italy, Japan, Romania and Greece – and finally America – joined Britain and the Allies while the Ottoman Empire and Bulgaria stood behind Germany and the Central Powers.

Robin reflected on the rise in tensions in his memoirs. He remembered '*how the pot boiled and simmered alternatively all over Europe during that month of July, with mobilizations and threats of mobilizations, moves and counter moves in the political worlds of various countries*'.

If this domino effect was the immediate cause of war there were numerous nationalistic, anarchistic and militaristic niggles that came before. The downward slide of the Ottoman and Austro-Hungarian Empires attracted the avaricious gaze of other powers. Russia was struggling with internal division. France was looking for ways to avenge its defeat by Germany forty years previously. England had been suspiciously eyeing German naval ambitions – just one of numerous rivalries. Also, there were economic and technological imperatives as well as a need for honour to be satisfied.

So when war was declared on Tuesday, 4 August, it came with more of a thrill than a sense of foreboding.

The day before had been a warm Bank Holiday and many people were still buoyant because of it. Most heard about it in the same way as Robin, by the echo of a newsvendor's call through an open window. Even the most momentous news was still utterly dependent on the printing presses for its public circulation.

At the beginning there was hope: that it would be a short spat, that Britain would triumph, that its Empire would remain economically unrivalled.

A conversation between Robin and cousin Reggie Sterndale, who apparently possessed some 'advanced democratic ideas' according to Robin, gave voice to the notion that war was clunky and outdated. Many felt the treaty that protected Belgium, made some seventy-five years previously, was a flimsy excuse. Reggie believed that people would not stand for war and it would not last three weeks, let along three months.

Wiser heads like Robin's agreed to differ. He perhaps took his lead from Secretary of War Lord Kitchener, who was himself derided by cabinet colleagues when he suggested the war would last years and that millions of men would have to be mobilised.

'*It shook* [Reggie] *when a little later Kitchener said it would last three years,*' observed Robin. But Reggie – along with miscellaneous parliamentarians – believed war would not be tolerated by such a vibrant British society.

After all, it was not a case of an acquiescent population being led by the nose. Before war broke out there was Suffragette militancy, unrest in Ireland and a General Strike was planned. There were nearly 1,500 separate industrial stoppages in 1913 as workers began to flex their considerable combined muscle.

Yet war with Germany struck a euphoric chord in a way few could have predicted. It had campaigners for women's votes helping to recruit soldiers, trades unionists abandoning their immediate ambitions in order to improve Britain's military output and a private army ready to fight against proposed Home Rule for Ireland turning their enmity towards the Kaiser. As philosopher and pacifist Betrand Russell noted: *'average men and women were delighted at the prospect of war.'*

For its part Germany hoped for a quick victory over France in the west so it could concentrate its efforts on defeating Russia.

The British Army's top brass were also less convinced about the idea of a short war and for them there was a sense of forging into the unknown. Despite a largely peaceful era since Napoleon's defeat, Britain had been involved in campaigns in the Victorian era. The Crimean War of 1858 did not prove to be Britain's finest hour. Lessons learned included the importance of regular supplies and disease control to the fighting man. Happily the spread of a network of railway lines and step changes in the world of medicine would resolve this for future generations.

As for the Boer War, fought against angry but ill-armed farmers in South Africa, Britain's image was severely dented by its use of concentration camps, some dubious battlefield conduct and an inability to defeat inferior opposition. One of the greatest challenges on the home front proved to be finding sufficient numbers of healthy individuals to join the army's rank and file.

Although the Boer War ended little more than a decade before it wouldn't be the same army sent to meet the Kaiser's men at the Western Front. In 1907 there were wholesale changes made by Richard Haldane, the Liberal Party's Secretary of State for War, announced in a 190-minute speech to Parliament. Times were changing and Haldane wanted the army to respond. The days of privately funded militia forces and volunteers raised by county were gone and in their place came a small but professional army capable of defending Britain's interests overseas numbering 160,000 officers and men.

On the home front there would be a Territorial Army that could advance seamlessly into the front line in times of national need. Men in the Territorials for a four-year term typically spent two weeks every year at a camp where they were brought up to speed in military matters.

Ranged against them at the start of the First World War was a German army that vastly outnumbered that of the British, although all were conscripts. It seemed that Britain might overcome that numerical problem almost immediately when recruiting offices were overwhelmed with volunteers from a booming population. Streets outside the depots where names were being taken became a bobbing sea of flat caps, bowler hats and boaters as young men from all social classes surged forward.

Sir Arthur Conan Doyle, who created Sherlock Holmes, tried to enlist at the age of 55, convinced he would be a fine example for other men to follow.

The face and finger of Lord Kitchener, a highly respected old soldier, imploring young men to come and serve their country proved potent. In fact the famous image that galvanised so many, designed by graphic artist Alfred Leete and first published as a magazine cover a month after the outbreak of war, was mainly used in metropolitan areas to rally support. Much of the rest of the country was overwhelmed by a general and genuine fervour for fighting in a mighty citizen army.

The old spectre of ill health among the industrial poor had been all but eliminated. There was sufficient wealth and social care in the country – thanks to legislation that had brought in pension rights, national insurance and labour exchanges – to ensure that few were starving.

Doctors at recruiting offices were paid per recruit and accordingly many passed muster, so the harvest for the army was abundant. But once recruits were signed up there were difficulties arising from the lack of accommodation, uniform and equipment to address, not to mention the paucity of training. Men paraded in their own clothes and wielded broom handles. These men would become Kitchener's New Armies, who would be trained in due course while the regular army fought in the field. (Kitchener had little faith in the Territorials whom he dubbed 'weekend warriors'.) And it was Kitchener who ordered that volunteers like these should be treated well.

Then there was a lack of officers to govern men like these and those in the Territorials who would be next in line to make the journey to the front. That's where men like Robin came in. He had been a sergeant in the Officer Training Corps introduced at public schools across the country as part of the 1907 army reforms. This instilled military values into a large number of middle class boys who would come of age at a time when their country needed them most. With the six-year experience he gained at Bedford School on his CV he was ideal for the army and quickly earmarked for action.

Robin made his first enquiries with the War Office in Whitehall and was sent to the Inns of Court Territorial Battalion where he signed up as a recruit. '*They must have been short of material*,' Robin remarked drily, in his memoir.

Within a week of joining he was put at the head of a training squad. On 15 August 1914 he was appointed an officer in the Special Reserve, denoting that he had not been Sandhurst-trained. Although the status of being in the Special Reserve eventually rankled, he was at the time delighted that his wages doubled to two shillings a day.

He had no uniform although he was furnished with luncheon vouchers and enjoyed free travel in London until the perk was withdrawn.

When he was invited to become an officer, Robin had hopes of joining the Royal West Kents like many of his ancestors, but instead he was dispatched as a second lieutenant to the Essex Regiment, unaware at the time that one of his forebears, Colonel Alexander Monypenny, had fought under the Essex insignia in the eighteenth century.

Before he embarked for the continent there was a short spell spent on home soil helping to marshal a force together. When he arrived he was a second lieutenant in the Special Reserve of officers in the 3rd Battalion of the Essex Regiment. The word subaltern translates to subordinate and is a largely colonial term for junior officers ranked below captain.

ROBIN

In the middle of October, a large number of volunteers who had answered Lord Kitchener's call for his first hundred thousand, had been gathered together in Aldershot, Hampshire, and were drafted gradually to various depots. Five hundred were sent to our battalion; a canvas camp was prepared for them in a meadow just off the high road on the outskirts of Dovercourt. A Special Reserve captain was to take charge with four subalterns and some experienced NCOs to help him train these recruits. I happened to be one of these four subalterns.

We went to the station to meet these men off the train. They were of course all of them in mufti. They had very little in the way of their own kit with them and had apparently had rather a wretched time at Aldershot where everything had been done in a hurry. The staff had been insufficient to cope with them, they had been over-crowded in their tents and had not had enough blankets or food – and were therefore not in the best of spirits. But they were mighty glad for a change of scene.

We fell them into fours and marched them towards camp. They did look a motley crew, all sorts, sizes and shapes; some wearing what had been smart clothes, others in rags with a mix of cloth caps, bowler hats and homburgs on their heads. They hardly knew how to keep step or anything but a ragged column.

Just before reaching camp there was a large orchard on the side of the road belonging to a local farmer and, all of a sudden, there was a concerted rush with most of the 500 over the orchard wall, filling their pockets with apples. We had the time of our lives trying to round them up. Eventually we arrived in camp about an hour late, the men with pockets bulging with apples and all biting apples as hard as they could. I remember the sergeant major saying that we had some work ahead of us to make soldiers of them. But soldiers never were at their best on empty stomachs and these poor creatures were pretty hungry. England had indeed been unprepared!

We managed to provide them with a plain but hot meal, some blankets, and shared them out amongst the tents. The next morning they were turned out not too early and given a good, hearty breakfast. After this the real job of getting order out of confusion started.

They were divided into four companies of 125 men each, with names, addresses and particulars of each man taken. I was put in charge of one such company (one subaltern to each company). I remember sharing with a sergeant the job of taking particulars. One individual amused me: when asked about his occupation in civil life he replied, 'theatrical barber'. Not having heard of this before I satisfied my curiosity by asking whether he cut the hair of actors. He said he not only shaved actors but 'chorus girls' armpits'!

Most of these were London Cockneys; tradespeople, busmen, farmhands and so on with a sprinkling of better class business men and one or two university students, though most of the latter type had probably gone to corps that especially catered for them such as the Honourable Artillery Company, Artists Rifles, Public Schools Battalions and so forth.

They were a fine crowd generally speaking, and once they saw that things were being done in earnest for them, such as good and regular food, they became exceedingly keen and quick to pick up their work. After that there were regular camp routines and arrangements and not chaos, and the serious business of military training was taken in hand.

It is no exaggeration to say that in the evenings after all parades were finished, little squads of men were seen in odd corners practising drilling each other and arguing on the right or wrong way, and sometimes calling on some NCO to enlighten them.

I discovered that my batman – one of the new recruits – was a bit of a boxer and in order to have some exercise and keep my own hand in he and I donned some gloves on an occasional evening. We soon had some of the rest of the recruits as an interested audience with the result that I had to run the boxing and physical training of the camp, later getting up quite a successful boxing tournament.

I remember one afternoon a great big saloon car waiting at the camp gate with a chauffeur and as I walked out of the gate, an agitated lady stepped out of the car to address me. She wished to know why her husband, Private 'X', could not go home on short leave as some of the men had. The said Private 'X' happened to be in my company. Though an unobtrusive sort of man, he was obviously a cut above most of them, financially at any rate. A few men in each company had been allowed away on weekends and I presumed that 'X's turn had not arrived and, being unobtrusive by nature, had not pushed himself forward, or maybe he had joined up as one way of escaping from a bossy wife and was in no hurry to go back home. However, I arranged for him to have his leave the following weekend.

It was a real pleasure training these men whose sole aim seemed to be learning all there was to be learnt as quickly as possible before heading out to the scene of the action – just splendid fighting material. But red tape and officialdom would for a while stand in their way.

Suddenly we four subalterns heard that we were to rejoin our old companies prior to going out to the line battalions as reinforcements and new subalterns lately gazetted would replace us. How these new ones were to instruct men already considerably trained was a mystery. Perhaps the men were intended to instruct the new subalterns in the art of handling them. Anyway, a strange and, to us four subalterns, rather gratifying thing happened.

The new subalterns had arrived the day before we left. That morning, not a man would move on parade. The sergeant major shouted himself hoarse, but the men stood perfectly still and at ease with their hands behind their backs, although the SM had made several attempts to call them to attention. The captain called the NCOs up and told them to find the cause of the trouble. It appeared that the men were so keen on getting on with their training and getting out to the front that they did not wish to lose the officers they had grown used to and start all over again with new fledglings. Some sort of compromise was achieved and the authorities were prevailed on to allow us to stay till the drafting away of the men started and we ourselves went one at a time instead of all together. I should have liked to have gone with that lot as a whole unit but unfortunately they were only used as drafts in driblets.

CHAPTER TWO

'It was my first taste of any real sort of war atmosphere'

The Essex Regiment was already battle-ready when Robin was signing on the dotted line. Britain's army had been on alert since 29 July. The 2nd Battalion of the Essex Regiment was at Sheerness and was poised to mobilize when the order came at 5pm on 4 August. Proudly, it was recalled later, this was the first unit of the British Army to notify that its mobilization was complete. So swift was the operation that a staff officer was dispatched to ensure it had been done correctly. Happily, he reported it had.

Accordingly, the 2nd Battalion of the Essex Regiment was in France by 23 August and men found themselves quickly within the sound of the big guns involved in the Battle of Mons. The British Army had fought well but was seriously outnumbered. It retreated to counter the threat of being surrounded in a German counter-attack. The 2nd Essex joined the 4th Division which was charged with protecting the army's exposed left flank.

Three days after disembarking the men were fighting the Battle of Le Cateau – at a time when many felt they should be continuing a retreat. The Germans on their tail were vastly superior in number and had their sights set on Paris. Just 15km from the capital the German forces were sniffing victory while the French government made a hasty departure for Bordeaux.

Later, General Smith-Dorrien observed that the beleaguered 4th Division had no cavalry, cyclists, signallers, field ambulances, engineers, or heavy artillery.

> 'No troops to give warning, neither rapidly moving orderlies nor cables for communication, no means of getting away wounded, no engineers who are the handy men of the army, no reserve ammunition and no long range heavy shell-fire and yet the Division was handled and fought magnificently but at the expense of losses far greater than if they had been fully mobilised.'

But the Germans were ultimately stalled. In September the Battle of the Marne reversed German fortunes and marked the start of an enduring stalemate. From here forward neither side could fathom a resolution to trench warfare, with men of all nationalities developing a tolerance for it. The trenches would soon stretch from the Belgian coast to the Swiss border.

The Essex Regiment had already borne significant losses before Robin joined its ranks, with as many as 200 dead by the beginning of September, while Robin was embarking on his career. He was in a cohort of young officers whose paths began at the same point but knew various fates.

For example, Military Cross holder Alexander Blest was injured just sixteen days after joining the 2nd Battalion and invalided to the UK. His career in the army continued, however, and he was made a lieutenant in May and finally a captain in 1917. A second spell in France ended when he suffered a nervous breakdown. After the war he was in a re-formed Essex Battalion as a captain.

Robin missed the brief window of mobile warfare and only experienced the drudgery of the trenches when he was in Europe.

However, at the time the Royal Navy rather than the army was deemed most likely to win the war. Indeed, it was presumed without question that the Royal Navy – the world's largest – would keep the country's prestige intact. At the outbreak of war the Royal Navy had twenty Dreadnoughts which were larger and faster than any other battleship. Germany had thirteen and was intending to catch up fast. As a consequence, both sides had different tactics at sea.

The German fleet wanted to avoid an all-out engagement for fear of being outgunned. Its aim was to coax a small number of British craft into action, away from the protection of the bigger ships. Meanwhile, the British chose to move as a fleet, a powerful deterrent factor. Accordingly, the German naval strategy hinged on mobility while that of the British pivoted on power. It quickly became clear that the German navy would have opportunities to attack British shores with lightning strikes. More than that, they would target British civilians.

In Britain there was a widespread fear that the Germans would invade. Troop movements through Belgium had been quick and the Kaiser's soldiers were poised to reach the coast, which might provide a platform for invasion. There was an anxiety on the east coast particularly, that the war would come to their door.

On 3 November the fears of Great Yarmouth residents were realized when German ships bombarded the town. It was the first attack on home soil for some 250 years. Fortunately, most of the shells fell short and the raid caused little impact.

It wasn't the same story on 16 December when distant guns were unleashed on Scarborough, Hartlepool, Whitby and Hull. This time there were 137 deaths, almost all civilians, although some of the victims were soldiers. A great deal of fury was directed both at 'barbaric' Germans and at the absent Royal Navy. Certainly the attack spurred British Army recruitment which had already begun to plateau.

Yet despite these glimpses of total war the vast majority of soldiers and civilians had no idea how cocooned their existence was in the summer of 1914. The time spent inside barracks on home soil helped to forge a camaraderie that would endure the harshest of environments later on.

One popular pastime was football. Established in the latter half of the nineteenth century, football was a passion for many that crossed social class. It was so much an integral part of life that the Football Association, after consulting with the War Office, orchestrated the 1914–15 FA Cup competition. Some people were horrified. The Dean of Lincoln wrote to *The Times* in disbelief that '*onlookers who, while so many of their fellow men are giving themselves in their country's peril, still go gazing at football*'.

However, it was deemed by the government to be a morale-raiser. Certainly it perked up the fans of Sheffield Wednesday who secured a 3-0 victory over Chelsea.

There were still plenty of social activities to enjoy, too, although it was early days for cinemas and home entertainment from gramophones. Records made from shellac had only recently become available and the speed wasn't yet standardized at 78 rpm.

People flocked to theatres, music halls and pubs. Harry Lauder was among the popular singers who topped the bill. Music halls were aimed at mass audiences while there were West End shows for those in London. Lauder was a comic and singer from Scotland. He is best remembered for a war time song called 'Keep Right On to the End of the Road', which he wrote after the death of his son, John, in France in 1916.

Popular music spread not only through performance but via sheet music. Many homes had a piano in the parlour – and often a banjo in the cupboard – and those were the chosen instruments for domestic entertainment.

In his diary Arthur Maitland, who would serve alongside Robin, noted on 3 August 1914 that most civilians '*have not the slightest idea of the seriousness of the present state of affairs*'.

The following day his point was illustrated when a civilian, showing off in front of his girlfriend, disregarded military orders:

'*I was forced to put a civilian in the guard room for half an hour this afternoon, on being told to move on by the sentry he request[ed] him to come out to be hit over the head. Just a cheap buck in front of his girl. However he was very apologetic after his solitary confinement. These civilians want waking up a bit. Our sentries have had great trouble with people disregarding their challenging. Someone will get shot one of these days I expect.*'

Among others, Robin had a lucky escape.

ROBIN

I had rather a narrow squeak one dark night when there was a howling gale and it was pitch dark. I was visiting the sentries as orderly officer; the order to the sentries was challenge once, then shoot if no reply. In the gale, I did not hear a sentry's challenge. In the interval of his hesitancy to fire I had moved considerably nearer to him and heard the click of the bolt driven home. I dropped flat just in time to hear a bullet whining away into the distance. I did some shouting myself then to make my presence known.

Gunfire on British shores was not unknown. There was an outpost position away out on the seashore, as at this time there were strong rumours of a possible attempt on the part of Germany to try and invade the east coast of England. One night a terrific burst of firing startled us all at the farmhouse where we were billeted. Being the orderly officer for that night too, I took the section on duty at the farm house, prepared for just such an emergency, and we groped our way in the dark about a mile to the support of what we imagined to be a heavily-attacked outpost on the beach. As the firing had ceased some time before we reached there, we assumed the outpost must have been over-whelmed and we wondered what sort of reception we would get. However, on reaching it all seemed quiet. As it happened a new naval searchlight had been playing towards the beach and had caused running shadows along the sands. As all presence on the sands was forbidden the NCO in charge had thought that the shadows must be a landing party and had opened fire. As nothing further happened he had sent men out to investigate and naturally drew a blank.

As the winter was early that year a considerable amount of wet weather kept us indoors a good bit. We were supposed to have lectures and be taught tactics etc., by our company commander but probably our smart friends from Sandhurst knew more about that than he did. At any rate as the afternoons wore on we generally finished up with a raucous party playing the card game *Vingt-et-un* or roulette, to be joined occasionally by others from other parts of the surrounding defences, and our farmhouse seemed to become quite a rendezvous of an evening.

In the daytime, when off duty, we used to play football with the men or have an occasional concert when it was wet. Our young Covernton was very popular with the men, he had a good voice and sang Harry Lauder's and similar songs very well, as well as others not so well known but a bit more ribald. He was also a bit of a conjuror on the stage. He was no soldier but had a way of being friendly with the men without being too familiar, a manner impossible in a ranker or one of that type.

Two or three of us who were fond of shooting used to go out on the marshes with our shotguns after snipe or woodcock and thus supplement our menu. An amusing incident occurred once. One of us had gone out and was stalking some game bird in a ditch. About this time there had been enrolled a number of very zealous special constables. A party of these arrested this officer as a German spy and locked him up for the night in spite of all his protests and explanations. Evidently to be seen hiding in a ditch was hardly in keeping with a British officer's status. (Poor chap, I helped to bury this officer in Flanders months later.)

Joe Ashley, a thin, wiry, jockey-looking man of uncertain age (he used to train race horses), was a curious being. He had a thin, dry sense of caustic humour and in a friendly way would pull each of us to pieces with his sharp tongue. I took a great liking to Joe, though I disagreed with most of his views of life, yet he would drink or gamble or flirt with the best or worst of us.

Towards the end of 1914 I received orders to proceed to France with a draft of 200 men. They were mostly from the old reserve battalion. We entrained for Southampton after having 24 hours leave to go home.

From Southampton a troopship took us by night to Havre. The following day we sailed in the same boat up the River Seine right up as far as Rouen – this part of the journey was quite like a pleasant excursion of ever changing scenery. I had in pre-war days lived both in Le Havre and Rouen and across the Seine in Honfleur, when I do not think such a thing as an excursion steamer as far as Rouen used to run.

> *28 Jan 1915*
> *2nd Essex Regt., 4th Infantry Base,*
> *My dear Aunt Ethel,*   *Bruyeres Camp, Rouen.*
> *This is where I am & not at Havre; the steamer came all the way up here. We are under canvas & it is awfully cold, everything frozen, we shall probably be here a little while. There are two other Essex subs here. We are some way out of town & only occasionally allowed down there.*
> *   Awful job to get a wash here, otherwise fairly comfortable. Could you send me a sponge & an extra dry battery for my pocket electric lamp, just the ordinary pocket size about 2½ inches long & 2 inches wide. I don't have news, this is just to let you know where I am.*
> *   Your loving nephew,*
> *   Robin*

At Rouen we went into camp on the south side of the river, well away from the town. I was only there for a few days before being sent up the line. It was my first taste of any real sort of war atmosphere. Everything so far had been in the nature of a big joke to me, but here the recently arranged row of bell tents and the half dozen army huts (very little comfort beyond the bare necessities of life), the arrival of fresh drafts, the departure for the front of others, seemed to bring the war close up. We were allowed out of camp by special pass between certain times in the afternoon. I tried to find the family I had once stayed with but they had apparently moved away from Rouen. Nor could I contact any of the young Frenchmen I used to play rugger with as they had all been conscripted. (I once played for Rouen against a Swiss town, in those days the French had not really got used to the game yet and it was one long scrap.)

29 January 1915
2nd Essex Regt., 4th Infantry Base,
My dear Aunt Ethel, *Bruyeres Camp, Rouen.*
Thanks awfully for those footpads or whatever they are called & for your letter. Yes I should like a pair of fisherman's boots if possible, several have them here. A great many also what they call trench boots, a kind of boot & gaiter combined made of leather, but I think the fisherman's boots will be best, get me a size 10 if you can. I don't know how long I shall be here, perhaps two or three weeks or may be only two or three days. Am just off to ask for leave to go down the town. It is frightfully cold. Some of our men are to go off to the front soon, I don't know who is to take them, I don't suppose I shall, as there are two other Essex officers here.
   Goodbye for present.
   Love from,
   Your loving nephew,
      Robin

31 Jan 1915
The Expeditionary Force, 2nd Essex Regt.,
My dear Aunt Ethel, *4th Infantry Base, Rouen*
Just a line to thank you for that warmer etc, it will be very useful in the trenches. I shall keep it in my pocket & use it as a hand warmer & occasionally as a foot warmer or rather a sock warmer when the opportunity occurs. I hope you got my wire from Southampton & also my letters from here. I have no more news; one of our subs is off with a draft today to the trenches, so that leaves two of us here in our regiment. I hope you can get me a pair of fisherman's boots, they say they are very much needed. It is still very cold here, & it was snowing about lunch time. By the by, could you send me some of that stuff for the ears to prevent deafening? I saw it advertized. I think it is a kind of plasticene. It is called Fibrous Plasticene, I think it is Harbutts Fibrous Plasticene from Bath. I saw it in an advertisement of Jan 23rds Land & Water but can't find it again. If you could get me some, it would be a great comfort as I know a big noise rather deafens me. This is an awful pen, hence an awful scrawl.
   Blest has gone to the 2nd Batt. So leaves two of us here now. It is a bit warmer today, as it rained hard all night. Goodbye for present.
   Much love,
   Your loving nephew,
      Robin

CHAPTER THREE

'There's a tremendous din going on, like a huge thunder storm, as there's just now an artillery duel over our heads'

On 6 February 1915 Robin began life in the trenches. At first the Germans and the Allies believed the rudimentary ditches they dug after the Battle of the Marne would be temporary. As time seeped by it became apparent trenches would become a permanent fixture of the conflict. Construction and the defence of trenches became uppermost in the minds of officers and soldiers for almost the rest of the war.

Although they varied, trenches usually had a front wall or parapet some 10 feet tall and lined with sandbags. A wooden ledge or fire-step enabled soldiers to spy or fire through tiny holes in the barricades. The back wall or parados was also clad with sandbags. For safety, trenches weren't built in long straight lines which would have eased the forward passage of any encroaching enemy. They were dug in a zig-zag pattern, with a front trench closest to the enemy – probably only a matter of a few hundred yards or even less ahead.

In close proximity there would be a support trench and a reserve trench, for back-up troops. Then there were communications trenches, linking commanders and their front line. As time went on more additions were made to trenches, including wooden supports, shelters and duck-boards. However, shell fire would quickly reduce even the best made trenches into squalid dirt.

Deluges were another on-going problem and in 1915 soldiers at the front suffered far higher than usual rainfall. Weather in northern France is similar to Britain and Meteorological Office monthly rainfall records show that February 1915 remains the eighth worst on record with 116.6mm of rain falling. July that year is the sixth worst, with 119.9mm while December 1915 has the second worst figures ever recorded. A hefty 168.8mm of rain poured down, a figure still only beaten by that of 1914.

At times the mud became so treacherously glutinous that men would drown in it. Forced to stand for hours in foul water sitting at the bottom of the trench, many soldiers contracted trench foot, in which the skin was eaten away.

Although rats are rarely mentioned by Robin they were a further burden of life in the trenches. The rat population soared during the war, with the vermin feeding off dead bodies abandoned in no man's land.

Companies were replaced every fourth day. An experimental period of swapping on every second day was abandoned by the 2nd Essex in January 1915 at the request of soldiers.

Some trenches were better than others. In his diary Arthur Maitland talks about the poor condition of trenches he was posted to in November 1914 that had been occupied by the Inniskillings:

> *'They've been here some time and haven't done one hand's turn of work to them except to bury their dead actually in the trenches themselves. We have consequently got about 10 days real hard work before us.'*

It was, he realized, his birthday. A day later he wrote:

> *'I spent a miserably cold night in these awful trenches with my platoon digging a communication trench all night and bullets knocking the mud off the top of the parapet continually, and it has been the same all day today. The frost still holds and it is bitterly cold.'*

The following description from the regimental diary of the 2nd Essex gives a different insight, recording what troops found on 24 July 1915 after relieving a French territorial regiment near Auchonvillers.

Here, B, C and D companies were in the front line and A Company were in reserve in the village.

> *'July 25th. The trenches are most extraordinarily clean. Nearly all trenches are floored with bricks. There are a certain number of completed bomb proof shelters capable of holding from 25 to 30 men. These are roofed with tree trunks and from 3–4ft of earth. The telephone system is excellent from the way it is laid out it is obvious that the signals must be trained electricians. There is very little revetting. What there is, is done with brushwood bundles.*
>
> *The front trench has a large number of loopholes in very fair state of repair. The top of the parapet is hardly thick enough. There is plenty of barbed wire in good condition and there are some 6 to 8 saps forward from 20 to 50 yards long for listening patrols. The German trenches are from about 200 to 500 yards away and are below ours.*
>
> *Drainage is arranged for into:*
> > *(a) deep sump pits away to the side of the trenches*
> > *(b) smaller soak pits dug actually in the floors of the trenches and covered over with wooden gratings.*
>
> *The communication trenches lead right back into Auchonvillers. No fires are lit or cooking done in the trenches. The reserve company carries all cooked food from the cookers to the front line.'*

But evident delight at the fine condition of these trenches did not last:

> '*Aug 11. Owing to the heavy rain which fell the other day the trenches are exceedingly wet in places and it has shown that the large sump pits are going to be useless for draining in the winter even though they are dug down to the chalk. Aug 26. The battalion took over trenches by day from the 5th and 6th Batt Royal Warwickshire Regiment, a frontage of some 1,500 yards. These trenches are partly old French line, old German line and line hastily dug by the French after a successful attack.*
>
> *The front line is in a disgraceful condition, being very badly traversed and the parapet being undercut both front and back, no attempt has been made to provide adequate draining. The relief was a bad one, chiefly owing to the fact that the guides had been badly instructed and either lost their way or did not turn up.*'

As Robin arrived a looped-shaped trench dug by the Germans to within 25m of the British line had been spotted.

It wasn't long before Robin saw for himself the vulnerability of soldiers trapped in trenches. Two days after he arrived his unit was mourning the loss of an officer who was trying to tackle the monumental problem of drainage.

Although only 19, Lieutenant Philip Christy, from Ingatestone in Essex, had already fought in the Battle of Aisne in September 1914. In January 1915 he gained special permission to attempt a drainage scheme, obviously with thoughts of improving the lot of the soldiers who inhabited the trenches.

Although his company was relieved on 7 February he asked to stay on to complete the task. He was killed by a sniper, as he was '*doing useful work*' according to the regimental diary, and is buried at Calvaire, the regimental cemetery established at Hainaut in Belgium in November 1914.

Afterwards, every man in his platoon was presented with a duralumin war knife – just a few years after the aluminium alloy had been introduced – engraved with the stirring message 'Carry On', followed by the name P.A. Christy. The gift was made by his father Archibald. Christy was one of thirteen killed in the battalion in February, with a further fifty-one being wounded.

Robin probably didn't meet Christy. But there were many men with whom he crossed paths, who enjoyed varying fortunes during the war.

Major Jones, a Welshman, born in Abermule, Montgomeryshire, was an old boy of Winchester School. Lumley Owen Williames Jones was affectionately known as 'Lumpy' and was held in genuine affection by everyone who worked with him. A career soldier, he won the DSO as well as French and Italian honours, and had served with the Essex Regiment in the Boer War. Curiously, he commanded both Robin and his brother Phillips during the First World War, having been promoted to lead a brigade in November 1915. He died of pneumonia in France two months before the conflict ended, aged 41, at the rank of brigadier general, with his condition exacerbated by exhaustion.

Arthur Edward Maitland, a machine-gun officer, was the diary writer who has helped to illuminate Robin's story. Despite ill health, he became a temporary major in the autumn of 1915. He won the DSO and Military Cross. He married in London in 1916 when he was 25. Much later in his career, he was in charge of soldiers sent to the disputed territory of the Saar to help police a referendum. The area had been taken from Germany by the Treaty of Versailles which ended the First World War. In 1935, with Hitler in power, a vote to determine its future was won overwhelmingly by the Führer. When he witnessed the behaviour of young Nazis on the streets, Maitland was filled with a cold realization that another conflict was inevitable. Worse still came the knowledge that the sacrifices of the First World War had been in vain. On the way back to England he suffered a nervous breakdown.

With him in the Saar was Captain R.V. Reid, wounded in action as early as 13 September 1914. He was promoted to captain in October 1915. Before the war ended he had been awarded a Military Cross.

George Rowley joined the battalion in France a matter of weeks before Robin. In a gas attack described later by Robin he was so badly affected he was sent back to the UK. By the start of 1917 he was made captain and remained in the regiment after the war.

Basil C.N. Wilmott was also gassed at the same time as Robin and Rowley. Having spent some time in the UK he was made a captain in 1916. After returning to France he fell ill with trench fever and was once again invalided back. On 28 March 1918 he was taken prisoner when Germans overwhelmed the trenches at Arras after a four-hour bombardment.

Earlier Ernest Raphael Capper had became a prisoner of war and died on Christmas Eve, 1917. Before he was wounded and captured his courageous conduct secured him a Military Cross. The citation reads:

> *'After the enemy had secured a footing in a portion of our trench he organized a bombing attack with his platoon and cleared them out, and when his original bombers had sustained casualties and were too tired to throw bombs accurately he collected a fresh squad of men from another unit and attacked again. His excellent leading, clear orders and great coolness under fire very largely contributed to the success of the attack.'*

In November 1914 he had changed his surname, Friedlander, by deed poll to Capper, presumably in response to its German connotations.

Sergeant Edmond Richard West is one of the few men in the ranks that Robin names. Although born in Essex, he was stationed in Quetta, then in Imperial India, before the war.

He died on 4 January 1918 in an enemy attack on the Essex trench which included a heavy barrage. German heavy artillery fire like this usually came before a raid and, although the incursion was not in the Essex sector, West was one of three from the battalion killed that day.

Unbeknown to Robin, on 15 February 1915 he was commissioned as an officer, finally losing the doubtful status of being in the Special Reserve.

ROBIN

A few days later, reinforcements of officers and men retrained for various units at the front. I was not in charge of any men this time, but simply went up as one of several officers. The train seemed to do a good deal of hanging about and shunting at various stations. There was, of course, no sleeping accommodation and for food we had to rely on what we had in our haversacks except at one place where I was provided a hot breakfast. We arrived there about 6am feeling very hungry and looking anxiously for this breakfast we had heard so much about. The train had stopped some hundreds of yards away from the refreshment room and the orders were not to leave the train. On enquiring as to why we had not drawn up opposite the restaurant we were told that we had to wait for the Rail Transport Officer. Shortly afterwards, somebody in our party found that the said RTO had a sleeping car on our train and we were waiting for him to rise, bath, shave before appearing to order our breakfast. There was an immediate rush for this sleeping car and our friend the RTO thought it politic to hustle without his bath and shave.

As the train neared the scene of operations we gradually began to hear the thunder of the guns though they were still some miles away. I disembarked at a station outside Armentières and was met by the Regimental Transport Sergeant and his transport horse and cart for my valise.

After a ride of a few miles in the transport cart I arrived at the village of Le Bizet right on the boundary of France and Belgium. A smallish river passing through the middle of the village was the actual boundary. The village was only 2½ miles from the front line trenches, and my unit, part of the 2nd Battalion of the Essex Regiment (The Pompadours), was quartered there in billets. It happened to be their turn for a week's rest out of the trenches when I arrived.

7 February 1915
2nd Essex Regiment, 12th Brigade,
My dear Aunt Ethel,   *4th Division, British Expeditionary Force*
A few lines to let you know, or at least to give you a foggy idea as to what is happening to me. I am now up at the firing line with the regiment, of course I mayn't mention whereabouts.   I arrived here yesterday, and from the

railhead I had the pleasure of a ride on horseback with the second-in-command several miles to the firing line. It wasn't long before I came within the sound of heavy guns. Artillery was shaking the place all yesterday and occasionally at night. I have been posted to my company. Last night one of our coy's officers, Blest – who was at Rouen with me – was wounded by a hand grenade and so we are minus one. We are in billets at present, and we go up to the trenches in a couple of days or so. It is pretty lively up there as far as I can gather, plenty of excitement & lead flying about. A few shells drop here occasionally; two did yesterday but no damage beyond digging up the roadway. Snipers are the difficulty, always somebody hit by them.

The billets are fairly comfortable considering the proximity of the enemy. By the bye, could you send me another pair of drawers & a vest, also if you could do so, please send me once a week a Daily Express *Tuck box? They are supposed to be the very thing for the trenches. No need to open them until right in & then very handy both to carry and to keep there, no difficulty then of arranging for grub there, otherwise it is rather difficult about the rations. Papers do talk rot, we have a stiff job before us, very nice for those who criticize from arm chairs at home. Fairly warm at present though murky trenches still have plenty of mud & water. Met Symonds Taylor at Rouen the other day, do you remember him he was in the crescent in Mr Symonds' house? He is in the Shropshires. Well good-bye for present.*

Much love from
Your loving nephew,
Robin

There apparently had not been a great deal of heavy fighting round here of late and the village seemed fairly intact, a few signs of shells having damaged a building or two. I suppose the fact that the land was as flat as a billiard table belied the feeling that one was so near the front line, since three miles on the flat is the average man's horizon limit. One could hear occasional bursts of rifle fire and a shell exploded now and then. The officer commanding the battalion was a fairly junior one as peacetime soldiers went. At the outbreak of the war he had been the junior captain and adjutant with about ten years service. He was now temporarily in command with rank of acting major. I soon found he was an excellent soldier. He had been looked upon during peacetime as a bit of a bad lad and not too good a worker so had transferred to the West African Frontier Force to escape the pinpricks, but war had brought out his true merit. I presume he was a Welshmen, his name was Jones. The original colonel and senior officers had become casualties sometime previously. The last man to be in command had been a certain major who apparently had been an absurdly strict disciplinarian. For army purposes I believe in strict discipline myself but tempered with reason; there are limits to every-thing. I believe he used to expect the men to parade absolutely spick and span, as if on a general review in peacetime, and this after leaving the mud and blood of the trenches. He used to punish with a very heavy hand anyone not coping with it. I heard a rumour that it was well for him that he had become a casualty when he did or perhaps some exasperated soldier might have mistaken him for a German.

Major Jones, however, was a different case entirely. I found a vast difference between the general atmosphere pervading a battalion of a regular line regi-ment than some of the new ones with which I had come in contact. The officers of this regiment took the war seriously and looked on it as the great opportunity of their lives, in quickening up their rise in their profession and a chance to put in practice all the tenets of their careers. Most of them, how-ever, soon ended their careers in the mud.

To a slight extent I felt myself at a disadvantage being only a Special Reserve Officer, and a wartime one at that, though there were two or three others similar to me with us.

The adjutant at the time was a Captain Maitland, one who was after the type of the major previously mentioned and appeared to emulate his harshness and discipline. He was, however, a very capable soldier, to give him his due.

Major Jones shook hands with me when I reported at his office and asked me a question or two and, though not exactly effusive, was quite pleasant. Maitland, however, never offered to shake hands but must have regarded me as another nuisance to keep an eye on, having to steer my erroneous course by strict handling.

I was attached to No. 15 platoon of D Coy. I say attached though I was really in charge, because No. 15 had lost their officer and had been in the quite capable hands of Sergeant West for a considerable time. Under the circumstances he obviously knew more about the handling of the platoon than I did and he knew the general routine in the trenches. So I said to him, '*Look here Sergeant, though I am officially in charge and responsible for the platoon now, yet you know more about the ropes than I do at present. Therefore I want you to carry on as you have been doing and I will pick up the thread of the game as I go along, and you must tell me everything and not mind me asking questions.*'

I found that he responded to this way of looking at it immediately, was very helpful and loyal and it was not long before I found my feet. Had I taken an attitude of complete authority straight away, like some did, my path, I am sure, would not have been so smooth.

I remember my first night in the trenches. Sergeant West fell in the platoon after dark on a misty winter's evening. He called the roll, checked off the men's equipment, rifles, bombs etc. (Lewis guns had not arrived then). There was a machine-gun detachment of two Maxims with two sections attached to each company directly under the OC Company. We moved off at the word of the company commander, at five-minute intervals between platoons and all of us in single file along the edge of the country road, almost walking in the ditches.

Our OC Coy was a tall lanky individual called Captain Reid, I did not take to him much. Our second in command of the company I was rather inclined to bracket with Reid, but I got to like him better later. The three other platoon commanders were Rowley, Wilmot and Capper.

For my first tour in the trenches D Coy went into a support line, some 150 yards behind the firing line. I remember distinctly going up that night. West led the way, as he knew it and I did not, and I was just behind him. After going for a mile we began to hear close overhead the flip-flop of passing bullets. When a bullet passes close to one at near range the speed is so great that it causes a vacuum behind it and the refilling of this vacuum by the atmospheric pressure causes the sharp cracks one hears so close to the ears, though it is probably some feet away. It was distinctly uncomfortable to know that these little winged messengers of death were flying indiscriminately close overhead and all around us, as we went down the straight road. In the dark it seemed more eerie than it would have in daylight, but in daylight the bullets would have claimed more fatalities as we would have been an easy target.

We soon passed an estaminet, or café, at a crossroads; here we had to hop across the corner of the building, one at a time in a rush, as a German machine gun, trained on this point by daylight, continually played on it all night long in bursts. My platoon crossed over safely but a few yards behind us a ration party going the opposite way had a youth shot in his side, the first casualty I had cognizance of, not helping to make me feel happier in my baptism of fire. We eventually scrambled into a trench and relieved a platoon of another regiment. West, checking, taking over, and signing a receipt for small arms ammunition, bombs and various trench tools.

He posted the necessary sentries and I reported the platoon in position to the company commander, who in turn would telephone battalion head-quarters on the field telephone line when his whole company was in position, and the relief taken over complete and correct.

12 Feb 1915
2nd Essex Regiment, 12th Brigade,
My dear Aunt Ethel,   *4th Division, B.E.F.*
Am writing to you from a dug-out in what was once a large farmhouse, but is now in ruins after a heavy bombardment by the Germans. We were in a trench on the 10th, then moved to a farm under heavy fire, had to work on a redoubt

under fire in broad daylight. Then yesterday evening came to this farm under fire. It is under fire at this moment, the German trenches being only 30 yards away.

The reason we have to move under fire in the open is because our communication trenches are flooded out, so we are not always safe behind a bullet-proof parapet or trench as some people might imagine. It is pretty safe in a trench except when bombs are thrown, but it is the moving to & fro from one to another etc. I felt a bit queer the first time under fire but am getting quite used to it. One can see that nobody is very happy while under fire, I mean when not fighting (i.e. replying with fire) but when moving about and working under fire. When fighting one thinks of the damage to the enemy & it is exciting, but it is not so when calmly moving about amid a hail of bullets. However I am really enjoying it, it's good fun & the men are very cheery. I think shell fire isn't really as bad as rifle fire when not fighting. There isn't really much fighting except when in the trenches where we keep bobbing up to fire & down again at once. The worst part as I said before, is going from billets to trenches or from trench to trench under fire & not replying at all. We have had one officer killed, one wounded since I came, of course several men. There's a tremendous din going on, like a huge thunderstorm, as there's just now an artillery duel over our heads.

I wouldn't miss it for anything, the only part I don't like is the pigging it in general & the mud, water, slush, smell and the rain which is coming down in torrents, however there are better times to come in regard to weather.

Could you send me a canteen, from the Army & Navy, a good one that's round with several parts to it, made in aluminium, with a khaki cover? I am rather at a loss without one. Also could you occasionally send me tinned milk, and cocoa, and a few odds & ends in the way of grub? The grub is rather a difficulty, much more than I imagined, & we can't buy any; the rations aren't up to much.

If you could send me some grub occasionally for my men, it would be a great help, both to them & me. If you know anybody who has shirts to send occasionally for them I should be very glad. Things are not very easy for them especially in this weather.

Although I have only been here a few days, I am getting to know my men quite well, they are quite a nice & very cheery lot, with good NCOs. One of them, a young fellow who is a sergeant is extremely well educated & refined, a good all round fellow, probably get a commission some day. Hope you got the spool of exposures I sent by my platoon sergeant who went home on leave. Get them developed please, as long as the press doesn't get hold of it. If you could send me one print of each out here, and keep the negatives. I have taken a few more which I will send by the next man who goes on leave.

We go into billets again to-morrow evening. I am going to try to take a photo of my platoon all together. If I succeed, I'll ask you to send me several copies of it enlarged to p.c. size to distribute among, if you could be so kind to trouble about it.

I'll let you have the money for all expenses. Must end now.

With much love, your loving Nephew,

    Robin

The first week and indeed for some weeks following, the life in the trenches was more or less a routine; glad I was too that it should be, to enable me to accustom myself to the general atmosphere of war and to get to know my men before anything desperate happened. I had heard of new men and new officers being plunged straight into a violent struggle and wondered how they could have stood it, let alone be of any use.

This particular trench line was dug out of the low-lying Flanders clay. Luckily the weather was just then fairly dry and we did not have mud and water added to our discomfort; but we knew that the wet months lay ahead and it was up to us to improve the trenches the best we could, even though it generally seemed to happen later that somebody else benefitted by it. There were half a dozen, not 'dugouts' in our platoon's portion of the trench, but merely hollows scraped out in the parados and roofed over with a bit of corrugated iron and perhaps one layer of sandbags on top, with a bit of sacking in front as a curtain. It would keep out light rain but hardly keep out shrapnel bullets, to say nothing of bombs or high explosive shells.

At this particular time rifle grenades were all the vogue, that is a grenade, similar to a hand grenade but with a shaft which you put into the muzzle of a rifle and fired with a blank cartridge – and terrible destruction it could deal too. Both we and the enemy, who here were about 100 yards distant, kept up an incessant play with these things, and even in the light of my later experience I think I hated them more than any other weapon. You couldn't see them coming as a rule and you might occasionally hear them when they were almost on top of you, making a sort of irregular humming sound. We had a fair supply of these and though I disliked them, they had a weird fascination for me and I used to try and outdo our opponents, that is to send two or three for every one the enemy sent. I was told later that that was the right spirit, that the men were sometimes inclined to leave 'Jerry' alone in the hope that Jerry would leave them alone instead of making them fed up with the proceedings. I was probably more inclined that way myself later when I had begun to get tired of the war.

My second day in the trench I had a bit of a sickener. One of those grenades landed right on a man's shoulder and split him open right in half – that was my first gruesome sight.

A good deal of sniping went on at this time. In this the Germans had the upper hand, both in mechanical aid and in skill and practice. To start with, they had telescopic sights which none of us had ever seen. They had also a special armour-piercing bullet and the half-inch thick armoured loopholes that we had fixed in among the sandbag parapets were death traps. They were easy to spot and these bullets would go through them like butter. Germans had also been better trained in the art of sniping.

We discovered one day later on that a German who had given us a lot of trouble in sniping, and whose position we were unable to locate, had come out into a field of mangel-wurzels, a type of beet. He had dug a trench behind a large mangel and used the vegetable root as a kind of mask by making holes in it. At a distance of 80 yards we had not spotted it. He would only fire at odd intervals so as not to give away his direction and when he had a sure target.

Most of our time at this period was occupied in improving the existing trench, strengthening the sides with sandbag walls, cleaning out the bottom and enlarging and strengthening dug-outs. Everybody worked about 16 hours a day out of the 24 as well as taking their turn at sentry duty.

Another regiment relieved us at the end of the week and we welcomed our arrival in billets though this did not mean total rest. We were always relieved at night because there were very few communication trenches in those days and above ground by daylight meant almost certain death. Also we could move more quickly above ground than in a trench so night relief meant a considerable saving of time.

The next day we took the men for a hot bath and to have their clothes fumigated. A large laundry at Neuilly was fitted up for this. The officers had their baths the best they could in their billets. The afternoon would be devoted to a thorough cleaning up and the following day would be a CO's inspection and everything was required to be as clean as possible, buttons bright etc. The rest of the days in billets would be filled up with arms drills and musketry in the mornings and football in the afternoons. The officers were pretty busy in the intervals between the above with reports, defaulters parades at the orderly room, checking equipment and ammunition and so on. As a matter of fact at this village of Le Bizet we were generally subjected to more shell fire than in the trenches at that time, all a part of the Boche's policy of unnerving us, though a great deal of damage was not done and the shelling was not heavy. A house would be struck now and then, although most of the shells were landing in open ground. This shelling also was very often at certain fixed times, at other times a battery would be fired just to empty the guns for cleaning and four shells would come over at the same time.

17 February 1915
2nd Essex Regt.,12th Brigade,
4th Division, B.E.F.

My dear Aunt Ethel,

I am sorry to hear about Rex & hope he will soon be all right again. This must be a short letter as I am off tonight to dig a trench all night & I ought to get in a little sleep beforehand. I have received the boots, underclothes, battery, sponge which I thanked you for in my last, but not the cork soles nor tuck box yet. I would rather you sent them made up yourself as you suggest, as you know what I like. If you could include a very small box of preserved fruit every time it would be very nice. Could you also send me a packet of pencils?

As regards to papers I should like Land & Water *every week and* Illustrated London News & an occasional daily paper. I seemed to be asking for a lot but it will be awfully nice of you if you do, I shall appreciate it most. Especially as life is dull here while in billets if we have no work. I can pass the papers on to my men when I finished with them.

By the bye if you know anybody who has any old spare shirts or socks or underclothes of any sort my men would be most grateful, as they are shockingly badly off for warm underclothing, especially shirts.

I have got hold of a most excellent servant, a good cook & experienced man. I must end now so with much love

from your loving nephew,
Robin

There was one obvious occasion of deliberate shelling. Aeroplanes (they were not in large numbers as yet) came over and spotted a large field where we were playing football. A few minutes later a salvo of shells landed, digging up great holes all over the field. Luckily nobody was hurt but we thought it wisest to postpone our game. The enemy was not going to allow us to enjoy some recreation.

CHAPTER FOUR

'The parapets and parados here were thick with dead bodies'

With the advent of war came a barrage of propaganda. The depths of German depravity knew no bounds, as far as the British public was concerned. There was plenty to fuel the fire of enmity.

The fate of Nurse Grace Hume in a Belgian hospital overrun by the Kaiser's army made headline news. In a letter apparently penned by her and delivered to a sister in Dumfries, she told of a patient being beheaded and her own right breast being severed. The woman who conveyed the letter confirmed Nurse Hume's left breast was also cut off before her death.

It seemed to confirm the general view of German barbarism. Unfortunately for those implacably opposed to German ambition it was entirely untrue, having been concocted by Nurse Hume's sister, Kate. The nurse in question – safely at her home in Huddersfield – was as shocked as everybody else to read reports of her violent death.

But stories like this cannot have been entirely unwelcome news to the British Government. While there was general fervour for war it was proving difficult to conclusively explain why the death of a distant European aristocrat had led to British soldiers laying down their lives on foreign soil.

In fact, there was ample evidence of German killings in Belgium during the first months of the war that gave cause enough for outrage. An estimated 6,000 civilians were slaughtered by German soldiers marching towards France in what the British press dubbed 'the rape of Belgium'.

For its part, the German army claimed the killings were done to stem guerilla attacks. Many of Germany's soldiers were no doubt subject to their own side's propaganda.

The first of eleven German spies, Carl Lody, was executed at the Tower of London as early as 6 November 1914, instilling into the public consciousness the perpetual threat of German infiltration. A twelfth was hanged at Wandsworth Prison.

Then there was the execution of British nurse Edith Cavell on 12 October 1915. Cavell was a distinguished nurse who worked in Belgium prior to the outbreak of war. Her hospital belonged to the Red Cross and thus treated all nationalities. She was charged with treason, having helped 200 British and

Belgian soldiers to escape the country once it was overrun by Germany. She is also thought to have helped injured Germans flee. Remaining breathtakingly honest in custody she insisted she would do the same again, saying: *'Patriotism is not enough.'*

When the sentence was passed both America and Spain, two neutral powers, pleaded her cause, warning Germany the execution by firing squad of a nurse would damage the Kaiser's image overseas. Indeed, it not only inflamed British passions, but also helped to shape American opinion about the German character.

But in addition to the facts there was fiction, like the story of Nurse Hume; so-called atrocities that were manufactured to heighten the hatred of Germans. The story of the crucified Canadian soldier whose bayoneted body was discovered on a barn door was commonly recycled. The existence of peddled myths ultimately tainted the stories rooted in truth.

Newspapers, pamphlets, posters and postcards were the tools at the disposal of the British Government. The message that 'the Hun' was a dastardly threat was constantly re-inforced.

To keep a tight grip on public opinion the government passed the Defence of the Realm Act in August 1914, which permitted the authorities wide-ranging powers.

No one was allowed to photograph military bases or elicit information from servicemen, for obvious reasons. However, it was also now illegal to own or use telegraph equipment without a government permit. Permission was also needed to keep homing pigeons. Flagpoles – which could be used for signalling the enemy – were felled. The military were given the power to appropriate land without the permission of its owner. Local councils were likewise able to take over privately owned plots to grow food.

Against this background it was only a matter of time before soldiers like Robin were compelled to return their cameras so only official prints and footage of the war were available for public consumption. For weeks afterwards he regretted the loss of his Kodak Autographical, known as 'the soldier's camera' for its widespread use in the conflict.

At home the sale of alcohol was strictly controlled, in the belief drunkenness could cripple the war effort, and lights had to be put out or heavily curtained, even though the risks of night-time attack by air were as yet unknown.

It all served to stoke public feeling against Germans. There were numerous attacks made on those perceived to be German – and their related businesses – on British streets by angry mobs. Olympia, the roomy events centre in London, became a concentration camp for German 'spies', with some 300 detained there within the first week of the war. By contrast, recently jailed Suffragettes and strikers were now released without conditions.

Germany was waging a propaganda war of its own, hoping to persuade its people that the nation was a victim rather than an aggressor. Consequently, the men on both sides believed they were fighting for freedom and had God on their side.

Given the heightened tensions it is impossible to tell if the Belgians Robin believes were spying for Germany were indeed traitors, or merely in the wrong place at the wrong time.

ROBIN

When we returned to the trenches our brigade was in reserve, that meant taking up position about half a mile behind the front line. Our company found itself in and around a little old farmhouse and its outbuildings. To my amazement, an old Belgian woman and her married daughter were still living there. The husband was away in the Belgian army, they apparently had nowhere else to go and philosophically braved it out there. An occasional bullet would find its mark on the walls. One day, when two of us were seated having a meal at a table in one room, a stray bullet came in through the window and knocked a mug off the table between us. The extraordinary part was that the place never seemed to be shelled, though shells would fall nearby fairly often.

Another farmhouse occupied in a similar manner by another of our companies had one or two male inhabitants; that place was also not shelled. I could never understand how these men were allowed at large and in a country where practically every male was mobilized; these chaps did not seem too old. Soon it was discovered that one of these men – who used to assiduously plough his fields – was ploughing certain code signs which were read by enemy aircraft. Needless to say he received short shrift when found out.

23 February 1915
2nd Batt. Essex Regt., 12th Brigade,
My dear Aunt Ethel,   *4th Division, B.E.F.*
Thank you for your letter, glad to hear Rex is really all right again. We have got a new sub from Harwich, he is in my company, Wilmott is his name. Three others have been warned.

I hear that they may have been asking for volunteers at Harwich, both officers and men, for the West African Frontier Force, a permanent job, to start on £300 a year. If I had been there I'd have snapped at it at once, Covernton volunteered, but I think he was told he was too young as he is only 18, and he must be over 21 to join.

By the bye I got a letter from Jack dated 18th January. He could give me no news of himself & his doings as he said the censorship was most rigorous, but he said that they were just getting their communications put right. Doesn't sound very good, does it? He said he would be pleased to ask for me to join his regiment

& said he would do his best. He thought I was luckier than he, to be going out to the real show in France instead of his minor affair. But I think they are having a harder time almost than we at present though of course much better weather & fighting conditions.

I received the tuck box yesterday; not bad at all, although your idea would be better of making it up yourself. Put what you like in it, just for guidance I'll make a specimen one.

1 Tin Nestles Milk

1 Tin Cocoa

1 Tin Café au Lait

1 piece of currant cake

A few biscuits or shortbread

1 tin preserved fruit

1 packet very plain chocolate, the plainest to be had

If you could put the above in every time, anything else you could vary, such as Bovril, potted meat, sausages or anything you might think of. If you could send me one a week. You might drop in a small tin of sweets, like drops, occasionally.

We are in different billets, lost our nice French friends and we are with some Flemish people who talk rather poor French.

No news I'm afraid, I am just going round to my men's billets so goodbye for present.

Oh, could you send me a pair of my pyjamas?

With much love, your loving nephew

Robin

On another occasion when the battalion was again in brigade reserve, D Coy was stationed with Batt Hqrs at a larger farmhouse. That meant that D Coy officers messed together with the CO and his staff; the adjutant, 2nd in command, doctor, signal officer and so on. At this house were two grown up girls, one fairly passable looking and so of course a certain amount of mild flirting went on. Being fairly new and very junior I naturally took a back seat in all this, but one day one of the girls tried in a sort of sign language to say something to me about some domestic matter concerning the house. Of course, I spoke to her in French to her considerable surprise and pleasure. She chided me as to why I had not spoken up before seeing that the others could scarcely speak a word of French. She then insisted that I tell them what she had been trying to convey to me. After this I was in considerable demand as an interpreter, after being told I was a dark horse, poor me only really having kept in the background through modesty. I think from then on Jones took a bigger interest in me and I gradually got to know him better and Maitland also, although I believe secretly annoyed with me, was a little less unbending.

A recently promoted Captain Irwin was rather a favourite of Jones. He was OC A Coy and was often dropping in at Batt Hqrs. He was interested in the two girls and was always at me to interpret for him.

This Hqrs farmhouse, though within easy range, was also not touched by shell fire and we used to feel quite safe there. It was later found out that the old father was in league with the enemy. He used to play a harmonium occasionally and it transpired that it was electrically connected underground to a German listening post half a mile away and there was a code arranged between them.

At another time in this neighborhood we discovered another clever ruse of the enemy. There was a haystack somewhere near the reserve position and it had been hollowed out inside; two German officers lived there with a telephone connecting to their lines. They used to come out to reconnoitre at night and report back.

We did not always go back to the same billets at Le Bizet. Rowley and I used generally to share a room together; he was rather a haphazard chap. I remonstrated once with him for leaving his revolver about loaded, because he had the habit sometimes of raising it and snapping it off in any direction when unloaded. I was thinking of my own skin. If I had to be slain by a German bullet – well! Pro Patria, etc.! But I did not feel like being the victim of an accident so I thought I would cure him by giving him a fright. I found his revolver lying on the table of our room, loaded as usual, so I picked it up and deliberately fired it in his presence at a bottle standing in the corner of the room. Of course, in such a confined space it made a fearful din and put the wind up him properly. He started to call me all the names he could think of. When he stopped for his breath, I chipped in with my say. After calling him a few things I said, '*it is entirely your fault, I have often spoken to you about unloading your gun. I took it for granted that by now you had the nous to have done so – and to think I might have pointed it at you.*' Needless to say that revolver was always empty henceforth in the billet and never pointed indiscriminately.

Occasionally we could get an afternoon off while in billets and two or three of us would get mounts and ride into Armentières. The Divisional Follies used to be one attraction and excellent they were for an amateur show. One day we were riding through Neuilly and we got off to have a drink at an estaminet. At the counter appeared a rosy-cheeked girl. I stared at her for a bit and then I said in French, '*Mlle, I seem to know your face, where have we met before?*' I had not met her, but it turned out that she was one of the two girls acting in the Follies.

Armentières at this time had not been badly damaged, though occasional ugly reminders would come over in the form of 8 inch or 5.9 shells. [Common shell sizes in the First World War were 150 mm (5.9"), weighing about 50 kg and 203 mm (8″), weighing about 100 kg.] They used to be the bane of our lives. But there were plenty of civilians and the shops were open. There was a nice little café where some of us would foregather and meet others of different units and discuss the general news.

At one time in this sector we were holding a part of Ploegsteert Wood; the weather was bad and the trenches had been awful with mud. And I saw a pathway about three miles long & a yard wide leading through the wood paved with full bully beef tins. Somebody made a fortune out of bully beef. It was a fine thing as part of our ration when nothing else could be had but Tommy soon got tired of it when there was plenty else available. However, the bully beef kept on being served, irrespective of how little was eaten, and in consequence it became used in this manner. If the Royal Army Service Corps had shown themselves in the firing line occasionally they might have discovered it and put an end to this waste.

In Ploegsteert Wood we were instrumental in repulsing one or two minor attacks and the Germans did not get beyond our barbed wire. Two such attacks were in broad daylight and I think were meant to be more in the nature of a feint – not seriously driven home – the serious attacks being further along the line.

There were a few pheasants in Ploegsteert Wood, we used to try and pick them off with the rifle firing over the parados. I don't think we ever got one, though the anticipation was good.

This was the sort of life we led during January, February and March of 1915. Late in February and early in March the weather became atrocious with continuous rain and the Flanders clay became very glutinous and persistent. As luck would have it some of the trenches we had worked hard to drain and make comfortable were handed over to another unit and we had to start all over again with a fresh spot of dirty ditches, where we stood for hours at a time in water up to our knees. Gum boots and even thigh boots were very necessary and as for getting anywhere a dry spot to lie down on to snatch an hour's sleep, that was an impossibility. So we lay down in the damp, while our lucky successors inherited our hard work. Why the higher ups must either bungle things like that or, if deliberately, try to make us mutinous, goodness knows. It would not have been surprising if there had been a mutiny.

Fritz and ourselves were too damp at this time to have much metalled vituperation at each other. Everything was extremely uncomfortable and having partaken of a billy of tea one day, we found a dead German in the hole out of which we had drawn the water to make the tea. I hope it was well boiled.

The parapets and parados here were thick with dead bodies. Wherever we dug to improve the ditch we dug through dead bodies. It must have been the burial ground of a fight that had happened a few weeks before. As for the stench and rats, well, we won't go into that.

At one so-called rest period out of the line, two of us officers and a hundred men were detailed for a digging party. We started off at dusk. By the time we reached our destination, a few yards behind our front line, it was pitch dark and pelting with rain. We had to dig a communication trench 200 yards long, six feet deep, two feet wide at the bottom and four feet at the top, and we had to finish it by daylight. Of course it was an utter impossibility under any conditions but under such conditions we managed just over half the task, which was good going. (We very often were assigned impossible tasks, whether this was on purpose to get the most out of us or just sheer damn incompetence on the part of the staff, I don't know – most probably the latter.) We got away at daybreak almost dead to the world, two of our men already dead with bullet holes and that was all on top of a week's tour in the trenches – and this was supposed to be during our rest period. Rest my foot!

During the digging of the trench, a staff officer came along and told us we were digging in the wrong place, we were to follow him and he would show us the right place. This seemed an irregular sort of proceeding. My brother officer and I discussed the matter and finally I said I would only take orders direct from my own O.C. That same night this man was arrested as a disguised German. He spoke English perfectly. Of course I should have arrested him immediately myself but I was as yet a bit green about this sort of thing. A few months later I'd have done so unhesitatingly.

I had to take a party two days later to finish off this trench by daylight. We had got down to a depth sufficient to give us some cover to work by day. I was standing talking to a corporal wearing a woollen balaclava helmet. This cap had a tassel on the top. The tassel must have just shown over the top of the roughly made and still narrow parapet. Some sharp-sighted Boche drew a bead on it and, allowing for the depth of his head, shot into the parapet. The bullet went clean through the corporal's head and grazed the skin on the back of my neck. The sniper nearly got two birds with one stone. Luckily this trench was along the side of a slight slope so that water could be made to drain away to some extent down the slope otherwise in the thick clay this job would have been almost impossible.

My dear Aunt Ethel,
Thanks awfully for all the parcels, the tuck parcel from Army & Navy Stores, the canteen which is excellent, the socks & handkerchiefs etc and the Land & Water *of two weeks.*

Very nice contents in the grub parcel, only worst luck I opened it when there were two other subs in the room & the result was a big hole in the preserved fruits box. I'll have to open these parcels when I am alone. Also thanks for your letters. I came back from the trenches last night. We had two officers wounded this time: Captain Watkins, poor old 'Beery,' and 2/Lt Round, one in the head and the latter in both arms, neither very bad although knock outs for several months. I got a parcel from Margaret with all sorts of things; soup cubes, honey and matches & candles galore. And as for Mother she sent me matches and candles to last a whole company the whole campaign, I should think, so if anybody thinks of sending me any more matches or candles, you might tell them will you? I was very glad to get them, tho'. I didn't expect it would be so lavish. I got a pair of mittens and a helmet from Cousin Jessie, I will write to her. I will also write to Phil.

I would give you a routine of what we do as you ask, only I don't think it would be passable [by the censor]. However I'll give you a rough idea, although there isn't much in it. We go into the trenches and relieve another regiment for four days and all we do is stay there; keep up at sniping, get shot at, shoot back, keep building and making the trenches better, get the mud and water out where possible, throw bombs or have better ones thrown back and get blown to pieces & of course a very sharp watch has to be kept in case of attack.

Then we have occasional nasty jobs like putting barbed wire out in front. There isn't much sleep to be had – the men, of course, have practically none. Everybody is wishing for the advance to start and is simply longing to charge those trenches we see day after day in front of us and look so easy to take, except for trip wires, barbed wire and heaven knows how many machine guns tucked away somewhere. They seem to have four to our one, and they use them too, while we keep ours quiet in case of attack. There isn't much knowledge or skill wanted for the present phase of the campaign, but rather stamina and no nerves. When they are hit the men get killed in cold blood, as there's no excitement of an attack or charge or movement or even firing at all. In fact most of the casualties occur on the way up to the trenches & back again.

The singing of the bullets very close to one's ears isn't very pleasant until one gets used to it. I don't mind it now. It is all luck whether one is hit, unless one shows oneself by day when, of course, a German sniper with a match rifle or a telescopic sight gets you for a cert.

Well, I must be closing as it's bed time. I have given my men the shirts socks etc & the herrings, they are very pleased with them.

Yes, I can get my washing done here, By the bye, could you send me two pairs of stockings – thick heavy ones, like footer stockings only heavier. I would try & see Major Ensor & Col Alexander, only one isn't allowed to go more than ½ mile away from here.

Well goodbye for present
With much love, your loving nephew
Robin

With the advent of March, the weather improved slightly and signs of spring appeared. With its coming the army generally seemed to be more hopeful. There were rumours of a spring offensive, talk of marching to Berlin and so on. It was merciful that we did not know what and how much trench warfare was ahead of us.

5 March 1915
2nd Essex Regt., 12th Brigade,
My dear Aunt Ethel,   *4th Division, B.E.F.*
Thanks for your last, and for the clothes for my men; please don't send any more as the men have been issued out with a new lot of clothing so they won't need them now. I am doing my four days spell in the trenches now, but this time my company is in reserve. We are resting in a farm behind the lines and doing digging work on certain trenches by reliefs.

I got all the stuff you sent me, except in one parcel where you said there were five shirts, there were only two.

Thanks awfully for the cake and fruit salad. I am going to have some of that roast turkey for lunch today. I think the compressed milk & compressed cocoa is great stuff so do send me some more of it, was it you who sent it or am I mixing it up? You sent me the compressed milk & bivouac cocoa & I think Margaret sent me the compressed cocoa. It is all awfully good & much more handy & lighter to carry, especially the compressed milk. I enjoyed the preserved fruits very much. Don't send me any Bovril or Oxo as I don't care for it much, but I could do with one packet a week of those different soups, like the turtle soup you sent me. Somebody – I think it was Mother – sent me a whole lot of Oxo, I hardly ever touch it and plenty can be had from rations, & I think it is too concentrated.

There was a list in your parcel of campaigning things to be had at the Army & Navy. I thought at the time it was a good list but have since lost it unfortunately. The Canteen I asked you for is awfully handy & so light.

Excuse rather a scrappy sort of letter but I am very sleepy as I hadn't a wink of sleep last night working in the trenches.

Well goodbye for present, will write again very soon.
With much love
Your loving nephew
Robin

CHAPTER FIVE

'It was a roaring, raging, swirl of destruction'

When the men arrived at enemy trenches a bloody tussle lay ahead. At close quarters anyone who used a rifle or revolver risked killing a comrade. So they resorted to bayonets, the sword that slotted on to the end of their rifle that transformed it from gun to savage blade. There were some advantages, especially early in the war. Bayonets economised on the use of ammunition and, with muddy trench conditions, there was always the possibility that rifles would jam.

Although the advance into the trenches was invariably orderly the hand-to-hand fighting that followed was chaotic. The bayonet was designed to cause fear and panic. In the confusion German soldiers were likely to flee or surrender.

During the First World War the British Army was using a 1907 bayonet designed for a Lee Enfield rifle that measured 17 inches or 42cm. When it wasn't being wielded in anger by soldiers, it could be used for chopping wood, opening cans and even hanging clothes.

In training men were told to aim for the throat, chest and groin. One can only guess at the brutalizing effect that bayonet combat had on the men involved. However, it ultimately became commonplace for a well-sited machine gun to mow down the owner of the bayonet before he could do any damage and the use of bayonets diminished.

There was another casualty for the battalion in March. Second Lieutenant Robert Johnson, 21, from Billericay, was buried at Calvaire after being killed on 13 March.

The next action, heard rather than seen by Robin, was the Battle of Neuve Chapelle, when the British and French demonstrated that German trenches could be breached in a sustained onslaught. However, it also amply illustrated the difficulties of capitalizing on any gains made as no significant ground was captured.

On 9 March Robin wrote to his aunt. The letter contained little news although it did indicate he still had his camera as he mentioned sending home spools of film. He praised the compressed cocoa and tablet milk from the Army & Navy Stores for being useful in an advance. He asked for apples, tinned fruit, new waterproof puttees and a Trenchoscope costing 10s 6d.

'I seem to have asked you for a terrible lot lately. However I want to get absolutely prepared in case of an advance which may come at any moment now, I want to be able to carry as much as possible with as minimum of space and weight as possible, if we advance it will be a matter of going from trench to trench, business all the way.'

ROBIN

Early in the morning on 10 March, away to our right, a great number of guns started, which kept growing louder. This was the first sign of the spring offensive. It was General Rawlinson's Fourth Army Corps and the Indian Corps. For half an hour 300 guns strove desperately to pour in the greatest number of shells in the shortest possible time. Though we were not actually in the offensive's front line we could see at a distance of about a mile and a half, as dawn broke, the thick, pale yellow lyddite smoke, the continuous burst of shells, trench machine guns and human bodies flying up into the air.

It was a roaring, raging, swirl of destruction. In half an hour the guns suddenly ceased and the infantry poured out over the top and across the hundred yards of intervening space, disappearing into the blanket of smoke. Then broke out the rattle of machine guns as the Germans, waking up from their first daze, got to work. After varying fortunes, the trenches and the village of Neuve Chapelle were captured.

In the meantime the enemy artillery had replied and throughout the day grew louder and louder as more guns were brought into action. On our part of the front the support given to the attack was by heavy gunfire and I suppose our troops were consolidating what they had gained. The shells passed over our heads, hour after hour. A further advance was made in the afternoon and at night things simmered down to a desultory fire. The next morning was very misty, which was rather unlucky, as it had been intended to push the attack further but except for heavy gunfire on both sides, nothing much occurred.

My dear Aunt Ethel,   *11 March 1915*
Just a scrawl to say I received the clothes from Miss Down & Mrs Robertson, will write to them as soon as I can, I can't always promise a very punctual letter as we are always pushed for time. I said in one letter don't send any more clothes, well wash that out. Send some more if you are given any by other people, only send them in smaller parcels as it is a job to carry them about especially if they arrive while we are in the trenches.

By the bye, could you send me some opium pills made up to the proper strength, in case any of my men are badly wounded, to send them to sleep? Sometimes 12 hours pass before medical aid can be given. Also if they are wounded in the morning we can't take them away from the trenches till night.

If I am badly hit I might take one or two; a good many use them out here as
they are safer than anything else. If you could, get them from a doctor.
   I haven't received your grub parcel yet. Could you send me a packet of Bronco
toilet paper?
   Love from Robin

On 13th March we relieved the London Rifle Brigade. A perfect inferno of
shells poured down all day along the line, including our piece of trench, and
we stood to arms from daybreak onwards, with the earth trembling all around.
Earth fountains spouted everywhere but we seemed fairly lucky as not a great
many actually landed in our trench, though there were plenty of them unpleasantly close. I had two men blown to bits and another had his chest torn
open with shrapnel. In one case there was a shrapnel burst unpleasantly close
above my head. I instinctively ducked. I happened to be wearing rather a
baggy pair of riding breeches and later I discovered eleven holes in them, in
the baggy part. A shell landed in front of one unfortunate private of mine. His
body whirled up about 40 feet into the air and as it turned to come down, his
limbs parted from the body coming down in several bits and the amazing
thing was that his feet were blown clean out of his boots, which were found
unharmed and still laced up!

Two days later as a sort of reply to the British attack at Neuve Chapelle, we
heard the heavy rumble of guns again, this time to our north where the enemy
attacked with some success at St Eloi, where they exploded a mine, stormed
the trenches and a part of the village; some of the lost ground was retaken in a
week's desperate fighting.

As a counter blow to this, a mine which the Monmouthshire Miners had
prepared just opposite us was blown up one morning. Here we saw a great
upheaval of earth go up in the air for several yards; dug-outs, timber, men,
machine guns etc., went hurtling into the air and at the same moment there
was a short but intense bombardment by our guns to clean up any living thing
that might still exist in the spot. Then as the guns lifted their range to smother
the German supports, the company that was in support just behind us, and
who had been prepared for this little affair, moved up and over in a rush and
occupied the front lip of the mine crater, posted machine guns and then proceeded to consolidate the position with spades and sandbags they had taken
up with them.

Needless to say it was not long before retaliation came in the form of a
stream of high explosives all over them and us, causing those in the mine
crater considerable losses, owing to their position being still somewhat
exposed. Their expected infantry attack did not develop that day and two
platoons, including my own, moved up that night to help in consolidating the

position with extra sandbags and spades. It was no joke trying to shape out some form of trenches on the steep edge of a crater, especially while the German artillery were still playing on us intermittently, and quite a considerable part of our time was spent in digging out men who had got partially or wholly buried by 5.9s.

While I was doing my little best to superintend this chaos and confusion I felt a fearful shock as if my bones had been blown right out of my body, I went hurtling down the side of the crater with what seemed a ton of earth on top of me. I was dug out, however, feeling nothing more than badly shaken and bruised and with a fearful headache for a part of the night. Having got the place into more or less of a defensive state, a fresh company relieved us before dawn and we went back to their position to try and get some rest and food, neither of which we had had time to enjoy. Again the expected attack did not come, which gave time that night for a party of engineers to wire in our new front. The Germans must have been too busy with their efforts at St Eloi.

> 19 March 1915
>
> *Dear Aunt Ethel,*   2nd Essex Regt
> *Just a note as I wrote a letter yesterday. This is only to say I am sending you a German Death Head Hussars helmet to keep for me. We are not supposed to send things home but I am chancing it. I have put some odd bits of warm stuff to try & make it pass such as gloves, scarf etc. Let me know when you get it, also when you get those photos. Could you send me out another three films, also one pair of 'Lotus' thick boots size 8, a broad 8, as if we have to march far I have only one pair and they are size 10 to allow several socks for winter. I shouldn't want to wear more than one pair in the summer.*
>
> *If you look at the* Illustrated London News *of March 13th, page 324–325 (about the fourth in the paper), at the long top drawing. It is where the Essex has been for a long time, just now we are about ¼ mile out of the wood on the right and to its right. There has been fighting for months & still it goes on. I must end now.*
>
> *With much love*
> *Your loving nephew*
>   *Robin*
> *P.S. You will find in the parcel, a Princess Mary's gift box, it belongs to my servant, will you send it to Mrs Curry, 12 Eve Road, West Ham.*

After this there was about a month of comparative calm though, of course, every day took its toll in terms of dead men: killed by snipers, rifle bombs, machine guns and the intermittent shelling. The off days were more deadly than the battles of previous wars. Just about now we had some new reinforcements in the way of drafts, which were sadly needed by us as each company and platoon was considerably under strength. I suppose the New Armies had as yet had hardly enough training and organization to come out, and drafts were also still short. Quite a number of these new reinforcements were mere lads, some of whom had not had more than about six weeks training. Also at this time it was rumoured that munitions were none too plentiful. The First Battle of Ypres, Neuve Chapelle, St Eloi and such fights had used them up and Lloyd George and his munitions campaign had not yet got into its stride.

26 March 1915

My dear Aunt Ethel,   *2nd Essex Regt.*

Thanks so much for your letters and the parcel of food & the underclothing, both of which I found on my arrival in billets this time. No, don't send me out any more clothes for the men now, as all my platoon have got plenty and also it is getting warmer so they won't need them so much; also we may move any minute and any surplus stuff the men have to chuck away. By the bye I am sending my camera home, as a strict order has just been issued that no officers are to have them. Any we've got we must send home. Let me know when you get it. I am writing on my company commander's note paper block; could you send me out one with some envelopes? These fancy campaign letter books etc. are no good. We have had no excitement the last four days in the trenches and it's been raining hard and everything is in an awful mess. We had two days warm sun to start with but it is like November now. I think it is the calm before the storm and it won't be long before we meet the Germans face to face.

Mother has been sending me The Tatler. *I got three papers the other day but they were all the same numbers of* The Tatler. *I was awfully sick about it.*

Please thank Margaret for her papers, I'll write to her when I get time.

I am afraid I have no news.

I had a rain of Jack Johnsons [slang for 15cm artillery shells, named for the US heavyweight boxing champion between 1908–15] *all round me the other day. I was just going to play football when they shelled us. The footer field was ploughed up with great huge holes & the mud flew yards up in the air ...*
[A second sheet appears to be missing.]

3 April 1915

2nd Essex Regt.,12th Brigade, 4th Division,

My dear Aunt Ethel,   *III Army Corps, First Army.*

Thanks awfully for all your parcels & letters. Yes, I have received everything up to date. The periscope is excellent, the best I have seen out here. Please excuse a dull letter & if it is nonsense occasionally, because I am awfully sleepy. I haven't slept a wink the last four days as we have had a lot of work etc. day and night, I may fall asleep over this one. You see I have received the writing pad. It's a

*boon. I got the boots. I rather wish I had asked for size sevens, as I think these
are a slight bit large for one pair of socks. I got the last grub parcel all right
with the tea etc. I don't remember everything to acknowledge just now, but
I know I have got everything up-to-date. You say that my name is no longer on
the Army list as being on probation, were there any other on the list who were
on probation? At any rate it is about time I was off probation considering I have
been out here over two months.*

*Awfully funny, do you know I find myself the senior 2nd Lieutenant in the
company now. I am in D Company here, my platoon is no 15. Captain Reid is
Company Commander, Lieutenant Irwin is 2nd in Command. There are two
Sandhurst officers who were out here before me, and one of them about three
months before me, and I am senior to them. I don't know how, however, I don't
mind.*

*I was in charge of the company for 12 hours in the trenches & today I took it
out for a route march. I was offered a horse to go on, but preferred to march
myself as one gets more exercise that way than sitting on a horse at a slow pace.
I am going out for a ride tomorrow with another fellow if we can get two horses.
Yes, I got the puttees, opium pills, in fact I am sure everything up to date. I wish
I was with you enjoying the sun on the sands of the seashore, slightly more
comfortable than out here. However, the weather is improving considerably &
fighting is beginning to get more lively. On the night of April 1st just before we
came away from the trenches, it being Bismarck's birthday, the Germans kicked
up a huge tamasha [commotion], with drums beating, bugles blowing, all sorts
of fires lit, singing & cheering & firing like blazes. We came out in a perfect
hail of lead. My platoon did an awful lot of work in the trenches this time, as
the weather was quite fine. The London Rifle Brigade had left it in rather a
bad, smelly & cramped state. After four days hard work one would not recognise
it as being the same place. We widened the whole trench, had the floor boarded
and revetted the sides with wood, made good drainage and sanitary
arrangements. Afterwards the men said it would be like walking in Hyde Park
if it weren't for the bullets.*

No, I have not received father's letters yet.

*I wish I could speak German, it would come in most useful later on. My
French is extremely useful, they have gradually got to know in the battalion that
I speak French well & if there is any difficulty they send for me.*

*Do you think you could send me out those German pamphlets of Hugo's
Institute that Rex used to have; have you still got them? If so, could you send me
out the first dozen of them? I will try to teach myself some in odd moments. If
you haven't got them, could you arrange to have some sent out?*

*If there is anything you could send out to me for my men, or anybody else
could it would be awfully nice. Don't send anything more in the way of clothes,*

but anything in the way of food, tobacco, cigarettes or papers. It makes a lot of difference both to the men and to myself. I like to be popular with the men, but it is not easy to be both popular and a good officer at the same time, because to be the latter one has to be strict which, of course, is not popular. However I mean to try & combine the two, and try & show them I like to look after their interests. Yes, we have football occasionally when the Germans don't feel inclined to shell us. We had quite a good game this afternoon.

Well I must box up now. So goodbye for the present
With much love
Your loving nephew
  Robin

CHAPTER SIX

'Hour after hour the tempest raged as huge shells tore the earth up'

With static warfare came the opportunity to revive an ancient art of battle. For centuries tunnelling was used to infiltrate a siege. During the First World War it was updated and became a method of delivering high explosives to the enemy's doorstep.

From March 1915 companies of men were organized to dig mineshafts down from the trenches and then beneath no man's land. It was dirty and uncomfortable work that could take weeks to complete. When finished, high explosives would be delivered to the tunnel end and eventually detonated to kill enemy soldiers and wreck their trenches and trench defences. Ideally it was men who had worked as miners at home who were assigned the treacherous task. However, 'clay-kickers' who had helped to build the underground tunnels in London, and Manchester men who laid the city's sewage system, were also employed.

Of course, tunnelling wasn't the preserve of the Allies. German miners were also heading in the opposite direction. Sometimes men from opposing sides met in the middle, having broken from one tunnel to another, and a fight would break out underground. Men in the trenches on both sides became alert to the sounds of tunnelling, fearful of certain death if it was successful.

When the mines were perfectly executed the results could be extraordinary. An estimated 450 tonnes of British explosives laid in twenty-one mines beneath German lines during the Battle of Messines in June 1917 killed 10,000 Germans. It was said the explosion was heard in London.

Tunnellers were hidden underground and could work night and day. On the ground it was only safe to move at night, although the trenches were frequently illuminated by Very or Verey lights – flares from a specially-designed gun named for inventor Edward Very (1847-1910).

The number of casualties in the Essex Regiment was escalating. On 8 April the unit lost another officer when Captain Gerald Binsteed, 30, was killed looking out at the observation hole half way up the back wall of a battleground farmhouse. Binsteed had been among the first to be awarded a Military Cross, which were first announced on New Year's Day 1915, having distinguished himself during the retreat to the Marne the previous year. Before the war he had taken a notable collection of photos on four visits to Mongolia – at the time something of an uncharted wilderness.

Captain Bruce Swinton Smith-Masters had been in the first deployment to France on 23 August 1914, having been in the regular army since 1912. After being wounded in October he convalesced in England until March 1915. He was made captain in November 1915 and won the Military Cross in June 1916.

On 1 July 1916 he died on the first day of the Battle of the Somme, aged 24, leading D Company into enemy trenches – one of 22 officers and about 400 men from the Essex Regiment to perish that day.

His brother George, 20, a second lieutenant in the Bedfordshire Regiment had died the previous year. Both are commemorated in Stewkley Church, Buckinghamshire, on a specially commissioned altar frontal made from the wedding gown of their sister. Incorporated into it are the figures of two angels with hair from the boys' mother and sister sewn on to their heads.

Lieutenant Covernton – the talented singer who had hopes of joining the West African Force – was discharged from the army before the end of the war.

On 1 May 1915 Second Lieutenant Philip James Barrell, 34, was killed by a sniper in a day marked by heavy shell fire and a largely fruitless attack from Essex trenches by the Sirhind Brigade. Barrell's brother Harold, a corporal in the 1st Battalion, Essex Regiment, died ten days later in Turkey.

For decades after the war, the British Army's top brass came in for stinging criticism for the perverse orders that were routinely issued. 'Lions led by donkeys' was the term coined to sum up the plight of the foot soldiers – the lions – who were controlled by asses. More recently there has been new examination of the difficulties posed to the higher commands that put them in a kinder light.

ROBIN

On 17th April began the fight for Hill 60 at the south-east of Ypres. A huge British mine exploded the hill and the infantry stormed it. There was a desperate bayonet and bomb struggle and in spite of a terrible bombardment the British held until the fight died down. Here for the first time the Germans experimented with gas and some of their shells contained the poison.

I learnt afterwards that Lieutenant Covernton, whom I had known in England, was one of a new draft and that he was pitchforked straight into a bayonet charge from the train at the railhead after arriving from England for the first time. He was wounded in the body and went temporarily off his head. The terrible experience was too sudden.

About now we went into the line for the first time that year in the neigh-borhood of Armentières. There was no serious fighting, but we worked hard at repairing another dilapidated portion, the only outstanding event being the poisoning of a few men who had made tea with the water from a small stream running towards us from the enemy lines. The Germans had put arsenic in the stream. Luckily nobody died though they had very violent pains in the stomach.

On the evening of 22 April we were relieved and I remember feeling so thankful as we had had very little sleep in the past week. The CO had promised us a good rest when we got out and had told us to redouble our efforts to get the trenches in good order because a new territorial battalion was taking over and he wanted to show them how regulars kept the line. We seemed to have been showing many others too, for this was not the first time we had improved the trenches of other units and then handed them to someone else. All very nice, but these extra efforts so often seemed ill-timed, though of course nobody could foretell anything a few hours ahead.

However, we handed over the trenches, reached our billets in Le Bizet and after dismissing the men Rowley and I simply tumbled in, both on the same bed, just as we were; uniform, boots and everything. We were too tired to take anything off.

Just as well we didn't waste any time disrobing, for we had barely been asleep a couple of hours when, after desperate efforts, an orderly managed to wake us – and then it was quite a time before we could gather our wits to understand. Finally it gradually dawned on us what he was saying. '*The alarm has gone, Sir, all troops to stand to arms.*' I said, '*But, orderly, we are not in the line, what the devil do you mean?*'

'*Sorry, Sir, but that is the order from the Brigade, something about a break-through by the enemy.*'

We rolled out of bed, tumbled outside and with the greatest difficulty got the sleep-weary troops to fall in, all bewildered and wondering who had gone mad. We waited about, standing in the street for what seemed a long time which showed that somebody had panicked for we could have slept for at least another hour. We heard rumours that the Germans had made a big break-through up north and were rolling us up. Somewhere around midnight we started our long, long trail. March, march, march, we never seemed to stop. We stumbled along half asleep. I am sure I was fast asleep for several miles, my legs moving automatically. Quite a number of men were so absolutely done up that it was quite impossible to get them along. They had to be left behind to be picked up later. We passed through villages looking ghostly in their devastated silence with here and there a house still burning. Dawn came and still we marched.

The need must have been great but what use would such tired troops be? All very well for the staff, they had cars to travel in and I bet they had had their regular quota of sleep, to say nothing of decent and regular meals – and they got more kudos and better pay for it. No wonder many of us said to ourselves, I am getting out of the infantry into something else if at all possible. The day turned out hot and dusty, which added to our trials. Still we marched on until at last at midday, somewhere near Poperinghe, a long overdue halt of two hours was made. We had covered 26 miles without a stop having started off fatigued and drowsy. It is amazing what the human body can do when pushed. During this two-hour break we were issued a meal, but I do not think much was eaten; nearly everybody went off to sleep.

It behoves me now to explain a little of what had happened to cause this sudden forced march of a whole division. On the northern Ypres front from Bixschoote to Langemarck, the French territorials and African troops held a position about five miles from Ypres itself. On their right from Langemarck to in front of Zonnebeke was a Canadian division.

On the evening of 22 April a furious bombardment descended on the French and the Canadians and at the same time from the German trenches issued a yellowish green vapour, forming a great bank. Impelled by a northern breeze, it swept over the French lines and to the left of the Canadian lines. Some of the French threw up their hands to their throats and fell down writhing in agonies of asphyxiation, others rushed madly out of the mist and made for the rear. Back to Ypres and the Yser Canal poured thousands of gasping, choking African troops.

Meanwhile the Germans advanced and occupied the trenches wherein lay the dead garrisons with gas-blackened faces and burst lungs. Several thousand prisoners, many French guns and four Canadian 4.7s which had been supporting the Turcos [French Algerian troops] in Turco Wood fell into their hands. There was a gap of five miles in the Allied front. Had the Germans had a cavalry division handy to hurl into it, there is no saying how the war would have fared with us but they wasted time in consolidating the position.

A German force tried to roll up the Canadian flank which, though suffering heavily, had not broken, only bent back to cover its exposed flank. It was to fill that great gap that troops were rushed up from all parts of the line – the column thus formed and tearing along was called '[General Herbert] Plumer's Flying Column' (they should have added 'half-dead').

Well, after our two hours hard-earned rest, we pulled ourselves together the best we could, collected many stragglers and started off again in a column of fours up through shell-shattered Vlamertinghe into the holocaust of 'Wipers' [slang for Ypres].

By now it had got dark and as yet we could not see the fearful destruction of Ypres. Here, there was a great movement of troops, with the rumbling of artillery wagons, supplies, etc. They seemed to be moving both ways and we could not follow what was happening. All the time there was an intermittent shelling and we could see our way by the light of the shell bursts and burning houses. Here every now and then we had to halt for some other moving column, either troops or wagons that seemed to have converged on us or were trying to cut across our front. To me, all seemed confusion, though apparently there was some scheme in this chaos.

After a while we emerged out in the north of Ypres and our brigade marched up in columns of fours, along the road towards St Jean. Whether the wily German got to know of our column or guessed at reinforcements coming up that road I don't know, at all events we walked up it in a perfect rain of shrapnel. It was a cobbled road and the shells were bursting about 20 feet above the road surface and, right along it, men were falling like flies. All of a sudden there was a blinding flash and a terrible crump and a great gap appeared in the column near me where eleven men were killed or wounded. I thought I was hit. I was bowled right over on to the road but got up no more than very dazed and deaf in one ear. A corporal who was walking along side of me was dead. Later the medical officer who had examined him told me that he was not hit but had died of the shock of the explosion, so close had the shell been.

We re-formed the column as best we could and moved on along the road somewhere towards the gap and expecting to run into Germans at any moment. It seemed madness to me to go up like that in fours, but it was pitch dark, we were new to this district and any other formation would have meant losing touch with each other and gave us no means of control over the men.

I suppose somebody in charge knew more or less our objective, because as soon as we came under heavy rifle fire and machine-gun fire, we were deployed out on both sides of the road and told to dig in for all we were worth.

Dig! Poor chaps, we had no spades or shovels, just the men's entrenching tools, miserable little things to work with on a pitch dark night when one is already exhausted and sleep-drugged. I had to rouse the men time and again, for as soon as they got down on their knees to dig they were apt to roll over and fall asleep. I kept telling them: '*Come on boys, dig like hell or else you will never get a chance to dig again, we shall be shot like rats in the daylight. The enemy can look right down on us here, we are well below him.*' We were down a bit of a slope and I could only surmise that he was somewhere near the top and only a couple of hundred yards away by the sound of the rifle cracks.

Later on it started to rain as if we hadn't already enough misery, and the difficulty of digging in mud became worse as it turned to glue. By morning we had a series of mud holes varying in depth from two to four feet according to the weariness of the various men. I, of course, did not carry an entrenching tool, and, as it was my job to see that others kept on working, I was exposed all night to the constant rifle fire and had to be more or less upright above ground and walking about while the men were close to the earth. When dawn came I had to look for the biggest hole and share it with its occupant. Naturally it was not the deepest, its owner had worked too much sideways instead of downwards which was just as well for me.

That was a miserable day and it rained for most of it. We had nothing to eat as we had already consumed our rations during the night to keep our strength up, having had nothing since the midday previous. Now we found ourselves without any near supports and no hope of getting ration parties through till that second night. We dared not show ourselves or make any movement and, to cap it all, the Boche, apparently annoyed at finding the gap filling up, started his gunners busy and the rain of shells kept on most of the day. Luckily for us visibility was poor due to the drizzle and they had not yet the range very exactly. We slept in snatches where and how we could and during the waking moments tried to widen out and join up the holes.

That night a small party was sent off and managed to get back with some spades but the ration party appeared to have got lost, so we still went hungry. We continued to struggle on with the now rapidly shaping trench and by the next morning we were fairly well dug in. We gained in that way but we lost in another. The visibility had improved and the night's work with spades had brought up a lot of new earth (or rather yellowish clay) which said in loud tones to the Germans, 'Here we are, an easy mark for your guns.' And my word, we got it hot that day.

Hour after hour the tempest raged as huge shells tore the earth up, crumpled the newly made parapets and buried the men, who had to be continuously dug out only to be blown to pieces the next moment. This is where the terrible shelling first began to tell on my nerves.

All that day it kept on and we seemed to live in a sort of terrified daze. And after coming on top of our wearisome march with no food to speak of, no supports that we could see anywhere, the Germans only had to walk over. I don't think we were in a condition to give much resistance. Why did he not come? It was a mystery to us. A well-pushed attack would have swept right through us, but the god of battles must have been very much on our side. After what seemed an interminable rain of steel, welcome night came – welcome in that the guns generally eased off a bit and there was a chance of moving about and getting food. At last food came up the third night. With that inside us, and a quieter night, our spirits seemed to rise and we managed to shake off some of the dazed lethargy that had gripped us in the past forty-eight hours.

When the men had eaten we re-organized them a bit, made out a casualty list and got them to have a thorough clean up and oiling of their rifles. It was the only really vital thing to keep clean, though we tried also to clean ourselves, which was very difficult. Presently the second in command of the company – (Smith-Masters) – came along. I had not seen him or any of the other officers, since arriving in this position, movement had hardly been possible to that extent and we had been too busily occupied in trying to get the men underground.

After having a chat with me, asking me questions and answering some of mine he concluded, '*Nobody seems to know anything, we seem to have no reserves and no support from our guns, why the hell the Boche has not walked over us beats me. Where is Wilmott?*'

'*I suppose he is on my left, his platoon is there all right,*' I replied.

'*I had better go and find him and, now that we are more or less awake, make sure to keep in touch with your flanks.*'

He returned in about half an hour looking a bit worried and told me that Wilmottt and his platoon minus his casualties were all right but their left flank seemed to be in the air as they could not contact anyone; Smith-Masters was returning to report to Reid, the OC Company.

Half an hour later still S-M returned to me and said that Reid wanted me to take a small patrol to investigate Wilmott's left flank, my platoon being in the centre I could be spared more easily than Wilmott whose job it really was.

I left my platoon in charge of Sergeant West and, taking a corporal and four men, passed through Wilmott's trench. After a word with him we moved out into the open, feeling along to the left (of course this was at night, it couldn't have been done by daylight). We had to move very cautiously for we were liable to be shot, even by our own side if there were any that way. We spread out in a close diamond formation only a couple of yards between each of us and must have gone about 400 yards without seeing or hearing a soul. Then we bumped into a trench running across our path towards the Germans, so we followed this up towards the enemy. I was in the van with one man when I heard voices. Approaching almost on all fours I crouched and waited and, to my surprise, I heard French being spoken. I was lucky that I understood French and could appreciate a genuine French accent as opposed to a German-French accent or else I do not know how we should have fared. I said in a loud voice, '*Nous sommes des Anglais ici.*'

A voice told us to approach one at a time. I went forward to find a French NCO who in turn called his officer. I explained my errand. He said he had heard that we were supposed to be on his right but had wondered where we had got to and the shelling had been so heavy that he would not send a patrol. They had only taken up their position twenty-four hours before. '*Good heavens!*' I thought, '*We had had our flank properly in the air previous to that with apparently no one there within miles; it was bad enough to have a gap of 400 yards.*'

We returned by making a detour as near as we dared to the German line. We could see by the Verey lights which both the French and the Germans were sending up that the enemy had plenty of wire in front of their positions and it appeared to be just over the crest of the rise on the opposite side of the slope to us. We nearly bumped into a working party who were busy knocking in posts for additional wire and were making too much noise to notice us. Stealthily we withdrew in our own direction.

This information was sent by Captain Reid to Major Jones who was holding a trench some 200 yards behind us with his battalion headquarters and the reserve company. Major Jones came up with Reid to tell me what to discuss with the French commander, and to report back the result. The latter I found a dear old chap and very pleased that at least one Englishman in his neighbourhood could talk his language. He sat me down to share a meal they were just having and, being French, also a bottle of wine; it had been months since I had tasted wine. Then he suggested that we each spare a few men and thus make a couple of intervening posts in the gap between them and us. This we did later on that night after I had informed Major Jones of the discussion. They were withdrawn at dawn because they had not had time to make cover for themselves by the arrival of daylight.

During my meal with the French colonel we discussed the war generally. He seemed anxious to know if we had plenty of reserves in England for he said France would be bled white before the war was over (he was not far wrong in his prophesy) and their only hope was the rapid expansion of the British armies. I asked him his personal attitude towards the war and he made a very striking reply.

'*Well Monsieur le lieutenant, this is Belgium and I am a Frenchman, yet it happens that my home is only a mile on the other side of these German lines opposite. I married a Belgian girl and that is her property. Under these circumstances there is only one attitude I could have and that also is the attitude of every Frenchman in France and every Belgian in Belgium. Vous autres, you have come gallantly to our rescue, but the war can never be the same to you as it is to us.*' I am sure he was right.

During the meal a French artillery officer came in to see the French colonel who asked him to join us in a drink, and here again was an odd coincidence. It turned out to be Capitaine Le Bon whom I had known and met previously in Le Havre. This livened things up a bit and we almost forgot the war over our reminiscences.

The following night a working party was formed to link up by means of an oblique trench from our left to the French right, oblique because as will be remembered the French trenches were forward of us. By daylight it had not properly been completed. Though it was the required depth the parapet and parados were as yet only roughly thrown up and not worked down hard or leveled.

So hide bound had been the training in the British Army that even the good soldier Major Jones wanted me to occupy the position with my platoon, the other platoons stretching out to occupy the vacancy this caused. I was not at all keen on this and thought it was unnecessary for I knew what it meant. The platoon would be annihilated by high explosives and for no purpose. The trench was so obviously new, the bright yellow clay subsoil showing on the top and so easily within range of the enemy who would enfilade it with gunfire.

I was there to do as I was told. However, I thought a strong hint would not be amiss and we might still live to fight another day. I am glad for our skins that the CO agreed with my suggestion not to put us in there till the following day for my fears were only too well founded. That day we watched in silence our new trench being blown sky high and barely a trace of it was left by night-fall. Imagine my feelings, had the CO been obdurate we would have died. But that sort of thing had happened before and would happen again, and during four years of the war our casualties were in this fashion more than double they should have been had our staff and senior officers used a little more common sense and not been quite so parade ground efficient. I pride myself a little that even Major Jones learnt something from a beginner that day.

We went into that trench again the following night to set about rebuilding it, the CO saying that we were to stop there the next day and only return to our original trench if our casualties were heavy from shelling. At this time of the war there was still a stupid idea amongst the regular soldiers that every yard of ground must have a man to hold it when, with a bit of judgment, a series of little strong-posts in these awkward cases would have saved count-less lives. I was not a regular soldier at that time, I could only see it from a common sense point of view. In my longish life, I have come to the conclusion that clever or highly trained people very often have very little common sense. Personally, if I could not have both, I would rather have common sense than be clever or highly trained.

Well, there we were the very next day and the jolly old shells came down heavier than ever and we started to go sky high in bits. It was left to my dis-cretion when to clear out, a discretion which I should have been glad of but in the army as it was then I did not like at all. I would rather have had a definite order one way or the other. However after enduring a tremendous crushing and several casualties, and having been buried alive three times myself and nearly every man having had the same experience, we withdrew into our old line feeling pretty battered. We had done no good at all and made the army weaker by the loss of several good lives.

Irwin, the adjutant, came along to see how we had fared, the next day. He said, '*Well, Monypenny, I am sorry you had such a rotten day yesterday, but you can console yourself that it has cost the Boche a pretty penny in ammunition. Each of these HE shells cost several pounds.*' How comforting!

About now we started to hear a new sound amongst the German guns. Every now and then there would be a tremendous boom ending up in a sort of metallic twang and miles overhead would rush what sounded like half-a-dozen express trains. At the end of it there was a terrific roar and away in Ypres somewhere a great hole would be torn. This was a new 17-inch gun the Germans had produced and it was fired regularly every afternoon.

'*There goes the "Wiper's Express"*,' the men would say, '*it must be somewhere near four o'clock.*'

Later on, down in the outskirts of Ypres, I came across one of these shell holes and it must have been 50 feet across and 30 feet deep. You could drop a fair sized house in it. Imagine standing somewhere near one when it landed.

18 April 1915

My dear Aunt Ethel,   *2/nd Essex*

Thanks so much for letters & parcel & please thank Mrs Hunter for her portion of it. I am afraid you have been some little while without a letter, but I just found one in my pocket which I thought I had sent off. I also have been very tired lately & somewhat fed up. I sat down once or twice to write but my brain wouldn't work. We have been working frightfully hard lately & everybody is more or less tired. I think it is about time this regiment was taken away for a rest, at any rate before the advance begins as the men have had a long tiring time of it, more so than many regiments.

I wish I was home in a way, to get some nice exercise in the way of running & football and a decent bath & change of clothes. Here, when we play football we have to play in uniform & we get nasty & sticky, I don't like staying in the same clothes, days on end, however these are really trifles compared to what we get accustomed to. I must not grouse any more. I must say we are all looking forwarded to the invasion of Germany, if such a thing ever comes off. Please don't send me any more of that compressed milk, I don't think I care for it. I find it does not make very good milk, it is more like melted butter. If you could, send me tins of café au lait and cocoa au lait & an occasional tin of Nestles Milk. Could you send me two pairs of summer pants & summer vests? I seem only to be asking for something, I am afraid I am going to ask for some more. Could

you send me some more Bronco Paper, Carbolic soap, Colgate's Tooth Paste &
Shaving Soap? Could you send out a Daily Mail *for about a month from now?*

   Yes, Captain Binsteed is a frightful loss to the regiment and to the British
Army. He was the cleverest officer in the Division & a very nice man too, could
speak about seven languages & a very clever soldier. Yes, do send me out some
more cigarettes for the men, as they are getting short of them. Keep a look out in
the papers, for movement of the Fourth Division or any regiments in it as there
will probably be something worth reading about.

   I have got a little puppy, I have had it about three weeks now. Topping little
beggar, he comes to the trenches with me. He is going to be a huge dog.

   Love from Robin

On 26 April our guns, which up to now in this sector had been singularly quiet,
started a vigorous bombardment from seven o'clock in the morning until two
o'clock. At that moment, lines of our men were advancing down the slope
towards us. An attack was being launched over our heads, on a front of four or
five miles. Several waves of troops came up in extended order, in perfect lines
as if on parade. Away to the left we could see the dark blue of the French
attacking. Just behind us came the Highland Light Infantry and Indian Corps
consisting of Sikhs and Gurkhas. Of course, the German guns opened up
searching for these lines of Infantry. I remember seeing a tall bearded Sikh
through my field glasses. Suddenly a shell landed at his feet. His puggri
[turban] went sailing up in the air, but there was no sign of him – and his
comrades on either side automatically closed in the space a bit and moved on.

   Two battalions of Gurkhas passed over us and made for the German lines,
but such a withering fire of machine guns opened up they were mowed down
in lanes. Apparently the wire protecting the enemy lines had been scarcely
damaged by our guns. After a vain attempt the Gurkhas had to fall back with
heavy losses to our trench, where they reformed under cover of our fire. To
the immediate left of us the attack had also failed owing to a cloud of poison
gas, of which we got a slight sniff. Our first taste of it. Further on to the left
still the French had had some success.

   The next day there happened again one of those unaccountable things
which makes me think that our Staff were prime muddlers or so hidebound in
their out-of-date training that they were just guessing at new warfare and not
trying to think it through. Also, as they seldom appeared near the front how
could they learn anything? Some of those dates such as 27 April 1915 are
indelibly stamped on my mind.

   The previous day I saw a whole brigade consisting of two battalions of
Gurkhas and one of HLI being decimated. A heavy bombardment failed to
even reach the German position in front of me and this was repeated over the

whole of the divisional front which attacked. Well, the next day, I received orders from battalion headquarters through Reid that – with two platoons under my charge – I was that afternoon at 2pm to attack the German position. I was dumbfounded as I could see no reason for such an outrageous order. I know it has been said, '*theirs not to reason why*' – etc. I was ordered to do so and I was prepared to attempt my little futile best on this utterly forlorn and hopeless quest, for I knew that not one of us would reach halfway across no man's land and most of us would die there. How could we when 2,000 men, as part of a big general attack, after a heavy gunfire utterly failed? How could about seventy men with no preparation or artillery support succeed?

I was prepared to try but not without protest. I discussed it with Captain Reid who agreed with me that it was a hopeless task. I queried a possible blunder but he showed me the message on a telephone form. I asked him to have it re-confirmed and he gave me the telephone to ring up myself. I got on to the CO. who said it was a brigade message which he himself had already queried and had been told to carry on with it. I suggested to the CO that if I would be allowed to make the attack four or five hours later after dusk, we might have some chance of reaching the German trenches, making a silent raid on them and perhaps be of a little use – but to carry out what I was asked to do would simply mean wasted life. I hardly dared face my men with such a proposition.

However, I got them together and explained matters the best I could. I might as well have told them they were all going to be put against a blank wall, including myself, and be shot out of hand by a firing party. Still, I made certain orders for formation attack, the whole thing seeming so utterly futile with such a minute force. Had it been a sort of night trench raid there might have been some hope of doing something slightly positive, such as killing a few Germans or even capturing one or two for the loss of most of our men. We resigned ourselves and got ready knowing full well we had no chance of coming back.

About half an hour before the time set for this ridiculous business a message came through cancelling the whole thing. Talk about a sigh of relief. I was furious and tried hard to get to the bottom of this order but could never get any further with it. Somebody had made an awful blunder and corrected it only just in time, his or their conscience having been stirred by my insistence on querying it. I feel that day at any rate I had saved the lives of seventy men including myself. Had the thing happened only those in the immediate vicinity would have known about it, and it would soon have been forgotten in the fog of war. But what of us poor devils so utterly sacrificed on the altar of crass stupidity. We did not make a song of dying, sooner or later most of us there would be dead, but we would rather have died doing something to help win the war not help to lose it. I was always a bit sore with Reid about this. He never even attempted to remonstrate about it nor try to clear up the mystery.

That night we had to find some burial parties, for the HLI and the Indian left a lot of dead behind them and, as the weather was rapidly getting warmer, matters would be pretty unpleasant before long if these corpses were not underground. I had to go out in charge of these parties and scour the neighbourhood – not a pleasant job, though I was glad enough for a chance to stretch my legs. At that time the organisation that was later built up for the disposal of the dead had not come into being and each man was just buried where we found him, after his identity disc and papers were removed. Quite often he was so mangled that these methods of identifying him were totally obliterated.

Some way to our left we found quite a lot of men whose faces had gone black with gas poisoning. I suppose the cloud had been thicker in that direction whilst we received only a whiff of it. In one spot near the edge of a wood we found a great stack of dead bodies, a bunch of men must have been caught in a fierce cross fire of several machine guns. But the astounding fact of it was that there were Scots, Frenchmen, Sikhs and Gurkhas all mixed up together in a heap. How they had thus come together to meet their death mystified us. There they lay huddled over each other.

Though it was night-time we worked with the aid of electric torches when it was necessary to see anything properly. Going along I happened to stumble over a dead body. I stopped and saw it was a dead Gurkha. I stood up to point him out to the burial party then I heard a slight groan. On closer examination he appeared to be still alive though unconscious. He had a great hole in the back of his head where a bullet had blown it out after going right through from his forehead. On our way back to our trench that night we carried him and deposited him in a dugout. We reckoned that he might have been lying out there for at least thirty-six hours with that awful wound and few men could have survived. There was no chance of sending him to the rear then for no stretcher parties were available and we could not spare any men. We were holding the line too thinly as it was. The casualties of the previous days were still being dealt with and I had not seen a medical officer about the place for a week. That Gurkha must have lived through the gas attack while unconscious for we found him near where there were several gas victims. It was not for another two days before we could get him away. He appeared to be in the same condition. I often wonder if he lived but I do not think he could have survived.

Things seemed to be simmering down again, though at all times there was much more liveliness up in the Ypres Salient than we had had down at Armentières.

28 April 1915
2nd Essex, 12th Brigade,
4th Division, B.E.F.

My dear Aunt Ethel,
Just a few lines to thank you for the papers and the parcel which arrived safely
& for the German grammar.

Things are getting very lively. I should like to tell you a lot of things but they
would not pass the censor. We are going to have a very warm time because we
shall be drawn in to the greatest battle of the war; it has been pretty quiet here
but we are to have some warm work elsewhere. No doubt you will guess after a
time where we shall be.

The weather is grand just now, though it is still a bit cold at nights in the
open, though I daresay I would sleep quite well in an open field with a British
warm coat on; my feet will be the only difficulty.

If you get hold of a map of Belgium & follow the names in the papers of the
places and the different corps & regiments etc you will be able to discover roughly
whereabouts we are.

You may not hear from me often now but I will write whenever I get an
opportunity.

Things don't seem to have been going extra well in East Africa, have they?
I wonder how Jack is getting on.

Please thank Mrs Robertson for being so kind in sending me Punch, *I haven't*
managed to write her yet but will do so if I get a chance. But letter writing is no
easy matter now. I must end now.

With much love
Your loving nephew
Robin

CHAPTER SEVEN

'I know a little more about chemistry now'

It was the beginning of a sustained period of action for the battalion. The use of chlorine gas – against the rules of The Hague Convention which began setting down the laws of warfare in 1899 and 1907 – added a new dimension to the horrors of warfare.

The first to feel its noxious effects were the French, as witnessed at a distance by Robin. Correspondent Will Irwin, of the *New York Tribune*, described the attack on 27 April.

'The attack of last Thursday evening was preceded by the rising of a cloud of vapor, greenish gray and iridescent. That vapor settled to the ground like a swamp mist and drifted toward the French trenches on a brisk wind. Its effect on the French was a violent nausea and faintness, followed by an utter collapse. It is believed that the Germans, who charged in behind the vapor, met no resistance at all, the French at their front being virtually paralyzed.

Everything indicates long and thorough preparation for this attack. The work of sending out the vapor was done from the advanced German trenches. Men garbed in a dress resembling the harness of a diver and armed with retorts or generators about three feet high and connected with ordinary hose pipe turned the vapor loose towards the French lines. Some witnesses maintain that the Germans sprayed the earth before the trenches with a fluid which, being ignited, sent up the fumes. The German troops, who followed up this advantage with a direct attack, held inspirators in their mouths, thus preventing them from being overcome by the fumes.

In addition to this, the Germans appear to have fired ordinary explosive shells loaded with some chemical which had a paralyzing effect on all the men in the region of the explosion. Some chemical in the composition of those shells produced violent watering of the eyes, so that the men overcome by them were practically blinded for some hours.

This new form of attack needs for success a favorable wind. Twice in the day that followed the Germans tried trench vapor on the Canadians, who made on the right of the French position a stand which will probably be remembered as one of the heroic episodes of this war. In both cases the wind was not favorable, and the Canadians managed to stick through it.'

The French forces were cut down that day when the thick gas fumes turned into hydrochloric acid on contact with the moisture in men's throats. The effect was vomiting, diarrhoea and powerful internal spasms which were often fatal.

By May the Essex men had been issued with mouthpads made of flannel or wool that were soaked in hyposulphite of soda, which acted as an antidote. This was the only, limited protection against gas at this early stage in its use.

The Essex Regimental Diary recorded a later attack that Robin experienced like this.

> '*May 2 – Enemy attacked with gas, a thick wall of gas some 60–70ft high of a greenish yellow colour was seen all along the front of the trenches held by the 12 Bgde.*
>
> *The gas appeared to be thickest in front of the trenches held by the Lanc Fus on the right and by this Battalion on the left. Our trench was held by B and D coys and one platoon of A Company.*
>
> *Both the French and our own artillery kept up a magnificent covering fire on the enemy's trenches and absolutely prevented him from leaving them. After the trenches had been re-occupied the enemy twice left his trench opposite our right but was driven back each time.*
>
> *A hostile aeroplane also came over flying low and was brought down by the battn but unfortunately fell just in his own lines.*
>
> *A large number of men were missing, these had been gassed and were admitted to hospital.*'

Unknown to Robin, a dozen men – mostly from B Company – held the Germans back after the gas attack until they were eventually forced to retire.

Then Lieutenant Noel Mackintosh Stuart Irwin, from A Company, led his men into the fray, almost certainly saving Robin's life in the process. It was the same Irwin who Robin had interpreted for during flirtations with two French girls earlier in the war. Irwin's bravery earned him a Military Cross, which he received at Buckingham Palace in March 1916. During the conflict he was mentioned in despatches no fewer than four times. A Sandhurst graduate, he went on to become the battalion commander and then left the Essex to lead the Lincolnshire and Leicestershire regiments in the First World War.

In the Second World War he was a commander at the retreat from Dunkirk, helped to orchestrate the defence of India and, later, was posted to West Africa. By the time he retired as a Major General in 1948 he had a host of military honours to his name. Twice married, Irwin died in 1972.

The Regimental Diary records that there were 23 killed, 67 wounded and 175 missing after the gas attack, of which Robin was one. And his 'resurrection' caused some humour.

In his diary Maitland – who was himself wounded that day – records:

'*Monypenny was missing for a long time but at 9 pm suddenly rose up from the bottom of his trench where he had been lying gassed and demanded to know where the hell he was!*'

Also among the missing were Rowley and Wilmott, both of whom were later found to be suffering from the effects of gas.

ROBIN

Another memorable day dawned on 2nd May. At 4pm as we were watching the German lines, a huge yellowish-green vapour was suddenly ejected at high pressure and, with the favourable breeze behind, rolled over us. This was the first time we had seen this chlorine cloud. We had had a whiff of it in the previous attack, but it had not been thick enough to be visible and had only made us a bit uncomfortable. The only protection we had was a small square flannel issued to each man, dipped in some ammonia solution but it was ineffectual. The first instinct of the men was to blaze into it, but this soon stopped as the cloud reached us. Everyone was coughing and wheezing, fighting for breath. Men began to roll down into the bottom of the trench in their agony, the worst place to be as the heavy gas tended to collect there.

Suddenly it was too much for some of the men who tried to avoid the gas by climbing out of the trench at the back. Seeing this, I suppose others followed suit. In a way this was the best thing to do, to get one's head in the upper layers of the gas where it was thinner, but to me it began to look like a panic and I was afraid of a retreat as some of the men were running back. All I could do was to grab the nearest man to me who was leaving the trench. I could not shout or even speak, I was fighting hard for breath which became shorter and shorter. I noticed the nearest machine gunner doing his best to work his gun. I happened to look over the parapet to see what he was trying to shoot at and to my horror across the mist I could see forms approaching. I stumbled to the gunner's aid but by this time we were both far too gone to use the gun. I felt as if my lungs were bursting, being torn out of my mouth. Everything swam in front of my eyes, I reeled and then there was merciful oblivion.

It must have been three hours before I came to. It was pitch dark and at first I wondered if I was alive. I looked up and could see the reflection of Verey lights in the sky. I could hear an occasional shell and the crank of a rifle. But a great lassitude seemed to hold my body. I could scarcely breathe, the breath coming in short sharp gasps and with every gasp a stab of pain. I could scarcely move my arms or legs. I must have lain there for another hour when a slight bit of strength seemed to come back to me, with some power of coherent thought.

The first thing I remembered was those advancing forms through the fog of gas. What had happened? They must have captured the position, there was scarcely any resistance. In fact, they must have broken right through. Perhaps by now they were in Ypres, perhaps beyond. How long had I lain there? Was it that night or the following night? I must be in German occupied territory now so was I a prisoner? I seemed to be in a trench of sorts, was I still where I fell unconscious? If I could only collect enough strength to get up. Had the Germans used the bayonet and cleaned us up, and had they missed me thinking me already dead? If so I might still have to undergo that unpleasant operation, there was no trusting them!

Presently I managed to turn over. A Verey light went up and I was startled to see the form of a sentry a few yards off. Was that a German? It must be. What was I to do now? Just lie there and hope for the best or should I make a noise, would he help me or would he finish me? Then I heard a voice in a low tone speaking to a comrade. Was it German he was talking? It did not sound guttural. I strained my ears and caught an English word or two. What a relief, I lay exhausted again with the reaction of it.

A few minutes later I tried to make a noise through my mouth. I could not as yet formulate any words and heard, 'Say, Bill there's som'ut down there a-moving, have a look will yer?' The said Bill came groping along and, as the reflection of a Verey light showed my face for a second, said, 'Hullo, Sonny, are yer all out or is any of yer a-kicking still?' I do not know if I grunted or not, but he bent low. 'Lor' blemine Alf,' he called to the sentry. 'Blowed if it ain't an orficer got that there blasted gas I reckon, he's a breathing like a gas engine. Pass the word along to our orficer will yer? How are you, Sir? Say Alf, I reckon he's in a bad way, looks like that young fellow in D Coy what the boys call "Baby".' (This was the first time I had heard my nickname, I used to be taken for about five years younger than I was.)

It turned out that this was our reserve company, now holding our trench. Major Jones had counter-attacked and re-captured the trench. I was carried down to battalion headquarters where the doctor had a look at me and asked questions, which I tried to answer. His verdict was that it was best to let me rest there, moving me just then would do more harm than good.

Major Jones asked if he could talk to me and the doctor said that I was not to speak but just shake or nod my head to any questions.

The upshot of all this was that he had seen that we were in difficulties, having watched the cloud rolling down the valley. The gas seemed to hang at the bottom until after a while the wind changed and the gas appeared to disintegrate and disperse. Though the reserve company got enough to make it extremely uncomfortable, the gas did not incapacitate them. Just before dark he decided to re-take our front line with the reserve company and he took the Germans by surprise, bayoneting them in return for having bayoneted a number of our chaps when helpless with gas.

I think I must have fallen asleep for I woke up in the early hours of the morning before daylight and found myself bumping along in a stretcher. I was deposited at the Advance Dressing Station where the Medical Officer attended to me. All that I can remember of this is that he seemed to be at his wit's end as to what to do for us as there had been no provision made for gas poisonings. He would have attended to any sort of wounds but this was quite a new thing. There were several others there in various stages of poisoning and one or two had died after arriving.

I think I was given a hot drink and went to sleep for a long time, the sleep being very welcome as it seemed to relieve the fearful ache in my lungs. Next day I seemed considerably better and the second day I got up and walked about, though having to drag my legs as if they were weighted. I told the MO I thought I would go back on duty. He replied, *'I don't think you ought to, but I know they are fearfully short of officers up there. However, you had better come back here as soon as you feel you cannot carry on. You seem to be recovering very much more quickly than most.'*

So I struggled back and I think my kudos with Major Jones was considerably enhanced thereby. He let me take things easily for a bit. In fact it was three weeks before my lungs felt normal again.

I learnt that during the gas attack on 2 May, Irwin who was in charge of A Coy, on the right of us (D), put up a splendid show. Most of the men were either down with gas or had retreated, but he grabbed one of his machine guns and with the help of one NCO, stuck to the gun working it to the last minute and only withdrew to avoid capture or be bayoneted. I believe he was recommended for the VC.

My own Company Commander Captain Reid had his arm shattered. Rowley got badly poisoned and went home with it. Wilmott and Capper were both wounded and that left Smith-Masters in charge of the company and I his only officer. When we had collected and sorted out the remnants of our company, there were 52 NCOs and men all told out of about 200 who started from Armentières.

For some days all of us felt the effects of the gas. We could not have done much more than fire a rifle had the need arisen. Luckily we had at this time a number of splendid French 75mm batteries which continuously played on the enemy and nipped in the bud several attempted attacks. To our right, however, these attacks were more vigorously thrust home and quite a general retirement was caused, with us being the pivot that did not move.

6 May 1915
2nd Essex Regt., 12th Brigade,
4th Division, B.E.F.

My dear Aunt Ethel,

I am sorry I have had no opportunity of writing for the last ten days or so but conditions have altered considerably and there aren't many comforts for writing. I haven't slept in a house since nor seen one worth sleeping in, half a brick wall being as much shelter as one can find, and we keep clear of them as much as possible. You see the new kind of envelope they have issued us with, I suppose correspondence will be subject to a much stricter censorship, which in itself forbodes a stir. I don't get any correspondence from England of any sort until days after they are due and I haven't heard any news of matters in general for a week past.

You see I am trying to talk as much as possible about private and family matters as the envelope tells one to, but it is very difficult to know where to draw the line, taking it strictly literally one would barely fill half a page.

I am not feeling as well as I do as a rule, but am considerably better, was pretty near unconscious for three or four hours; however I am pretty fair again, my lungs being still a little queer. Wasn't bad enough to go away from duty, however. I know a little more about chemistry now. Excuse the bad writing but the ground is shaking as if in an earthquake and I am pretty near deaf. Well, I hope all is well at home, thank Margaret for the Daily Mirrors which I got yesterday but probably ought to have received a fortnight ago.

I got two letters of yours, also rather late in arriving. I should be glad of any eatables now, having eaten nothing but bread and bully for a considerable time. I have a different servant now, who belonged to Captain Reid my company commander, I don't know where my own servant is, I hope he is all right poor chap. Well goodbye again for present.

With much love
Your loving nephew
Robin

[The envelope referred to is a green Active Service envelope, No. A.F.W3078, with the following note on the front: 'Correspondence in this envelope need not be censored Regimentally. The contents are liable to examination at the Base. The Certificate on the flap must be signed by the writer.' On the flap: 'I certify on my honour that the contents of this envelope refer to nothing but private and family matters. Signature (name only)': It is signed R.G. Monypenny.]

CHAPTER EIGHT

'The continuous angry flash looked very ominous'

Robin remained at the heart of the action as the 2nd Battalion endured one of its busiest and most treacherous months of the war. After the gas attack that so memorably marked the start of May there was a tussle as Germany tried a land-grab and the Allies repelled the advance, to the pounding orchestra of bombardment and counter-bombardment.

On 13 May Lieutenant Colonel Jones ordered that Shell Trap Farm, also known as Mousetrap Farm, be re-taken by C Company and, despite heavy firing from the enemy, it duly was. Now the remaining companies were charged with taking back 1,000 yards of trenches extending from the newly liberated farm.

This counter-attack was swift and successful. According to the Regimental Diary, A and B companies' attack '*was splendidly carried out with great dash and determination. They were subjected to a very heavy artillery fire, both high explosive and shrapnel, and on reaching the ridge, to heavy machine gun fire. They never faltered in spite of fairly heavy casualties.*'

According to one account, men of the London Rifle Brigade in a nearby trench stood up to cheer as the Essex men strove forward.

The report submitted by the 11th Brigade said:

'*Yesterday attacks were made on Hampshires and Rifle Brigade, both being beaten off. Left company East Lancashires shelled to pieces and Shell Trap Farm taken. Counter attack by Essex restored the situation and Essex also retook trenches on our right vacated by cavalry.*'

In the evening a message was received from General de Lisle, commanding 1st Cavalry Division, conveying his thanks to the Essex Regiment for '*gallant and prompt assistance this morning. The Cavalry Division's opinion is voiced by the whole of the Fourth Division.*'

A message was also sent to 'Lumpy' Jones from 12th Brigade Brigadier, saying: '*Just a line to tell you how delighted I am that the old corps have done so splendidly. Everybody is talking about it.*'

After the successful attack the Essex Battalion was relieved in the trenches and headed down the line. Any sense of euphoria was quickly dispelled.

The Regimental Diary recounts:

'On arrival at the support trench, wet and very cold, the Bn had the pleasure of finding that packs and great coats had been ransacked and many things taken, presumably by troops sent to occupy the trench when the Bn moved out.'

Casualties that day amounted to 37 killed, 94 wounded and 49 missing.

In the skies above the Royal Flying Corps was helping with reconnaissance in the same way that balloons had done at the outbreak of war. Manned flight had begun little more than a decade before war started and at first it was thought the main role of aeroplanes would be to take overhead photographs of enemy lines. Two of the five squadrons sent to France at the beginning of the war were led by former Essex Regiment men.

The military use of aeroplanes was still in its infancy in 1915 when radio transmitters for Morse code messages had been newly introduced into the cockpit.

At the time aerial combat was restricted. Those who fired at the enemy with pistols usually missed. Aeroplanes were not sufficiently fast or agile to act as fighters. It wasn't until synchronised machine guns were the norm that aerial duels were routinely fought.

Strategic bombing was also a distant dream. The payload of early aeroplanes was tiny and hit the target by luck rather than judgement. However, and typically in times of war, advances were swift and the Royal Air Force, formed on 1 April 1918, looked a different creature to the Royal Flying Corps it replaced.

At the end of the Second Battle of Ypres Germany's gains were blunted but the Kaiser's army was now within shelling distance of the town, which was consequently obliterated. German losses of 35,000 stood at about half of those suffered by the Allies.

ROBIN

On 5 May we were relieved for a spell in Battalion Reserve, which meant that, though we were still in the front fighting area, we could get our boots and clothes off and take things a bit more easily. (ie we were the reserve battalion to the brigade, the other three battalions of the brigade holding the front lines and supports). There was no going back to billets as down at Armentières, there were no billets left for at least ten miles to our rear, everything having been flattened. But we were in a line of trenches and dug-outs where we could move about above ground by daylight, though we were still subjected to shell fire.

We had not taken our boots off since leaving Armentières and my feet were in such a state that I could hardly get my boots off and my socks were almost non-existent. That was from 22 April to 5 May, a period of thirteen days.

Our spell there was short lived for we had to move off in support of a portion of the line more to the right which was being heavily pressed. We moved up on the night of 7 May. Smith-Masters and I found ourselves with D Company in a support trench that was more a kind of ditch behind a hedge where a few bits of corrugated iron from a neighbouring broken down building were stretched across this ditch. When it started to rain we were glad of that iron. We did not, however, like the look of things. The front line ahead of us seemed to be very active and the big guns all around seemed to be extremely busy. The continuous angry flash looked very ominous. As the night wore on the thunder of the guns increased. In fact, for what seemed hours, there seemed to be a rising crescendo until all around a terrible storm of heavies broke out. All the powers of hell seemed to be let loose. We could scarcely hear each other talk, though we shouted.

The earth trembled continuously. Great big shells, and bigger, kept coming nearer. There is something particularly terrifying about a big shell on a dark night, for you can hear the deep drone of its flight for about two thirds of its trajectory, which is high and narrow in the shape of an inverted U. (I am writing of howitzer shells, naval gun shells usually have a much flatter trajectory.) During the last third of a howitzer shell's flight the sound is outstripped by the speed of the shell so that you cannot hear it until after the shell has burst. This means that you cannot really hear the one that is actually going to hit you, but you think you do because you hear the first two thirds of its trajectory. Even those that land 100 yards away sound as if they are making directly for you. What protection is a sheet of corrugated iron?

So often we held our breath that night waiting for that direct hit, till one moment we thought it had come. As a matter of fact we thought right, it did not land on the iron but just the other side of the hedge, a crack appeared in the ground between us and the big nose of an 8-inch shell showed itself, but the shell was a dud or else I would not be writing this now. The concussion of it hitting the bank bumped us up a few inches in the air as we sat there. After a moment's shock we cleared out and looked for another sheet of iron further along, just in case the 'dud' might have a delayed action fuse. [Shells were sometimes furnished with delayed action fuses or failed to explode if internal mechanisms jammed.]

This terrific bombardment was kept up for six days and six nights without ceasing, a tremendous blast of devastation. The enemy must have had several relays of batteries as well as gunners working round the clock. Hour after hour an inexhaustible downpour of huge shells fell with relentless fury. It was a contest of men on one side against material on the other. Trench after trench was obliterated. Down they crashed while men were either buried or blown into oblivion, or simply sat there, dazed, stupid and cowering, just waiting for the end.

During this storm the front line to our right was so utterly obliterated, that the Germans assaulted, passed through and took the village of Wieltje, their guns never ceasing but just lengthening range.

British reserves were collected and hurled into the break and still under that terrific downpour they regained Wieltje. To the right of Wieltje another terrific assault by German Infantry drove the Canadians out, but with the help of more reserves they reformed farther back. Other units were forced back on either side to conform with this movement. The terrible pounding by enemy artillery went on and so heavy was it that the efforts of our own artillery, which was hopelessly outnumbered, could not be noticed at all.

The British position was being gradually eaten away. Trench after trench was obliterated with not a soul left in them alive. The enemy just lengthened the range and walked into them. The troops were so thinned out, reserves so short, that the cavalry had to be pitched into them to act as infantry; and on 12 May – there had been in the meantime no break in the ceaseless storm of projectiles – the downpour if anything increased in fury and, to make matters worse, a gale and driving rain started.

This ceaseless shelling began to tell badly on us all and we had to grind our teeth to try and bear it. Our nerves were strung to an excessive pitch. Quite a number of men went mad. In my own platoon there was a man I had been watching. He had a peculiar wild look in his eyes and his teeth were chattering. Suddenly he pulled the bayonet off his rifle and came at me brandishing it like a dagger. I managed to seize his wrist, but he had the strength that madness gives. My sergeant tackled him from behind and we pinned him to the ground then tied his arms and legs with his putties. He was stark, raving mad, his brain had snapped. A shell landed on him later and his worries were over.

So far the line just to our front had managed to hold but that night we went up into it as the defenders were mostly dead. The line of the trench was scarcely visible, we could hardly see which were shell holes and which the trench.

This movement and action must have saved our brains from cracking. The next day came three more assaults, all in the hail of shells, and for the first time my revolver came into use. In the last assault some of the Germans got right into our position and there was a few minutes of violent struggle. Two had gone down before my revolver, when as a bayonet came at me I realised I had an empty gun in my hand. I hurled it at my assailant's face, this made him shift his arm up as if to shield his face, and I grabbed his rifle with all my might just below the muzzle. Just then a wild, cursing apparition with a British uniform and a bayonet dripping with hot red blood, plunged it into my adversary's stomach. We seemed to have gained the ascendancy and some of my men were hurling bombs as fast as they could at others of the enemy still approaching the position. I don't quite know how but this affair eventually simmered down and we still held the position, though the shell fire continued with renewed vigour.

The whole battalion, or what was left of it, was relieved that night and the brigade went into divisional reserve. It must be realised that at Ypres all these movements, front line to supports, supports to reserves and vice versa, meant that we were all the time in the area of heavy shelling. There was no such thing as going into billets. Even if there had been any houses left intact, the salient was too active a place to do anything other than get a temporary relief in a line of defences further back.

While in reserve this time, we received a few more reinforcements in the form of drafts. My company, in which I had been the sole officer to come back, had dwindled to about thirty men. These drafts brought it up again to about a hundred, or half strength. An officer who had been wounded previously and returned, took charge over my head as he was senior to me. There were in the drafts, some men returned from hospital and a few new lads, quite youngsters. I was sorry for them as their baptism of fire was not gentle.

Once again we had scarcely rested when we were required in action again. I remember just having had a wash and a shave – the rain had supplied the water – and a bit of a meal, when the stand to arms order came.

The cavalry who had, as previously mentioned, been put in line to do infantry work were being overwhelmed by a fresh assault. We were called up to rescue their left flank. So over the top we went in broad daylight, up a long slope for 2,000 yards, amidst an inferno of shells, the screeching of bullets and a downpour of rain. We moved up in extended order, keeping a beautiful line as if on parade, when within 500 yards of the enemy occupying the cavalry's left position, we were halted and lay down. This was either to give us a breather and collect more control over the men or perhaps some hitch had occurred elsewhere, I don't know which. Anyway I remember lying there with two new youths, one on each side of me at a few paces interval. Great shells were falling all around and machine-gun bullets spattered mud over us at intervals. One of those boys who could not have been more than twenty was sobbing hopelessly. I tried to cheer him up with a few words. The next instant there was a rush of air and sound and an 8-inch howitzer shell landed right on top of him. His worries were over. The blast of the shell displacing air at my low level rolled me over several times, but I was none the worse bar a shaking. The poor chap had completely disappeared, where he had lain was nothing but a reeking hole. The boy on the other side had fainted.

Presently we moved on, and just before the final rush into the enemy in our front line trench I grabbed a dead man's rifle and bayonet, having had a sudden feeling that a revolver might be inadequate. I do not know how much steel was crossed but as I moved up I was busy emptying the magazine of the rifle into our opponents and by the time I had reached bayonet distance there did not seem to be many of them there and those were holding up their hands in surrender. They must have been more terrified than us at the prospect of cold steel. So we collected the first batch of prisoners that I had handled and at the first opportunity, sent them back under a guard. Quite a number of them, however, didn't get very far as they got killed by their own shell fire.

I was looking around for the other youth who had been lying near me on the advance up the slope and who had fainted. I found him dead with a bullet through the chest, lying some 20 yards behind the trench. He never reached the chance of crossing bayonets with the enemy. When was my turn coming?

From that night the fighting died down temporarily. I supposed the enemy was getting exhausted as well as ourselves. The shell depots must have wanted re-filling after the millions expended in the last few days. Their guns must have worn out the barrels and wanted re-lining.

Aeroplane observers of this battle said that the whole landscape was one heaving, smoking, flaming inferno from end to end for six days without cessation and our gunners had found it impossible to make an adequate answer.

The next day our exhausted division was replaced by another and we got the first few days real rest we had had since about 14 April, more than a month previously.

> 16 May 1915
> 2/nd Essex Regt., 12th Brigade,
> 4th Division, B.E.F.
>
> My dear Aunt Ethel,
> I have written you several letters but it appears from yours that you have not received them yet. However here's another one, though I am afraid it rather what a Tommy would call a 'cadger' i.e. only asking for things.
>
> I don't know whether it will appear in the papers or not, but the regiment has been especially congratulated 'for saving the whole situation'; we have been somewhat hard hit and I myself am minus a good bit of my belongings. I have lost my canteen (I can do without that) I have found Captain Reid's overcoat, I am using it although it is much too big for me; but my Burberry, hat, razor and everything else except what I stand up in has been stolen, because we had to leave them behind on account of a sudden surprise attack and when the glorious remnants got back we found everything looted.
>
> Could you send me – put it down to my debit & I'll let you have the money when I can lay my hands on some – a waterproof coat, I saw advertised in Land

and Water, *a kind of a combination waterproof service hat with flap coming over one's neck and a mackintosh affair, I have tried to draw it but unsuccessfully. However if you look in the advertisements of* Land & Water *you will see it. Oh I have just found a copy; the cap is the 'Soft Service Cap' price 16/6 at Studd & Millington, 51 Conduit Street. And the mackintosh is called a Stormproof at Elverys, 31 Conduit Street.*

I am sorry to say another regiment pinched all our stuff, but we have made arrangements to mount a guard over all kit left behind in future.

You might send me a cheap safety razor, a cheap one is good enough out here.

Also will you send me out my brown revolver case? Please register everything you send, otherwise somebody might lay hands on them on the way.

My uniform is torn with shrapnel but I will carry on with it for the present. If it gets worse I shall have to send home for another pair of breeches from that breeches maker in town, I forget his name.

[The remainder of the letter is missing. There is no envelope. The paper has the crest of the 3rd Essex embossed on it.]

We moved out down past Ypres and bivouacked in a beautiful park at Vlamertinghe. Here there was a large mansion where some of the staff [officers] lived – the lucky chaps – catered for by a nice French, or was it Belgian, family. No wonder the staff did not really understand the war.

For the first time for weeks we got a good night's rest: a bath, regular meals and a bit of leisure to write home. That home, even the travesty of one that I had known, how far away it seemed now. What did people in England know? Were they taking the war seriously? Were the miners striking again? If so, they were stabbing us in the back and they ought at least to be made to go through what we had just gone through. They were drawing three times the wages of us poor cannon fodder chaps.

We had four days rest, four days in which we tried to forget the war but how utterly impossible. We knew we had soon to re-enter that hell and it was the worst for knowing what it was like.

Up we marched again through the shambles of Ypres, past the ruined Cloth Hall, out into the sea of shell holes and lacerated earth where there was a confusion of barbed wire fences, shattered trenches criss-crossing here and there in all directions, gaunt splintered trees and occasional battered and smoking farm houses or an *auberge* – all other buildings having been leveled to the ground. And there were dead men and dead horses scattered everywhere. There had not been the time to bury the half of them, so great had been the slaughter and so dangerous the situation that at times even stretcher bearers, cooks, orderlies and anybody who could hold a rifle had been thrown into the fight.

As we moved up this time we noticed a dreadful stench. The weather was turning warm while the dead lay unburied. It was a ghastly miasma and it hung over the district for weeks, being ever present no matter where you turned or what you did.

This time we found ourselves in the line a bit to the right of where we had been first gassed on 2 May, and still on the nearer slope of the same hill.

20 May 1915
2/nd Essex Regt., 12th Brigade,
4th Division, B.E.F.

My dear Aunt Ethel,

Thanks for your letter which I received today. I believe we end our repose the day after tomorrow & shift back to the scene of the fighting.

I should like to tell you where we were, we were in the 2nd Battle for Calais near that much talked about place in Belgium which has been so much shelled with its famous hall.

I asked for a pair of breeches from Harry Hall, will you get them and keep them till I ask you to send them? Because it is no use sending them now as we go back to the fighting & it will only be in my way, but I will let you know when i.e. that will be the next time we get a rest. I should, however, like the other things, i.e. the stormproof mackintosh from Elverys in Conduit Street, & the Soft service cap from Studd & Millington & the Automatic Colt Pistol size 475mm unless you have already got another size & ammunition, 50 rounds. I enclose a cheque for £10, let me know if that does not cover everything.

We have got some Terriers attached to us for instruction for a week or two.

It has been terribly wet the last two or three days but is clearing up now & is getting warmer too. I wish I was home however, for tennis and sea bathing etc. This is no gentleman's war as one might call it, simply scientific cunning & bestiality. However I pity the German that comes anywhere near an Essex bayonet, the feeling especially since this gas is one of intense hatred.

I wonder if the War Office will give me a regular commission, my name has gone in for one and you might watch the London Gazette. *Could you send me some note paper & envelopes, similar to what I am writing on, it is much easier to write on than the pads. This happens to be some of Queen Alexandra's gift.*

By the bye could you send me a dog's collar with the following inscription on a little plate on it for my dog.

'Fritz'
2/Lt Monypenny, 2nd Essex Regiment

He is growing fast & will be a huge one I think, I keep him with the transport now. [Continued on a piece of squared paper] *I hope I manage to get him home later on, I shall try hard any rate if I go home any time, though if one is wounded one is packed off at once without delay & of course if one is bad there is*

no time in which to think about anything. I wish I had still my camera out here,
that is the most ridiculous order about not having them.

  Well goodbye again for present. I hope you get the cheque all right.
  With much love
  Your loving nephew
    Robin
We have a sub here who used to be great pals with Von Hindenburg & knew his
family well in Berlin!

The next few days it was fairly quiet although away to the right the thunder of
the guns had started again. Apparently, during the lull our foe had been piling
up the shells again and collecting fresh stores of poison gas.

At Vlamertinghe we had been issued with the first attempt at gas helmets.
These consisted of a woolen or flannel helmet, soaked in an alkali solution,
for pulling over the head and have two rubber and mica eyepieces and a
mouthpiece for blowing out the used air. They were not as effective as the
proper rubber and metal oxygenated helmets issued months later but never-
theless they mitigated the effects of the gas somewhat if you managed to slip
them on quickly enough and they probably saved a lot of lives.

CHAPTER NINE

'Then the downpour of steel started, a veritable drum-fire, almost blotting everything out'

British soldiers were fighting in the most relentlessly brutal war ever fought for the flag. With conditions ranging from fair to abysmal it was strict discipline that would keep men at their posts and obeying orders. Without it, senior officers reasoned, there would be wholesale mutiny.

The military punishment for cowardice, desertion and a whole host of other offences, including striking a senior officer, was execution. It was a sentence carried out on some 350 occasions.

For years after the war had ended it was felt a soldier who had been shot at dawn was the subject of stigma and shame. That all changed in 2006 when combatants shot for cowardice were pardoned, after a long-running campaign by relatives. The most potent plank of the argument for a universal pardon was the way warfare shredded the nerves of soldiers and caused a condition that would soon be recognized as shell shock. At the time, however, the evidence of mental stress played no part in the judicial process.

First to be tried, blindfolded and shot by a six-man firing squad was Private Thomas Highgate of the Royal West Kents. He died within an hour of his sentence on 8 September 1914, having fled the Battle of Mons. Formerly a farm labourer who enlisted prior to the outbreak of war, he was discovered in civilian clothing hiding in a barn. There was no one to speak for him at his hearing. Most of his immediate comrades were already dead.

Today there's no evidence men reported by Robin for their lack of metal in the face of battle action faced a firing squad, although they may well have gone before a military court.

Only one man from the 2nd Essex was shot at dawn during the First World War and the event was before Robin's arrival. Private Archibald Browne, 2nd Battalion, Essex Regiment was 26 when he died. He went missing in November 1914 after being ordered to escort a sick man away from the front line. After being found by French police in a house in Hazebrouck wearing civilian clothes, he was charged with desertion, breaking into a house in search of plunder and escaping from arrest – so briefly the officer in charge of him hadn't noticed he was gone.

His defence was that he got lost in a snowstorm and been captured by Germans, from whom he later escaped. Captain Arthur Halahan, from the Essex regiment, presided over the hearing, presumably mindful of recent orders for robust punishment for stragglers and deserters during the recent British retreat as a show of strength to the local French police. Browne, who came from Ingatestone, Essex, died on 19 December 1914 without having spoken at his trial.

During the First World War there were 3,080 death sentences handed down by senior officers but only 10 per cent were carried out. French, Canadian and New Zealand troops met the same fate. However, no American or Australian soldiers were shot.

There's a suggestion too that officers were treated differently to serving soldiers. On 30 September 1916 the 2nd Essex regimental diary reveals that a lieutenant was tried for being asleep in a dug-out during the hours of morning 'stand to'. He was duly acquitted.

Lieutenant Nigel Benjamin Bavin, who Robin replaced as the commander of B Company, was aged 19 when he died. His promotion to lieutenant was announced in the *London Gazette* only after his death. His parents, Benjamin and Alice Bavin, of Postwich, Norfolk, lost another son in October 1917. Lieutenant Antony James Bavin was on the destroyer HMS *Mary Rose* on convoy duty in the North Sea when it was shelled at close quarters by German ships which had been mistaken for British. Only five men survived.

ROBIN

On 23 May a shell exploded in the dug-out of the officer commanding B Coy, Acting Captain Bavin, while he was having a meal and it blew him to bits. A telephone message came through to say that I was to go and take command in his place. B Coy was situated in support about 150 yards in rear of the battalion's front line, in rather an isolated position by itself and rather exposed on the front side of a hill. It also had nobody on either flank and nobody to the rear for at least 500 yards. The line here was very thinly held owing to the huge casualties in the previous fighting.

I went over that night to take charge. I was sorry to leave my old comrades, though glad of the chance of some promotion. However, I felt a bit uneasy. I knew things were brewing up again and these men were strangers to me. In a tight corner one wants to know one's men well and they must have confidence in you. I felt it would be quite all right provided we had about forty-eight hours to get to know each other. Though we were of the same battalion, and some of them knew of me by name, we had scarcely seen each other owing to the peculiar nature of the campaign – and officially we had not come into contact at all. Added to this the last company commander had been a considerably older man than me and looked his age, while I still looked no more than a school boy.

Before arriving there I had a telephone message from the CO (Lieutenant Colonel Jones, now promoted to his proper rank), to send B Coy commander's body down to him as it had been decided to start a cemetery near Ypres. When I got to B Coy and asked about the late Coy Commander I was told that there was nothing left of him. On examining his dug-out, I found that this was probably true but there appeared to have been no attempt to try and find something of him or his belongings. I took this as a not very good sign of the spirit of the company. I asked who was the senior person left in the company? It turned out to be a very newly joined and very young 2nd lieutenant of about 19 who had had practically no experience of soldiering of any sort. The company sergeant major was also newly promoted and very young for his position, though he appeared a type who would cope when he had had some experience in his new job.

I gave orders for the late OC Coy's dug-out to be properly cleared and any remains to be collected together. In the meantime I tried to contact the colonel and found that the field telephone line had been cut by shell fire, and no attempt had been made to repair it from our end. I immediately went off the deep end about this and said it must be seen to at once. By the time this had been done, the remains of my late predecessor had been collected so I contacted the colonel about the body and he told me to send the remains down in a sandbag and they would be buried in the new cemetery. I am afraid there was more earth than anything else in that sandbag.

I had a chat with the young officer and told him to stick by me for the present, then I went round the position to have a look at all the men and chat with them, spending more time with the NCOs. I examined the trench and the two machine-gun positions. I had a gas helmet drill to ensure that they all knew how to put them on quickly – this was all during that first night of my taking over. I sent a patrol out to get in touch with our front line to make sure they knew we were there and to get to know the lie of the land, intending to go out myself for the same purpose later when I had seen to other urgent matters, and if the enemy gave me time.

Presently I heard voices and the colonel appeared with an orderly. He had come to see how I was faring, bless him, and it was no joke looking for people or places under those conditions.

Having showed his satisfaction at what I had done so far he said, 'Now, Monypenny, you are taking over a new company at an awkward time. Get to know your men as soon as possible and let us hope that nothing desperate will happen for a few days, but it probably will. You are rather isolated here and the heavy shelling will most likely cut the field telephone lines again and you will have to act on your own *initiative. The thing is to keep an eye on that front line, you are here to support those soldiers. As soon as you see them being hard pressed and in danger of losing their trench to the enemy, counter-attack immediately. Go hell for leather at them and do your best to hold that trench. If you don't know how things are going and in doubt, go all the same. Better to be too early than too late.'*

As soon as the colonel had gone, I proceeded to inform the company of his orders so that they knew where they came from. I felt I was still too new to them to be fully confident in my judgment. I explained that as soon as they saw me leap to the parapet and go forward, they must follow me. One machine gun and its crew only were to remain behind to cover our advance or our retreat later if we were forced back. The other was to come up with me with the rest of the company. Having seen to everything I could think of, I lay down for some rest and dozed off. I was up two or three times again that night to see if things were all right. Just before dawn we stood to arms. As the sky to the east was showing its first glimmer, we got a whiff of gas; then the gas alarm gong sounded in the front line trenches and we all pulled on our helmets.

Then the downpour of steel started, a veritable drum fire, almost blotting everything out. I walked up and down the trench a few times, telling the men to watch the front for the assault that would surely come and to remind them what orders I had given about advancing when I gave the signal. I explained that it would only be given if the front line defenders were being over-whelmed or appeared to me to be so. The din of the shell fire was awful and from inside the helmet it was almost impossible for one's voice to be heard quite close let alone by a whole company. Owing to the smoke of the shell bursts and the cloud of gas which was now thickening and even penetrating our helmets, visibility was very poor near and around us, but the front line trench on the crest of the hill up against the quickly brightening sky in the east stood in fairly clear relief.

Suddenly we heard the roar of musketry all along the front and we knew that the assault had started, then through the haze the advancing masses of Germans, company upon company of them. The roar of musketry and rattle of machine guns increased. The front lines of Germans wavered and fell, more took their places, stumbling over the dead and dying. On they came, the barbed wire holding them up for a while. But increasing numbers pushed their way over the hundreds that were falling. Then we saw some of our men get up out of their trench to meet them in the open. After a preliminary clash they were borne back. It was time for me to up and act.

We were still enveloped in gas which had penetrated somewhat more in our helmets and caused us considerable discomfort. The shells were bursting rapidly along our parapet, the Germans intending to prevent supports going up to our front line. Both the company sergeant major and I went up and down our trench shouting ourselves hoarse, saying we had to go over before we leapt on the parapet.

To my dismay I saw only a few men and the machine-gun team get up. I dashed up and down along the top of the parapet shouting, '*Come on boys, wake up, come on.*' Then in despair I wrenched my helmet off to be heard louder. Spluttering and coughing I dashed up and down, then finally I drew my revolver and threatened to shoot any man who did not move. This seemed to wake them up and I saw a more or less general move forward so I turned round and went ahead. We rushed up and charged into the front line just in time to rescue the remnants almost overwhelmed in a close encounter still going on up and down the trench. Our advent, however, turned the tide. Some of the Germans bolted back, a few surrendered.

God – I never felt so rotten in my life at the thought that we had nearly failed. Why the deuce had those men wavered? I had never seen any others behave like that before. Had it been D Company such a thing would never have happened. That was it, I suppose, we were too new to each other. I had been in command less than twelve hours and the crisis had come too soon.

When we collected ourselves and the remnants of the other company that had held the front line, I seemed to have a large number missing. We decided to hold the line and let the remnants of the other company occupy our old support trench that evening. I told the officer to send up to me the machine gun with its team I had left behind there and anyone else of my company who happened to be there in a fit state to fight. To my surprise two whole sections (half a platoon) as well as the machine-gun section came up. They had not budged. I got hold of the two NCOs in charge of these sections and told them they were under arrest with all the men under them and that I would deal with them as soon as we were relieved. I was going to telephone the colonel to that effect as soon as the linesmen had been out after dark to mend the lines.

As events happened I forgot about that business for quite a time. During the course of that evening (24 May) we were attacked several times, so it was lucky I had come up to their support. We also received from the enemy a pretty plentiful supply of tear gas shells. These were not as deadly as the chlorine gas, but made our eyes smart and water a great deal, interfering with our vision. If you happened to stir up a puddle of water by stepping in it, the stuff would come out of it again, it having been absorbed.

The brigade to our right was very heavily attacked that day. It had its right flank resting on a shattered farmstead called 'Shell Trap Farm', named thus because it was situated at the apex of a salient within the larger Ypres Salient. Consequently the Germans were able to enfilade it with shells from almost all quarters, even from the rear and also the trenches for some distance forming the salient on both sides of it. The torrent of shells was too much for the brigade on our right who got it even more fiercely than we did. The poison gas, followed by this bombardment which absolutely obliterated the trenches, had so weakened the defenders that they were unable to withstand the continuous infantry assaults and the few that were left were forced back to their support line.

Thus we found ourselves with our flank in danger and only protected by a few remnants of a single company of another regiment on our right under their colonel, who sent me a message requesting extra bombers as they were being bombed back along the trenches towards us. I sent a party of bombers and with their aid the Germans were kept at bay.

Just before dusk a panting and wounded runner brought me a message that the divisional commander had decided to launch the reserves in an attack at 7pm to recover Shell Trap Farm and that the rest of us were in the meantime to hold on to the last man. So I explained to our men that our job was to stick it out to enable our friends on the right to try and regain lost ground.

After dark, the colonel on my right with his handful of men and my bombers, were driven back to me and, in trying to have another bomb attack organized, he was badly wounded.

By now the enemy was beginning to work back round our flank with the aid of darkness. My last orders had been to hold at all costs, it was now past 7pm and I could neither see nor hear any signs of that intended counter-attack. I was in a bit of a quandary. If the attack did not come off within the next few minutes I would be surrounded with probably the loss of all hands as well as two machine guns and considerable ammunition.

Just then I received a message from the left flank that the attack was off and we must withdraw to the rear. A message like that on a dark night, with Germans round our right flank might very easily have emanated from a German source, so in order to make sure I went along to our left flank. I found the flank file who were supposed to keep us in touch with the next company had just got hit by a shell and both men were dead and on going further along there was no sign of anybody. We were literally left in the lurch, though not of course intentionally.

I hurried back, explained the situation to my NCOs, collected the machine guns, small arms ammunition and wounded and moved back in echelon formation, one platoon covering the next. We went back with our bayonets fixed and ready and as silently as possible. My left flank (facing the rear) tumbled right into some Germans and sharp short work of thrusting and jabbing ensued in the darkness. I edged my way off to the left to see how my chaps were faring and in the darkness nearly lost myself altogether.

After wandering about a bit feeling thoroughly scared and being entirely by myself, I suddenly stumbled into somebody and nearly got a British bayonet into me for my pains. He had just heard a good hearty British curse in time. Apparently my flank had taken the enemy by surprise and cut their way through them. We now wasted no more time and went back as fast as we could without losing each other and with luck, losing no more men. We seemed in the dark to have been going for ages and I wondered where on earth the rest of our troops had got to or whether they had been forced into a general retreat. At last we stumbled into more bayonets waiting ready and nearly got spiked by our own troops again. We were now about 1,000 yards back from our original trench as we discovered later, holding a well and solidly made line of trenches which had not as yet been wired.

The men whom I had told were under arrest had come up to me at dusk and had taken part in the bomb fighting and moved to the rear with me. They had behaved well since their previous failure, all except one corporal whom I had been watching as there was something shifty about him that I did not like. In fact, I had wondered how on earth he had ever come to be promoted. Instead of setting an example to men under him he seemed to take the tail end of everything. For the rest, however, I felt partly sorry. I knew I was only doing my duty as things like that could not be allowed to occur unnoticed. Even if I had wished to, I could not withdraw the arrests, because it is the law that only higher authority than the arrestor can do so. Thus on reaching the rear defensive line I had the unpleasant task of informing the colonel what had happened. The colonel dealt summarily with the men, but he remanded the NCOs concerned for a Field General Court Martial, which was held shortly after when we had had a few days in the reserve.

The sergeant major and two other NCOs supported me in my evidence as witnesses. One defendant NCO said that he had not heard any word of advance from me, the other said that his men would not go forward and the corporal I have mentioned with the shifty eyes actually declared that I walked up and down the parapet threatening to shoot any man who left the trench. This man was obviously extremely agitated, wondering what was going to happen to him, and I could only surmise that he lost his head in making such a statement. Anyway it just about queered his pitch in the face of all the other evidence.

In mitigation I put forward on their behalf the unfortunate circumstances that I had only just taken over the company that night, not having served in it before, and the men had scarcely seen me in the dark. Many of them probably did not know what I looked like, not having seen me at all before – though there could be no possible doubt as to what order had been given. But there is a vast difference in an extreme urgency of just automatically obeying an order and following a man you know well.

The NCOs lost their stripes in addition to field punishments for certain periods. It may be thought unnecessary for me to have brought up these unfortunate incidents, but if one is to chronicle the true happenings, the bad as well as the good must be put on record.

27 May 1915
2/nd Essex Regt., 12th Brigade,
4th Division, B.E.F.

My dear Aunt Ethel,

Thanks very much for the parcel which I received yesterday with cake, the fruit, galantine, chocolate etc. It came in most opportune as I had not anything for 24 hours & have had only bread & bully for some days. Could you send me out small parcels and oftener? If you could send me a very small one every day because we shift about daily & we are unable to take away food with us but have to leave what is not eaten which means I have to give away a lot sometimes, but if you could do as I suggest I should most days have something; of course the post does not always reach us. We have been having an awfully warm time lately and I haven't had any sleep for the past week. We got another dose of that gas; the respirators do a certain amount of good I think because I wasn't quite so bad this time, a good thing too as I had to make a counter-attack all on my own.

I am OC Company now, I think they ought to give two stars for it, because it is an awfully responsible job & none too easy. We have been shelled like blazes & it is terribly nerve racking to sit tight with those great Jack Johnsons dropping about in hundreds blowing people to bits & never knowing when one's turn is to come next. Somehow people at home seem to think trench warfare a soft job, I should much rather do the old open fighting. The men get their nerves absolutely broken & it is an awful job to control them especially as I have only inexperienced officers to help, the only one who has been a help being a captain in charge of one of my platoons who belongs to another regiment & is attached to us. I haven't had a shave for six days and look an awful sight.

Could you find out for me from Cox's what I have in the bank & whether I have been allotted any field allowance or any other sort of allowances, fuel & light for later on. I ought to get 6d a day command allowance for being OC Company. Had no letters from you for last three or four days. The weather luckily has been good lately or else I don't know what it would be like in this trench, it is bad enough already.

Could you send me a copy of a military book called Ceremonial *in the 'Imperial Army' series. It will help me with my company; get the latest edition.*

I have had no papers lately, only Land & Water, *no* Daily Mail *for ages.*

Well good bye for present

Your loving nephew

  Robin

In this company I discovered a corporal by the name of Clarke (naturally his nickname was Knobby, all Clarkes seemed to be called Knobbies), a big bluff ginger-haired individual. I could not understand why he had not been made at least a sergeant, he was one of the same rank as that shifty-eyed creature, but he was worth a dozen of the latter. The only thing that might have been against him was that he was not very well educated and had just a slight stutter, but he was a splendid soldier and as true as steel. During the fighting all day on 24th May he was splendid. In the advance in the early morning he and his men were the first to leap out and he had helped to rally most of the men. He had taken charge voluntarily of the bombers on our right front and led the men forward several times when they were inclined to be down hearted. I got him promoted to sergeant and also recommended him for a medal, but I never learnt whether he received the latter or not. I can only imagine that some of the earlier company commanders were not very good judges of men.

31 May 1915
2/nd Essex, 12th Brigade,
My dear Aunt Ethel,   *4th Division, B.E.F.*
Many thanks for your letter, and the parcel, with razor etc; as regards Fritz's collar, he is only a puppy at present but will be a great big dog, not fox terrier type, but you know these big creamy coloured continental dogs that draw carts. At present he is about the size of a fox terrier, but if you send me a collar for a larger dog with plenty of holes to insert the buckle strap so as to fit him at present. Don't forget what I asked to have inscribed on it: 'Fritz' 2/Lt Monypenny 2/nd Essex. I call him Fritz because I believe he came over from the German lines, souvenir fashion.

Send me out my breeches because we are going back for a rest & I shall be able to get these mended in the meantime & I shall be able to get at my valise so as to put one pair in. Also will you please get Harry Hall to make me a tunic (coat) of exactly the same material, because this one is torn and is rather shabby. I shall wear these in action but when we go back for rests I want something decent for parades, especially being a company commander. We shall probably be out of action till 8 June, so don't send me any clothes after a date which will reach me after the 8th. Haven't you seen anything of the Essex in the papers. See the 24th Daily Mail *& the 26th* Daily Express, *also I enclose the following which will give you our @@@@@@@ [position crossed through]. Did I tell you, I have found a very nice Kukri [Gurkha knife] in a scabbard?*

I have got three subs under me now and one captain of the Northumberland Fusiliers (Terriers) who is attached for a while.

I get a horse to ride now when out of the trenches.

Yes, do keep sending me the Daily Mail, *I miss it very much.*

Thanks awfully for Land & Water, Illustrated *& Margaret for* Daily Mirror *& cigarettes. Thanks awfully for the cap also. Very nice.*

Jolly glad Italy has joined in.

Yes, I got a letter from Jack. I'll lie low till I hear whether I have got a commission in the British Army & then perhaps I had better apply, but I doubt whether Captain Jones will allow me to leave before the War is over.

With much love

Your loving nephew

Robin

Shortly afterwards in the same neighbourhood we received a few more reinforcements by draft. We must have been hard up for men, for this appeared to me a very poor lot. One or two were of distinctly very low type, in fact two of them I am positive were not mentally balanced correctly. The result very shortly appeared in a startling manner. There was one morning a very sharp, short and violent bombardment and assault. To my amazement I saw two figures fling down their rifles and dash madly to the rear shouting, '*retire, retire!*' Nobody else budged, everybody looked back in blank surprise. For a moment I was bewildered but not so Sergeant Knobby Clarke. He was up over the back, cursing them and blazing at them with his rifle. I do not think he hit them, but the poor creatures were later rounded up by the battle police, and to be caught by the battle police generally meant a court martial resulting in a firing squad. I had to give evidence at their court martial. After the usual evidence I made a strong appeal that they should be medically examined as I was sure they were mentally unbalanced and had no right to have ever been recruited. I don't know what happened to them.

CHAPTER TEN

'There is a German sniper over there who has just parted my hair for me'

Heavy guns had moved from being a side show in previous wars to centre stage, as each side tried to blast the other out of its trenches. In northern France railways could deliver shells straight to the artillery. But more shells were fired in each daily bombardment than had been used in the whole of the Boer War and initially production could not keep pace with demand.

At the Battle of Neuve Chapelle in March 1915, 100,000 shells were expended – one fifth of the total supply – for limited gains. Two months later Sir John French complained bitterly that a shortage of shells cost him victory at the Battle of Aubers Ridge. Eventually gunners were limited to firing just a handful of shots a day.

The issue became a political hot potato after *The Times* and the *Daily Mail*, both owned by Lord Rothermere, decided that British lives were being sacrificed for want of shells. On 21 May 1915 *Daily Mail* headlines called the shortcoming 'Kitchener's tragic blunder'.

Although a staunch supporter of Kitchener, Asquith agreed to a Ministry of Munitions being established under the guidance of David Lloyd George. Swiftly he put the entire country on a more robust war footing than ever before. Production soared after railway manufacturers began making munitions. New factories were built and women were drafted in to staff them.

More than 1.5 million women helped the war effort on the home front. Not only handling toxic chemicals in the munitions factories, they worked in shops, offices, hospitals, alongside the police, on the buses and on the land.

A considerable number left domestic service to take up their new roles, an improvement in their prospects. But it was dangerous work, conducted in the shadow of fearful disease. Also, three major explosions at munitions factories, at Faversham, Kent, in 1916, at Silvertown in London in 1917 and at Chilwell in Nottinghamshire in 1918, claimed at least 312 workers' lives. And still, women received considerably less in their pay packets than their male counterparts.

Government also tightened its control of industry. The Munitions of War Act passed in 1915 prevented bomb factory workers from resigning without the express permission of their employers. There were strikes in both Britain and Germany by workers resentful at industry bosses making big money from the conflict. Governments moved quickly to quell them.

Shells were, after all, a critical phase of modern warfare. An initial bombardment was designed to soften up the enemy by disorientating the men, wrecking their guns and uprooting barbed wire. But this was not the sole effect of the prolonged shell shower. No man's land, lying between enemy lines, was destroyed by the barrage and became hazardously pitted. Consequently, attacking soldiers already burdened with guns and kit had an even more challenging route to navigate. The option of using cavalry was soon ruled out because of the craters. Inaccurate shelling also meant there was a threat of death from 'friendly fire'.

Spirits in the trenches rose when Italy declared war on the Austro-Hungarian Empire on 23 May 1915.

By May 1915 Robin hadn't received a single letter from his father in India. A letter to Aunt Ethel sent at the time requested small tins of jam from Fortnum & Masons, chocolate and café au lait. He asked for a little bottle of saccharin once a fortnight and a small tin of milk in every subsequent parcel. Again he asked for small parcels sent on a daily basis rather than large ones which were difficult to carry.

Brother officer Oscar Hornung, killed on 6 July 1915 aged 20, wrote his own letters home to his father Ernest William, creator of the 'Raffles' stories, and mother Constance. An Eton and Cambridge scholar, Hornung – nephew of Sir Arthur Conan Doyle – joined the battalion on 27 April and re-joined on 20 May, after the battalion had been in the midst of action at Ypres. He was sufficiently inexperienced to regret being part of the fray.

'*Nearly all the old crowd of officers are away wounded or worse,*' as Oscar put it. His captain, platoon sergeant, and servant had all been severely wounded. Robin, who had held a similar rank, succeeded to the command of B Company, and Oscar felt he had missed out. '*Oh, how I wish I had been in that scrap!*' he wrote, but added: '*Tomorrow I shall have my "blooding—"*'. It was an opportunity he was relishing. '*I'm as happy as a lark and a humming-bird rolled in one.*'

A few weeks later Oscar was hit by a shell as he bent beneath the trench parapet and his body was never found. It happened after Robin was injured although it is likely he subsequently wrote to Oscar's parents. Later, while Robin was convalescing in London, he was visited by them.

The following year Oscar's father Ernest William compiled his son's letters into a book called *Trusty and Wellbeloved*. Excerpts are included below.

Captain Henry Arthur Wyatt Peake, mentioned in passing in one of Oscar's letters when he was wounded in the middle of June 1915, was killed in action in France on 3 July 1916.

He and Robin's recollections differ in places as their letters will show.

dak Autographical used at the
nt by Robin Monypenny.

Robin Monypenny after serving in
the First and Second World Wars.

minute; and any surplus stuff the men have to chuck away. By the bye I am sending my camera home, as a strict order has just been issued that no officers are to have them, any we've got we must send home. Let me know when you get it. I am writing on my Company commanders note paper block; could you

Robin was furious when he was compelled to send his camera home from France.

Robin and his future wife Brenda at Highcliffe-on-Sea, 1916.

bin and Phil at Highcliffe.

bin's friend Joe Ashley in Felixstowe outside Hamilton Garden Billet, 3rd Essex, 1916.

Tommy Taylor, Joe Ashley and an officer Robin referred to as 'B' enjoying life away from the front line at Felixstowe, 3rd Essex, 1916.

Robin's older brother Rex, who was ambassador to Persia, seated in the middle.

x driving when he was in the Diplomatic Corps in Isfahan, Persia, 1917.

bin, standing second from the right in the middle row with a raised hat, during his time abroad
th the 64th Pioneers (Madras), Bangalore, 1922.

Phillips Monypenny joined the Royal West Kents in 1916.

The Monypenny boys at Bedford School. From left to right: Bert, Rex, Robin, Phil.

Robin in Bedford School's Cadet Corps in about 1908.

An official portrait of Robin as an officer.

with some envelopes

send me out one also. These fancy campaign letter books etc are no good. We have had no excitement the last four days in the trenches and its been raining hard & everything sludge is in an awful mess. We had two days lovam sun to start with but it is like November weather now. I think it is a calm before the storm and it won't be long before we meet the Germans face to face.

Mother has been sending me the Tatler, so will you hint to anybody else who might think of sending me a paper not to send the Tatler. I got 3 papers the other day they were all the same numbers of the Tatler I was awfully sick about it.

Theodore Please thank Mary aunt for her papers, I'll write her when I get time.

I am afraid I have no news. I had a rain of Jack Johnsons all round me the other day, I was just going to play football when they shelled us. The footer field was ploughed up with great huge holes & the mud flew yards up in the air.

though she was a stern guardian, it was to Aunt Ethel that Robin wrote throughout his time at the front.

Dear Aunt Ethel,

Here is a roll of 6 exposures which I have taken under fire; I send them direct from the trenches; as my platoon sergeant is going home on leave; he is going to post them in London. If you get them developed, at some insignificant place & take precautions they don't go to the press, they might be done straight away.

By the bye have you got my stuff from New Hall Farm. There was one spool of exposures I took, which I put in the red card bound box belonging to the camera; inside my leather suit case; could you please get them developed also.

The letter to Aunt Ethel, telling her about the camera film's imminent return.

March 26th 1915.   3/rd Essex Regt.

My dear Aunt Ethel

Very Thanks so much for your letter and the parcel of food & the underclothing, both of which I found on my arrival in billets this time. No don't send me out any more clothes for the men now, as all my platoon have got plenty now and also it is getting warmer & they won't need them so much; also we may move any minute, and any surplus stuff the men have to chuck away. By the bye I am sending my camera home, as a strict order has just been issued that no officers are to have them, any we've got we must send home. Let me know when you get it. I am writing on my company commanders note paper block; could you

Aunt Ethel sent numerous comfort packages, often in response to requests from Robin.

Weary figures on a bleak First World War winter landscape.

Trenches for shelter, communications and observation were dug with shovels.

bin's commission dated 15 February 1915.

illip's commission dated 7 April 1916.

Robin's daughter Sheila with his uniform and medals.

Thanks to his camera Sheila has had greater insight into Robin's experiences at war.

unnamed soldier brews up at the front.

apets and parados were sturdy with sandbags to protect against rifle fire. However, they were
effective against artillery barrages.

Before steel helmets were issued men favoured woolly hats against the cold.

To avoid sniper fire, sentries used periscopes to observe enemy activity.

Despite the hardships there was a great sense of camaraderie in the trenches.

Men soon grew used to the lack of comforts and apparent perils of trench life.

Phil was delighted when he won the Military Cross given to soldiers for 'exemplary gallantry'.

Phil's bronze commemorative plaque, also known as the Dead Man's Penny, issued to mark those who lost their lives in the conflict.

ROBIN

The artillery at this time were terribly short of shell ammunition. We had been sitting one day under a ceaseless thud, thud, thud of a shower of *Minenwerfers* and as we seemed to be simply grinning and bearing it for hours without any retaliation on our part, I rang up the artillery observation officer asking if the whole blooming artillery had gone on holiday or what? *'Very sorry, dear chap,'* he replied, *'We have strict orders not to fire a single round except in case of an enemy infantry assault, we have only six rounds per gun left for this battery.'* I felt pretty glum at that information, I could not see how it was possible to win the war as six rounds per gun would hardly be noticed.

We took over the trench in Turco Wood, just where the Canadian guns had been lost at the first gas attack. The gunners' camouflaged dug-outs were still there. They were above ground, in fact there were no trenches there as the ground was a low lying marsh and all defences were above ground – trench-like, parapets and parados started at ground level and were built upwards with sandbags. I took possession of one of these dug-outs as my company headquarters.

In a dark corner was a whole heap of weird bundles: jam tins, bombs etc. There was one peculiar contraption I had not seen before. The CSM declared that it was one of those French Verey lights with a floating parachute star light and he wished to fire one to show us his superior knowledge. When I declared it was a bomb he pooh-poohed the idea. However before firing it I insisted that he remove some serrated metal bits attached to its outside. He attempted to light it with matches but it was somewhat damp. Then he put a lighted candle under it. I said that the CSM was tired of the war and wanted to commit suicide and take us all with him. I insisted that everybody stand well away. Then the thing went off with a terrific bang and roar. The CSM looked very green as he had been holding matches to it. He did not question my judgement again.

A minnie (*minenwerfer*) had been worrying us a lot and we could not locate it for days. Finally, when I thought I had located it, I rang up my friend in the Artillery and said, *'Hullo there, have you chaps come back from your holiday yet?'*

'We have now a few more rounds we can expend on definite targets.'

'Good, there is a Minnie snarling over us from point so & so on the map,'

'Right, just observe the shots for us.'

After a bit, as one gun started, the telephone signaler below me was passing on my directions while I had my eyes glued to a pair of prismatic glasses just over the parapet. After a few shots, there was a crack and a rifle bullet parted my hair in the middle.

'Hey, artillery,' I said, 'don't waste any more of your precious ammunition today, thank you, or else the army will be losing my precious brains. There is a German sniper over there who has just parted my hair for me.'

> 12 June 1915
> 2/nd Essex, 12th Brigade,
> 4th Division, B.E.F.

My dear Aunt Ethel,

Thanks very much for letter & parcel with shortbread, milk, stewed fruit and potted meat. Did you get my letter with a second cheque of £10 and also asking for two watches, one an alarm-lever illuminated watch for £3/3 from Smith & Son & an Ingersoll (also illuminated if possible)? We are in the firing line again. I am in the spot where the Canadians lost and retook those four guns. There are some Canadian log huts here, I am living in one just behind our trench. We are rather close to the German line and in a somewhat warm corner, but worst of all it rained hard the day before yesterday and, being low lying, the ground is in a frightful state; inches deep in mud & water. A lot of dead French, Canadian and Gurkhas are buried close to the trenches & not very deep, and the flies are something chronic.

The French have had these trenches lately and they are in a rotten condition, I suppose they have put us here to try & improve them. Always the poor old Essex, put them in the tight corners. One of our generals is supposed to have said, according to the Essex papers, 'The 4th Division is simply splendid & the best battalion in it is the 2nd Essex, they never give ground and will remain in the trenches under the fire of the German big guns to the last man.'

I suppose people at home barely realise what it is like to be shelled like they do us, unable to reply and sit tight and watch our fellows blown to atoms. I wish they'd hurry up and make us enough big shells to return the Germans a taste of hell.

Yes, I should like to get a little leave but it doesn't look much like getting any yet a while.

Italy joining in will make a lot of difference and I hope Roumania & Bulgaria won't be long, but apart from that a good big supply of our own shells would make all the difference.

Could you find out for me about some waterproof boots, with canvas leggings coming up to the knees, they are supposed to be good both for wading and marching. The foot part is leather & from the ankle upwards is waterproof canvas; would you find out about them, if you can find them you might send me a pair size 8.

Well I am afraid I have no news and must end so with much love.

Your loving nephew

Robin

I had at this time with me as one of my platoon commanders the son of E.W. Hornung, the author who wrote *Raffles*. He was a nice boy, full of fun. He had picked out as his batman, a lad who had been educated at a very good public school, but he had been the bad boy of his family and had enlisted in a line regiment before the war. Even now he was inclined to be up to scrapes. One day he was sent with a ration party. He did not come back with it. Hornung was naturally agitated about this, wondering whether he had deserted. I told Hornung that I did not think he would do that, and that he was either wounded, killed or would turn up later in which case he must have a reasonable excuse.

He turned up two hours later with half a dozen bottles of champagne which he had found in some broken down cellar in Ypres. Of course it was not really a reasonable excuse, though he tried to make out that he was making up the officers' rations which were short in rum. It was against the rules to help himself to anything like that or to leave the ration party, but we overlooked it for once and I insisted that the champagne be shared out amongst the whole company, though it meant only a drop to each man. It was the only time that I ever saw champagne during the war in France. Some writers about the war depicted British officers as imbibing floods of champagne and whisky in the front line to keep their nerves up and have made statements that the men were doused with rum before an attack. Sheer mischievous nonsense. A tiny tot of rum was issued to each man only on very cold or wet nights and that only in the winter. Officers, except on rare occasions such as above, never saw champagne, and the price of whisky was prohibitive. No CO would allow his officers to take whisky to the line with them. Any heavy drinking behind the lines would soon have been dropped on. It is possible that the gilded Staff or the irregulars or the keep away from the line boys (RASC, etc.) might have indulged, I don't know, they needed something to help their courage against the thought of war ten miles away.

The batman mentioned above was eventually sniped through the neck and died, he had been trying to locate an enemy sniper but the enemy must have had telescopic sights against his open ones. His officer was killed shortly afterwards.

HORNUNG LETTERS

8 June 1915

Funny kind of day today – as quiet as the grave – hardly a shot fired this afternoon – our friend Fritz is never so crafty as when he is quiet – always up to some dirty game or other – so we expect some jollification soon!

There was a thunderstorm this afternoon which cleared the air a bit – it has been devilish hot – 'where the 'eat would make your bloomin' eyebrows crawl' our friend has it! The flies are awful now – suddenly come on – send me some of that 'Anti-Midge' stuff which Hardy's sell – My face is like St. Andrew's golf course now – and lots of bunkers at that!

Had a royal lunch today – potted meat and bread and butter – coffee (j: good) and cream – and tinned peaches and cream! I wish we had some more of the latter – just the thing in this crawling heat. We had my 'Barrack Room Ballads' out this afternoon, and Monypenny pored over them awhile.

My servant Crump is an extraordinary fellow – I am told he was educated at Charterhouse and enlisted at the beginning of the war!

MY DEAREST MUMMY AND DADDY,   *9 June 1915, 10pm*
No post last night so I daresay I shall get something tonight.

Another quiet day today – rained a bit this evening. Crump got me some fresh eggs and milk from a neighbouring farm behind the Canal – priceless servant, what? The flies are awful during the day here now – 'Muscatol' quickly please! Tomorrow night we go into the front line trenches which are barely 70 yards from our friends – There are no trenches to speak of and we are fired on from every quarter of the globe – but that is why they are sending the Essex there, remember! Tonight we are working away at the trench just in front of us – the men are working splendidly – and the whole place is swimming with mud and water already!

Monypenny and I and de la Mare lay and basked all day in our shirts drinking hot tea and cursing at the flies. This evening I had my Section Commanders up (remember – 4 Sections – about 10 men – to a Platoon) and told them a few things. It is by cursing the NCOs that one gets any efficiency out of the men – It is just like H. de H.'s at Eton over again – House didn't swing together if the younger members of 'Debate' didn't control their juniors – who were friends of theirs – So the young N.C.O. finds it hard to drop on the men from whom he has just been raised in rank – and 'the backbone of the Army is the non-commissioned man'. [A line from a poem by Rudyard Kipling called *The 'eathen*.]

Thanks to my worthy Sergeant Clarke – in charge of Platoon – my men are learning discipline and how to keep their heads – by degrees – but it is very hard work, as they are really all very young and inexperienced – straight from the home, so to speak – I am not quite sure how they would do if it was a case of 'no one cares to face 'em but every beggar must' – (R.K.) – however, as I told my Corporals tonight, we shall see their worth sooner or later. Peake was wounded last night – only slightly in the arm – will be back soon, in fact. I have got some glorious G: shells here – but don't know how I could ever get them on to the mantelshelf in the study!! Some more of that café an lait, please, and condensed milk and Menier Chocolate – keep you busy!

Well – I must go out again and have a look round – we shall have a great time in this trench out in front – it is in a swamp and there are fifty Canadians in the Parapet!

Toodle-oo! Much love to you both and everyone else at No. 7.

I so love your letters – both of you. 'Bon Soir!'

Your loving son,

OSCAR

MY DEAREST MUMMY & DADDY,   10 June 1915

No letter last night, but I expect something tonight – perhaps the bed! Today has been again uneventful and we go into the new trenches at 9.30 tonight. It is one mass of mud here now but will soon dry up with the sun. We shall be six days in the new trenches, and then probably straight back to billets. What was my surprise today but to see Monypenny suddenly open a ½ bottle of champagne! He had been given it down at Battalion Headquarters – a present from the CO!

Programme today has been 2am – flop into dug-out dog-tired and very sick at getting no letters by our midnight mail (?) – 2am – 3am 'stand to arms' – i.e. all respirators ready for instant use and rifles clean etc. whilst a mist slowly lifts from the dewy ground in front and the enemies' trenches become gradually visible. Directly they are well in sight the men are allowed to lie down and sleep – all except the sentries. 9.30am. awoke in frowsy, damp booby and had some breakfast made by the redoubtable Crump. 10am had a look round the platoon: saw rifles were clean etc: 10am onwards slept – or rather tried to, flies awful! Later in the morning Monypenny showed us where we were going tonight and what we should have to do there, then nothing more till tonight – just drowse and curse at the wet and the flies and read 'Michael Strogoff' – also listen to the Germans shelling buildings on our right and left and wondering for how long he is going to leave us alone!

Well – must stop now. I do hope these letters are reaching you – and not all in one batch! I still want something – and that is a revolver holster to fit that Smith Wesson revolver we bought together!

Much love to you all – You will now have an idea of what I am up to during the day – at night we simply work at sandbags and barbed-wire etc. so as to protect ourselves by day.

A rotten letter!

Ever your own loving son,

OSCAR

Saturday, 12 June 1915. 6.45pm

We have really 'upholstered' this 'booby' of ours very smartly – We have a table and 2 chairs (ammunition boxes) and have adorned the walls with pictures (of actresses) out of a magazine and the photo of a Frenchman's ma taken out of a rubbish-heap behind! The whole concern is only about 8 feet by 6 in dimension and de la Mare – myself – and my most worthy Crump live in it. . . . We sent Crump off on an expedition for food the other day and he was clever enough to buy us 18 eggs, 2 bottles vin ordinaire, 2lbs butter, 3 loaves bread, and a bottle of milk – and bring all these up through miles of communication trench without breaking an h'egg! Imagine him slushing through mud holding the bundle of eggs before him! . . .

This is really very cosy – and if undisturbed by our friends 150 yards off will continue to be so. We're going to ask for leave, 'Moneybags' and self, to bomb these blighters out of a small trench which they have jutting from their line – in other words a 'salient' in their line. This will be more to our liking than sitting being shelled, I'm thinking! After this rain – it will be a 'sticky wicket,' but a slow overhand bowler with a hand-grenade should beat the Teuton Batsman – at any rate the fielding will be good – although I shouldn't like to be silly – point!; that's my silly point!

Your loving son, OSCAR

17 June 1915

My dear Aunt Ethel,   *2/nd Essex, 12th Brigade, 4th Division*
Thanks for parcel and letter. I received my tunic here in the trenches, and the breeches, I sent them back to the transport for the Quartermaster to look after until we went back to rest again.

We have been in ten days this time and don't know how much longer. It has got colder again. I hope it does not rain as this place is a swamp when it rains. The Germans have been using dogs for messages from spies so we are on the look out for them.

If anything happens to any of the officers the Quartermaster writes to their people at once, however I'll see him especially about it.

I see somebody writing in Land & Water *says there is sure to be another winter campaign in the trenches (probably nearer Germany), I hope not at any rate, I don't feel like having another winter in the trenches, I doubt if many of us who were out here last winter could stand the strain of another one.*

I didn't look to see if the puttees were in with the breeches or not?

Do you remember the man who wrote to Miss Down, he has died of his wounds, was hit in the head. By the bye I have had no parcel from Mrs Rudd though I got some cigarettes from Miss Down & I got the 300 you sent. Well, I suppose I must close now

So with much love, your loving nephew, Robin

Saturday, 19 June 1915. 8.50pm

MY DEAREST MUMMY & DADDY,

You will be interested to hear I have been 'slightly wounded' – a mere touch under the ear which made me leave the trenches early this morning for the Dressing Station – just to take the necessary precautions, which are compulsory, against poisoning.

Yesterday the CO wanted a bombing-party to go out from B Coy to see what it could do. I had bagged that job weeks ago – and have been reconnoitering in front of our lines all this past week with a view to a 'scrap' some night. So last night I got a party – 2 NCOs and 1 man armed with Hand-grenades and myself with some of the new Hand-bombs – glorious things, just the size and weight of a Cricket Ball! Then at 12.30 this morning we got over the parapet and sailed over the intervening 200 yards. Of course I had planned the whole direction and spot to aim at etc. so we got up to 70 yards of the old Bosches without difficulty – going in single file – myself at the head ... and lying out in the long grass we could distinctly hear Fritz breathing hard over his spade-work – they were digging.

I had previously arranged with de la Mare that he should send a series of flares up to show me where exactly I was and so beat the Bosch at his own dirty game. The difficult part lay in getting within 20 yards of them – for the hand-grenades are difficult to hurl much further with any accuracy. As a matter of fact I could have got much closer up to their trench, if I hadn't been so anxious about the men with me – I would have done the whole job alone only the officer has to have 2 men and 1 NCO with him on these occasions. If we had tried to get any nearer than the spot which I eventually chose one of them would have given the show away I am sure.

At any rate we waited for a few minutes whilst more flares went up, and then after gauging the distance I led off with cricket – ball No. I – it was just like 'throwing in' from 'cover ' (a fast long hop!) – only this time I had 'some' batsmen to run out and there was a price on those stumps! I fancy 'things happened' in their trench – as there were howls – and a bit of lyddite flew back and hit me just under the ear – mere scratch – only it spoilt my old coat for ever and ever – amen! The others then stood up and 'threw in' – the wicket-keep put them down nicely – and we made haste back to the Pavilion! – it was a case of 'appealing against the light' – for it was 1.30am by then and getting uncomfortably light. 'Fritz' seemed so scared that he never fired a shot – only sent up a brace of flares – during which we lay down flat in the long grass.

When I get back Monypenny said I must go and have the scratch painted with Iodine and that sort of rot – so I went off with Crump (who – remember – is stretcher-bearer) to show me the way back to the dressing station at the Canal. We just got there before dawn. I then 'took car' (don't cher know!) to a place

2 miles back where I went to the Field Ambulance and had a sleep – then had the thing seen to and an injection v. poison put into me – then to our billets by Red Cross Car, as the Battalion comes back tonight and they said it was not worth coming all the way back. So here I am – alone in our little farm house again – and am off to sleep in the barn as usual! The Battalion won't arrive until early morning probably – so I haven't done badly!

I had a little jaunt with a R. Cross Captain in his ambulance Car and got some money from the Field Cashier, had a shave and shampoo and two excellent meals – in which we had STRAWBERRIES! – in the town close by here.

At first I was jolly sick at having to come back, but it has really been rather a 'jaunt,' starting with our escapade in the early hours – for all the world like those early rises up at Masongill – crawling after Rabbits: these were 'some' rabbits'!

Well – am dead tired – so good night.

I know you would like a description of this sort of thing – but remember that it is an every night occurrence – this bombing – and jolly sight nicer than sitting helplessly being shelled by invisible guns. It is the only relic of the old fighting left in this war – this bombing – none of your gas or shells – but just like our troops did at Badajoz etc: in the old wars – top-hole . . .

Your loving son, OSCAR

CHAPTER ELEVEN

'I scrambled back through the wire, tearing my clothes and my hands, hearing bullets whizzing past me'

Battlefield casualties were taken to safety by stretcher bearers, an agonizing and precarious journey for wounded men if the route was pitted with artillery craters. They were taken to a First Aid post and on to a field dressing station. Those too severely hurt to be dispatched back to the front line went on to a casualty clearing station where their final destination was decided. Those with the worst injuries went home to England by train and ship. Any with treatable wounds were kept in a base hospital.

In addition to battle injuries there were illnesses such as measles, mumps, typhoid, tetanus, stomach upsets and later, Spanish influenza, ripping through the ranks. There was trench fever, borne by the lice that infested uniforms, trench foot and shell shock.

It was when they were injured that men encountered women for the first time after many months of male company at the front.

Women played their part during the First World War, even if they weren't under fire in the front line. It soon became clear there would be a role for trained nurses and those from the Queen Alexandra's Imperial Military Nursing Services. But as the number of casualties mounted it became evident that there would not be enough.

The ranks were consolidated with Voluntary Aid Detachments, or VADs, founded in 1909 by the Red Cross and the Order of St John, who worked in hospitals, as ambulance drivers and as cooks.

Further, there was the First Aid Nursing Yeomanry, formed in 1907 to aid battlefield victims and who went on to treat the wounded and drive ambulances.

Initially, women who were not specifically trained as nurses were unwelcome. Edinburgh doctor Elsie Inglis had the same response experienced by many female volunteers when she offered her services to the Royal Army Medical Corps. '*My good lady, go home and sit still.*'

Her answer was to form the Scottish Women's Hospitals which, like the FANY, were welcomed by foreign governments when their services were turned down by the British.

If women arrived with only basic knowledge, it was quickly expanded by first hand experience as beds were perpetually filled with men suffering from serious injuries.

The conduct of women impressed the British hierarchy who had seen female labour transform the production lines on the home front. From 1916 more women were permitted to work in British army hospitals when previously they had been restricted to those run by the Red Cross.

In 1917 the Women's Army Auxiliary Corps was formed, renamed within the year as the Queen Mary Auxiliary Corps. Before the war had come to an end the Women's Royal Navy Service and the Women's Royal Air Force had been formed.

Robin sent two letters to Aunt Ethel, on 20 and 22 June, betraying how tired he was, although they were written during a four-day rest from the trenches.

From her he had recently received a watch, tunic, breeches, puttees, canvas boots, jam, Vaseline, two *Daily Mails*, one *Daily Mirror* and *Land & Water* magazine.

His dog Fritz appeared to be suffering from distemper. The battalion was about to enjoy an open-air concert before relieving the Lancashire Fusiliers at Turco Farm.

ROBIN

By now we were getting well into the summer of 1915, the days were hot and the nights clear and balmy, it was beautiful weather. Old England must have been basking in sunshine with its beaches lapped by sparkling waves. Beautiful girls would have been bathing and rollicking in the sea all by themselves or perhaps with a few wounded heroes, of whom they must have made much. Ah me, should we see anything like that, or were we the unfortunate ones who would leave our carcasses rotting in no man's land, perhaps not even get a few shovels full of earth over them, but be left to the mercy of the rats and flies. Oh yes, those flies were getting bad now. Such precautions as were possible were being taken to prevent contamination of food, and for the disinfection of the latrine and trenches, but were really hopelessly inadequate in the ordinary sense.

All the same, the amazing thing was that as far as I was concerned, I never felt better from a health point of view. My physique seemed good and I had even put on weight, though one would have thought that with nerves continually on edge that would tend to make a man thin and sickly. Certainly the occasional relief we got when taken back a few miles must have helped a lot, though we never seemed to get away from the shelling. Sometimes we rested on the banks of the Yser canal. Here somebody had built enormous great dug-outs, right under the banks themselves. No shelling could reach us there, about the only place on the Western Front. The canal itself used to get its share. We often had a swim in it and more than once while we were in the water German shells would come down and spurt great columns of water into the air.

We used to get our mail at the Yser. Somebody used to send me the *Daily Mail,* and the part that used to sicken us about the English newspapers in general was that they were continually extolling the valour of the Irish, Scotch, Welsh and Colonial troops – and scarcely ever made mention of the English, who after all were doing the bulk of the fighting as they were greater in numbers. But for some reason we all seem to praise others and denigrate ourselves. It certainly seemed to be a strong habit of the socialist party, judging every country as good except ourselves.

After the adjustment of the line on the night of the 24/25 May we, the 2nd Essex Battalion, remained for a while more or less in the sector of Turco Wood to St Julien. The work consisted mainly of improving the existing defences, erecting barbed-wire fences and continual patrolling by night. In order to foster the offensive spirit and show our foe that we still had fighting pep, an occasional raid was organized. This was also done to obtain information from prisoners captured. Night raids as such had not been done so far and we were one of the first units to inaugurate them. It was during one such night raid in which we took part that I received my first wound.

This was a silent raid, by this I mean it was not heralded by any preliminary bombardment or such special preparation. When the arrangements were being made, a preliminary bombardment was understood but I said, why wake Jerry up and alert him and why advertise the fact that we were up to something? So it was agreed to try a silent raid. It was carried out by two companies. After dark we crept out silently in two lines, armed just with rifles and bayonets and a plentiful supply of hand grenades. We went forward, creeping and crawling, without any accoutrements such as entrenching tools as they might cause too much noise as well as hinder free movement. The less we must carry the better. The first line was to do all the dirty work, the second line was more of a support, or cover for retreat.

As soon as things got busy and hot we were to be supported by the artillery opening up heavily on either side of us and on the German support line in front of us. This was called a box barrage i.e. boxing the enemy in. Two or three attempts had been made by silent patrols the night before to cut the German wire as well as to reconnoitre and fix with tapes and string any angled gaps the Germans often used to leave for their own patrols to come out by. Some of the men carried wire cutters and thick gloves in case they were needed.

We went forward and were nearly up to the German wire before they got the alarm. Then the first line made a rush into the German trenches, scrambling through and over the wire and hurling bombs. The second line stayed just before the wire and hurled a shower of bombs until a whistle was blown by the officer in charge who was to judge when the front line would be in danger from those bombs. This, of course, needed fine judgment and was a tricky operation. It is quite possible that some of our bombs did cause some of our own casualties.

Theoretically bombs were to be thrown over the heads of the first line into the German trench and most of them were, but there are always some panicky men who fumble things in this sort of pandemonium and hell was let loose. We had the advantage of surprise and the whistle was blown as soon as the officer realized that the men in front of him had entered the German trench. They were the first to do so as they had a gap in the wire in front of them. As soon as anybody had grabbed a prisoner he was to get to the back with him. It is a difficult thing to say afterwards exactly what happened. Guns opened up on all sides, bombs were bursting, the rattle of machine guns, the crack of rifles, shouts of excited men, yells of the injured, Verey lights pouring into the sky to light up the scene and the cries and groans of men in agony.

All I can remember is the sudden lighting of a dark trench by Verey light, me blazing my revolver at some forms just below me, then several of us leaping in amongst them. There was a terrified Hun in front of me with his hands up shouting '*Kamerad*'. I was pointing my gun with one hand in his belly, the other hand pointed over the parapet. I don't know what I said exactly, but I do know I was using most horrible language and the gentleman concerned seemed to understand and scrambled over as told, to be taken in hand by the other line waiting for us. Our bombs had evidently done good execution, for we stumbled over several moaning forms.

I ran into one of our NCOs. '*Got any prisoners?*' I asked. '*Yes Sir, two gone back that I know of,*' he replied. '*It's time,* I said, '*to get back ourselves, get along that way and yell them back, I'll go this way.*'

Then, after giving the return warning with a few others, I scrambled back through the wire, tearing my clothes and my hands, hearing bullets whizzing past me. Just as we got through the wire, the second line hurled bombs to cover our retreat. Here again there was the danger of killing some of our own men who may not yet have come back but that is war, it cannot always be helped.

After this we scuttled back as fast as we could, things getting hotter and hotter behind us. All of a sudden something burst behind me and I got a terrible whack on the side of the head, and one in the right shoulder. I rolled over and somebody grabbed me. I heard him ask for help, somebody else grabbed me and, after what seemed to me ages, I was dropped into our front line trench. Then I became unconscious.

I presume I was carried on a stretcher to the advanced dressing station. Anyway, after a time I came to, my head feeling awful and my shoulder feeling as if it had been torn off.

The MO came to me saying, '*You got some sort of a shell or bomb old chap. Successful raid, anyway; five prisoners but three of our men missing and seven hit. You are the only officer casualty. I can't say exactly how bad you are, but you are for Blighty, no doubt.*'

Relief flooded over me at that thought. Those months at Ypres had been a terrible strain, mentally rather than physically, though the physical conditions had been far from any picnic. Well, what a dream that was about to come true, unless some stray shell got me before I got out of range of any missile in that dug-out, or on the way down.

Presently I was covered with a blanket and two stretcher-bearers carried me away down a long road, an occasional shell bursting about. Then we came to a Field Dressing Station for the wounded. I was deposited in a dug-out again, an MO had a look at me and then tied a label on me. With three others I was put in an ambulance and whirled away. The rough cobbled stones jolted the car a lot, making my head and shoulder very painful. One of the others was very seriously injured and the poor fellow was screaming with agony, as we went along. I wondered why he had not been given morphine. The cheerful Cockney driver of the ambulance was doing his best to cheer us up, though poor chap he must have had to do this mournful trip hundreds of times.

The ambulance drew up at some sort of railway station. We were taken out and placed in a beautiful white Red Cross hospital train. How lovely it was to find oneself between nice clean sheets, nicely and neatly attired hospital orderlies to attend to us.

27 June 1915

Dear Miss Monypenny   'B' Coy, 2nd Essex, 12th Bde, 4th Div
I am very sorry to have to tell you that your brother* was wounded in the head & back by a trench mortar this morning. He has asked me to tell you that it is not very bad (flesh wounds), and as far as I can see I don't think it is. It is rotten luck for him. I expect you will have him back in England. Hoping for his speedy recovery.
* Yrs sincerely*
*   A. . . . . De la Mare*

[The writer's first name is not decipherable with certainty.]

---

* An error on his part as of course he was Ethel's nephew.

1 *July 1915*

My dear Aunt Ethel,   No 3 *General Hospital*

As you can see my right hand has taken a holiday for a while.

I hope you have already heard about me, the Quartermaster sent a wire and one officer wrote that day. Am not bad at all, fact won't take long getting all right; no big wound at all. A high explosive burst just behind me and two bits got my head, only grazes, a bit got my right shoulder, I can't use my right arm just now, a little piece went in my left shoulder, but I can hardly feel that. I am still in bed in the hospital which used to be a hotel. Treport is name of village but address is simply No 3 General Hospital B.E.F.

I suppose they will take the piece out of my shoulder & then send me to England for a few weeks, I hope so at any rate.

Could you send me a book to read, in preference one by Jack London The Call of the Wild *or* White Fang.

With love from
Robin

On headed notepaper with embossed address: Trianon Place Aux Terrasses Le Treport-Mers (Seine-inf^{re}) [this letter is labeled #27 by MBJG-M (presumed)].

I cannot remember how long we were in that train or where we were taken out, but wherever it was we were put to bed in a Field General Clearing Hospital in a ward with several other officers. Here there were nurses, at least the only one I remember was a dear old elderly soul.

Suddenly a voice from the next bed, after enquiring after me asked, '*How long is it since you have seen a woman?*'

I replied, '*Several months and then the last were only Belgian peasants.*'

'*Yes, is it not wonderful to see an Englishwoman again? It is not so much the length of time as the circumstances. This one is probably forty years old and not much to look at in the ordinary way but just now to you and me she looks lovely doesn't she?*' I agreed with him.

We were there three or four days, the bed cases being given a bit of rest before being moved on. Except for a continual bad headache and a very sore shoulder, I did not do so badly by day, but by night I used to have fearful nightmares; my chief one being that I found myself alone under a long narrow shed of corrugated iron and rifle bombs kept landing on this shed and I kept running up and down to avoid them. When I woke I found the nurse with her hand on my forehead. She said that I had been shouting something unintelligible, and sweating and panting as if in great distress.

The chap in the next bed turned out to be a staff officer of our corps headquarters. I asked him how one of the gilded staff managed to get wounded.

'*Yes, I know, you Infantry cannon fodder have not much time for us who see very little of the actual fighting. We do get long range shelling sometimes and it is usually pretty big stuff, however, you are right to a certain extent about us having a cushy time compared to you.*

'*In my own case I was actually wounded up near the front line and thereby got a pretty good rocket into the bargain from the General as well, for doing so. I have always hankered to see some of the real stuff and have managed to sneak away from headquarters a few times on some flimsy pretext. I did it once too often and here I am.*'

'*I congratulate you,*' I replied. '*What is your job in the staff?*'

'*I am afraid, rather a dull one, but quite necessary. I am in the personnel department and I deal with postings, leave, promotions and recommendations. I mean, I deal with the correspondence on these matters, I am no authority.*'

When he heard my name, he said, '*Yours is a very unusual name, that is why I remember correspondence about you in our files.*'

'*Oh*', I said, '*I hope it was nothing to my detriment. Am I allowed to ask what it was about?*'

'*In a way you might say it was to your detriment but one could not say to your discredit. Having gone so far, I'll tell you. Your Colonel recommended you for a decoration for some action concerning a counter-attack. It was agreed to by both brigade and division. But I am afraid that our old man held it up. Unfortunately due to the disturbed conditions, it was a bit late reaching us. By that time some trouble over some of your men in the same show had resulted in a court-martial, the papers arriving with us at about the same time. The Corps commander seemed to think that the two episodes did not mix well and would be queried higher up so he felt he had to turn it down.*

'*Seems rotten luck on you, I must say. But at the same time a strong recommendation from your Colonel arrived for granting you a permanent regular commission on the field. The general passed that one on, so obviously he had nothing against you but against the unfortunate coinciding of the other two matters.*'

'*Yes*', I said, '*Colonel Jones had told me that if I agreed to accept it, he would recommend me for a regular peacetime commission and a bit later I had to make a trip down to base to be medically examined which seems ridiculous. Here, I have been fit enough to take part on active service under most trying and strenuous conditions, yet I have to have a medical to see if I am fit enough for peace time. Talk about red tape, that is about the limit. Still, I shall be lucky if I live through this war anyway and it is hardly worth worrying now about what will happen after it.*'

A few days later we were both put into an ambulance and in this case there was a Women's Auxiliary Force driver, a WAF as we called them. I don't remember much about this drive except that it was a very long one. I could not see or hear very much; my head was well bandaged, I was deaf in one ear, slightly blinded in one eye and the right side of my face was partly paralysed. And of course I could not move much due to my wounded shoulder. We eventually arrived at a hospital at Le Tréport on the English Channel. We were put in beds next to each other. Our nurse or 'Sister' as we called her was another nice old thing.

I said, *'Why do they all have to be old or are we just unlucky?'* One of the other officers who had been there sometime said, *'They are not all old here, that one happens to be the oldest. The others are younger and the Sister on night duty just now is quite young and attractive. You'll probably see her tonight.'*

'There you are Monypenny, are you happier now?' My fellow casualty winked at me.

This night sister happened to be an Australian, the first Australian of either sex I had ever come in contact with except a very distant lady cousin of mine who was a Sydneyite but had lived many years in England. This nurse gave me rather a favourable view of Australians under the conditions of the time, though later I found that most of them tended to be a little long in the facial features to suit my taste. This one did not appear to have that failing.

> *1 July 1915*
>
> *Dear Miss Moneypenny*   *No 3 General Hospital, B.E.F.*
> *Your nephew Lieut. Moneypenny has asked me to write and tell you that he is having an operation today. He has been wounded in the head. It is difficult to say until after the operation how severe the injury is but I will send you a card tomorrow to tell you how he is getting on. He tells me his parents are in India so he thinks it will be better for us to write to you.*
>
> > *Believe me*
> > *Yrs sincerely*
> > *K.M. Carthew (Sister)*

[On the same headed hotel notepaper as R.d'A. G.M.'s letter No. 27 above]

> *OHMS War Office*
>
> *To: Miss Moneypenny, 288 Earls Court Rd, SW   Ldn 5 JY 15*
> *2/Lt R D A G. Moneypenny Essex Regt was admitted 3 General Hospital Letreport 29ᵗʰ June suffering from gunshot wound shoulder.*
> *Secretary War Office*
> *'Post Office Telegraphs' Inland Telegram*

At Le Tréport I had two operations, one on my head and one on my shoulder. In my head (in the skull) were two holes, the size of a penny and a half penny. Bits of metal were extracted and I was trepanned, which I understand means relieving pressure off the brain.

My friends used to say later, when they wanted to be facetious, '*relieved of a portion of the brain*'. Whether that was done or not I cannot say but ever since I have suffered from a poor memory of day-to-day occurrences, though I remember things well that happened months or years back.

10 June 1915

My dear Aunt Ethel,   *No 3 General Hospital, BEF*
Thank you for your letter & the books; I enjoyed the Call of the Wild *and* White Fang *but couldn't wade through with* Typhoon *or* M. Beaucaire. *The other lot hasn't arrived yet. If you could send any more after this letter, the* Blazed Trail *by James S. White and* In the Grip of the Nyika *by Lt-Col Paterson, but I expect I will be sent home before very long. I don't know when. The weather out of window looks simply glorious, the sea very calm, I wish we were at St. Jacut instead of wasting time this way. I wonder what has happened to my kit; the Quartermaster had it and said he was going to send it after me, it hasn't arrived here. I wonder if he has sent it home. One of the other officers says it will go to Cox's so could you ask Cox's if they have heard anything about it, I don't want to lose any of it?*
    My pack is supposed to be with my other kit.
    Well I am afraid I have no news,
    With much love
    Your loving nephew
    Robin

[Undated – postmarked 15 July 1915]

My dear Aunt Ethel,   *No 3 General Hospital, Tréport*
Thanks for your letter, I can't say I am coming, I keep asking & they don't seem to know, they say pretty soon, possibly in a few days by next boat. I am pretty sure to have to go to a hospital in London, I am not out of bed yet. But I don't suppose they will keep me long in hospital in London. I am getting out of bed & sitting in a chair in the room for a little while today. I should like very much to go to the sea side & am sure shall be quite well enough to do so in about three or four weeks from now, perhaps earlier.
    I don't suppose I shall be in a London hospital more than a week, you see I have to keep having my arm dressed after I am well enough to get up. I can move my forearm a bit but from elbow upwards it is useless at present.
    I am doing my best to make them send me home soon.
    Love from
    Robin

After three weeks at Le Tréport we were both were taken to England on a hospital ship. That was a nervy journey, we were expected to be torpedoed anytime on the way. We arrived at Newhaven without incident and were put into a gorgeous ambulance train. Our carriage must have been a transformed first class Pullman drawing room car, with great long plate glass windows alongside our berths. It was heavenly and it was glorious to see the lovely fields and landscape of old England. I had never appreciated it so much before, it was a revelation. Crowds of people waved to us at many places on the way. That night we arrived at Charing Cross where also was a great crowd of people, mostly women and girls, two of the latter had a long conversation with me through the window. My bandaged head and right arm were a very visible attraction, others with more serious body and leg wounds were covered under blankets, which was hard luck on them.

Presently a medical officer came along and asked us if we wanted to go to any particular hospital. We both asked for one in particular. The MO said that that was full up so he put us down for the 'Empire' hospital. Some of the others in the train chaffed us about this. *'My,'* they said. *'You are lucky. You'll be all right at the "Empire", all among the chorus girls.* Of course the only 'Empire' anybody had heard of in London was the old renowned Empire Theatre long since done away with.

OHMS *War Office*
To: *Miss E.M.C. Monypenny 288 Earls Ct Rd*   *Ldn 21 JY 15*
2nd Lieut R.A.A.G. Monypenny Essex Regiment admitted Empire Hospital
Vincent Sq July 18th
    Secretary War Office
    'Post Office Telegraphs' Inland Telegram

Well, we found ourselves at the Empire Hospital and we had a room each to ourselves. This was indeed luxury; in spite of the chaff it was going to be select, even better than we could have hoped, but sadly no chorus girls. Just as well perhaps, but we had a nurse to every three officers. Everything was up to date and beautifully arranged. It had been a children's hospital done up especially for us. What a bed, after having had to sleep for months on the wet ground of a mud hole. Was this a dream or would a bursting shell wake me up into that nightmare world again?

My nurse was a plump, not unattractive person of about thirty. *'Pity she is not a little younger,'* I thought to myself, for at thirty she would probably try to mother me, mothering was not so interesting. One day later she flung herself all over me. I am afraid I was astonished and not in a mood to reciprocate. I had certainly made no such advances. She went away looking rather sheepish and crestfallen and I think, annoyed with me: probably thought me slow as did some of the other chaps I mentioned it to.

Relatives and friends soon got to hear of my whereabouts and came along to visit me. My cousin from Coleherne Court appeared one day and, after she had gone, my nurse said to me, '*I am sorry I was so silly the other day. Now I know that that was your fiancée, isn't she a pretty girl?*' I smiled and thought it best to let her think it was. No one was more amused than my cousin when I told her.

At the Empire there were male orderlies to attend to the intimate necessities, which I thought a splendid idea. For we had found at Le Tréport a good deal of uncomfortable waiting about, due I suppose to a mutual modesty on the part of both ourselves and the nurses, though as the war continued that seemed to wear off. You could tell an orderly to hustle if he was still inclined to neglect you, and threaten to report him if necessary, though as a rule we found them excellent.

It was while at this hospital that Mr E.W. Hornung the author of *Raffles* and his wife came to visit me. It took my befuddled brains some minutes to gather who they were when they walked into the room. There followed some moments of embarrassment; he was obviously intensely moved by sorrow, while I was at a total loss as to what to say. I felt for them and any words I could say seemed too hopelessly inadequate. After a bit Mr Hornung started to question me and I could see that his imaginative mind was yearning for the minute details of his boy's life while with me and about his last moments. I endeavoured to comply to the best of my poor ability.

He told me that as soon as I was allowed out he would send me his car to go and see him and his wife in their house somewhere in North London. His wife was too overcome this day at the hospital to gather much from the visit – she was weeping most of the time.

One day the matron came in and told me that a chauffeur with a car at the main door was asking for me. She told me that, if I wanted to, I could go out for a few hours. I was already up and dressed in the mornings by now and had been out for an hour or two several days running. I put on my belt, but could not manage my hat as my head still had some bandages. With gloves and cane I went down to the front door. There stood a smartly liveried chauffeur and a Rolls Royce car.

'*Are you Mr Hornung's chauffeur?*' I asked.

'*Yes, Sir, I take it you are Lieutenant Monypenny, in which case I have come to take you to lunch with Mr & Mrs Hornung.*'

The chauffeur opened the door for me to sit in the back seat, but I said that if he did not mind I would prefer to sit next to him in front of the partition. I think he was a little surprised at this but said nothing. I wanted to talk to him. I told him how his boss had said that he would put him and his car at my disposal while I was in the hospital and if that were the case, would he, the chauffeur, help me in a little joke against the hospital and some of the other officers there? I wanted him to pretend that the car was mine. He seemed a bit doubtful at first and I said it did not matter if he would not, but to think it over.

I had a very nice lunch with Mr and Mrs Hornung and afterwards we sat and talked about their son until about tea-time. This was a bit of an ordeal, but I found it easier as time went on. After tea the chauffeur took me back to the hospital. On the way back the chauffeur said that Mr Hornung had confirmed what I had told him that he and the car were to be at my disposal till further notice so he was willing to agree to my request. As it turned out he enjoyed the joke nearly as much as I did. I suggested that he should come again the next day as I would like to give one or two of the others an outing.

During the next three weeks that I was at the hospital I took several other officers out in the car both in the day-time and in the evenings. Needless to say I was very popular, and they as well as the staff of the hospital thought that I was a lucky young man with a long purse. When I eventually left the hospital, I had not the courage to disillusion them. The chauffeur was quite happy because not only did I give him a big fat tip, but he received fairly generous ones from the others I had taken out.

About this time I received a letter from my father in India. This was a very rare occurrence. I don't think that in the whole of my life he wrote to me more than a dozen times. He never wrote to anyone much. I am not much of a letter writer myself but I am not quite as bad as that. His letters did not usually have much news, and when he wrote he had some definite reason for doing so. However, I used to be very thrilled at receiving such rarities. One thing I admired was his handwriting. My own handwriting is usually atrocious, and my mother's was even worse, though amazingly it was usually legible and of very good composition. My father's handwriting was so very neat, level, straight and of very uniform size. On this particular occasion he had two definite reasons for writing; one because he had heard of me being severely wounded and secondly, he had some news to impart to me which he knew I would be very pleased to hear, that he had in a small way touched his original ambition.

The Government Forest at Sukna abutted for several miles on the southern boundary of the Rhoni Tea Estate. Quite a number of government forest officers had either been called up in the Indian Army Reserve of Officers or had volunteered for the forces, and the government was hard put to find suitable people to carry on with the forest work. In this particular case my father was offered the temporary post of forest officer on a part time basis to take charge and keep an eye on the Sukna forest. Of course, this was in addition to his ordinary tea estate work and given the world crisis, the tea company could not put in an objection. As my father was responsible for quite a bit of forest on the Rhoni estate, he was more or less familiar with the work. Of course he had accepted it and had written to tell me about it. I certainly was pleased and hoped it might be possible for him to get gradually on to the permanent establishment if the war lasted long enough, though his age was rather against that.

CHAPTER TWELVE

'Fancy being shot at like this in England!'

Even in England Robin wasn't safe from enemy attentions. Felixstowe, the new base for the Essex Regiment, became a target for aerial bombing raids not only for its battalion headquarters, but primarily for the Royal Naval Air Service base established there in 1913. Its seaplanes sought out German U-boats prowling the North Sea. Before the war had ended it was one of the largest bases of its kind in the world.

Robin met a new array of regimental recruits. The outbreak of war had interrupted the studies of gifted chemist Thomas Weston Johns Taylor. The son of an accountant from Little Ilford, Essex, he was twice wounded after serving in Gallipoli and at the Western Front as a lieutenant. Afterwards he returned to Brasenose College, Oxford, to secure a first class honours degree in organic chemistry. His broad career as lecturer and chemist was disrupted with the outbreak of the Second World War, when he joined the Royal Engineers and spent three years in the Middle East. Later he worked in America and was knighted at the end of the conflict. When he died in 1953, aged 58, friends recalled his plain speaking and irreverent wit.

Meanwhile French-born Alfred James Morison perished on 20 November 1917, aged 30, while fighting for the 1st Battalion in France.

ROBIN

On leaving hospital I was granted six weeks' sick leave and as I had been more or less living in London before the war I had perforce now to make it my headquarters. What was the best way to spend six weeks leave under the circumstances? How could I cram into it the lost chances of the past, the chances of the future that might never be?

I went round and visited all my relatives and friends, did the theatres, spent freely of a bank balance that was fatter than I had ever dreamed. The trouble was that most of my boyhood friends were away at the war or had already gone 'beyond the bourne whence no return is possible'. I had to find new friends among those who were similarly situated as myself, friendships which could only be fleeting and shallow.

I visited my brother Rex at Cambridge. He was very sad at not being allowed to join up, but being trained by the Foreign Office they stuck with him. He should not have worried; he would not be where he is now – a retired ambassador on a good pension – had he gone to the war. Shortly afterwards I saw Rex off at King's Cross. He was bound for Central Asia and the only way then was across the North Sea, Norway, Sweden and Russia. I was not to see him again till well after the war was over, six years later.

Phil was still a boarder at Bedford School, but was hoping to go to Sandhurst. His housemaster told me that he was rather a handful and often in trouble. I said, '*Never mind, we shall be proud of him yet; that is the type I have found often turn up trumps in the darkest hour.*' I was not far wrong.

I tried to contact some of the girls I used to know before the war, but they seemed to be far away and scattered and not easily available. Marjorie Seddon was apparently engaged to some young man who was going out tea planting in India. He was apparently not fit for the services; had lost an eye or something as a child. I met Joyce Lloyd one day as she was passing through London to stay with friends or relatives somewhere in Suffolk, I took her out to tea at some place in Piccadilly. She was still very beautiful.

At the end of my sick leave I was given three months light duty and I found myself at Aldershot, attached to the 32nd Fusiliers, which was in the process of being formed. I found this very interesting work now that I knew something about it. I was attached as an instructor to one company, and also had to give lectures to new officers on trench warfare tactics as I had found them. There were a few others attached to this battalion in a similar capacity to myself. With two of them I formed a great friendship. The others used to call us the 'Holy Trinity', as we were always together when on leave, which needless to say, was almost invariably spent in London, whether a half day, weekend or longer. One of the two, poor chap, had a shell burst between his legs, and for a long time he had lain between life and death. A very eminent surgeon who had tended him had actually wept over him, such a dreadful case he had appeared. However, the surgeon's great skill and the lad's marvellous constitution had pulled him through. It had however left him, as the doctor said, not likely to become a father.

He had to report to this surgeon once a fortnight and after a while was told that if he did his best to arouse his erotic senses, he might recover. With that end in view he was to be as much as possible in the company of girls. On hearing this, the other two of the trinity decided to do our best to help him. My two friends were Watson of the Sherwood Foresters and Farmer of the Welch Fusiliers, but I won't say which was the one with fatherhood problems.

We were very happy with the Fusiliers when suddenly some malign influence rooted two of us up and sent us to another partly trained new battalion at

Milford Camp in Hampshire. Neither of us liked this at all; the men were all right, but the officers were an appalling lot. We took an immediate dislike to the CO who was an awful churl, and none of the officers seemed to know how to behave as 'befits an officer and a gentleman'. Their mess manners were gutter manners. No wonder that later, one sometimes heard that many of the officers were not what they should have been. I suppose in a mushroom army, where thousands of officers had to be created at great speed to cope with the demand, there were bound to be all sorts that crept in, and with no regimental or family tradition behind them. The results were sometimes unfortunate. But it was a marvel how so many of this kind happened to have gathered in this one unit. We immediately applied to be re-transferred to our original units. The unit staff did not help us exactly, but after repeatedly worrying them we got our way.

Once again I found myself back with the unit with which I had started my commissioned career i.e. the 3rd (Reserve) Battalion of the Essex Regiment. They were still on the East Coast acting as a depot battalion, but in a different locality. They had moved across Harwich harbour to Felixstowe. I was sorry to lose the company of Farmer and Watson but very glad to be back with the Essex. I kept up some correspondence with Watson and Farmer for some months till we all lost touch with each other in the general upset and fog of war.

The 3rd Essex had altered considerably; most of them were new faces to me but I was very pleased to find my old friend Joe Ashley. Poor Joe had had a bad knock in his head in Gallipoli, was rendered unfit for further active service and was marked for home service only. The battalion had increased somewhat in size owing to recruits and men returned from hospital after being overseas.

We were camped on the common right in the town of Felixstowe. There were about thirty officers in the mess which was held in a house called 'Aviemore' in Leopold Road, just off the common. The commanding officer at this time was a jovial middle-aged man, Lieutenant Colonel Crocker, a gentleman farmer cum country squire type. Owing to being a senior major in the Special Reserve in peacetime, his seniority had landed him in this job. He was conscientious and hard working but not a very great soldier. All the same he was a very nice man and popular with all which is sometimes better for leadership and contentedness among the troops.

For the first month or two I did not do very much as I was still supposed to be on light duty. Joe Ashley and I used to discuss our early days together, compare notes as to France and Gallipoli and wonder how some of our other friends had got on.

'*Well, Joe,*' I said to him one day, '*How is the feminine question?*'

'*No good at all,*' he replied. '*The place is very empty of civilians. We are on special anti-invasion duty here. The Germans are supposed to be going to try a landing and many of the civilians have been persuaded away; this is a special garrison. Of course fear of air raids and shelling from the sea had added to their nervousness. They haven't all gone, quite a few still seem to be about, but this place is nothing like it was in peacetime, especially at this time of year. It used to be packed, being a seaside holiday place. There are a couple of hospitals and some nurses. Perhaps I shouldn't say no good at all, but rather a limited choice amongst so many men.*'

One Sunday morning shortly after I had crawled out of my camp bed in the tent and was stretching myself in my pyjamas outside the front of the tent door the alarm sirens started hooting. I could hear a humming sound in the air, and before we could do anything, out of the blue of the sky appeared several German aeroplanes. The crash of bombs sounded all round the town, then bullets buzzed by us as they emptied their machine guns at our tents. One bullet tore through my tent canvas and made a hole in my enamel wash basin. Nobody was hurt in the camp, but a sentry on duty outside a store was blown to bits and two others injured. Two or three houses were damaged. It was over before we had time to recover from our surprise.

'*Humph*', I thought.'*This may not be a pleasant spot after all. Fancy being shot at like this in England!*'

Once a fortnight we used to muster as strongly as possible and man the defences as a practice in case of an invasion. There was a long concrete promenade just above high tide mark; below this the shore was all pebbles. Some of the pebbles had been used to make concrete trenches and gun emplacements just below the promenade. I was not much of an authority on defences, but after what I had seen of modern warfare it seemed to me very easy for enemy ships to get a range, and a perfect deathtrap with high explosives, as the shells falling on the pebble beach would shower the stones on the defenders like shrapnel at close range. To me it seemed the natural place to dig defensive trenches was just over the rise of the cliffs on softish, stoneless ground with no concrete that could be broken up to form extra missiles, which both the trenches and promenade would form.

One day Lord Kitchener came down to inspect the trenches. He condemned these concrete affairs and their position that had been built on the orders of the local brigadier, who had been resurrected from retirement. Afterwards we had to make the trenches behind the cliffs, and put barbed wire on the shore. I had not then thought of the barbed wire on the shore but I was very pleased with my own opinion of the trenches themselves.

About once a fortnight we sent a draft of men and officers off to the war and we all assembled at the station to see them off by train. The fresh men were all right, they were usually eager to do their bit, but I was always sorry for those who had already been out and were returning a second and sometimes a third time after recovering from their wounds. They knew exactly what they were going to, but it was marvellous how these lads, many of whom had never in peace time known what danger and discomfort were, took the matter philosophically. They personally had little to gain and everything to lose. Many did not know what the war was about. They had a vague idea that their country was in danger, and that was sufficient for them. There were all kinds and classes; some came of well-to-do stock, others of the very lowest grade, from Billingsgate and Limehouse and such delectable spots.

I was sitting in the ante-room of the mess one day, in a house at the west end of Leopold Road. The tents had been struck and we had gone into billets in the town in late autumn for the winter, moving our mess from the hotel to this building. One of our majors whom we used to call the 'Trout' (I don't know why and I have forgotten his name) suddenly said, as he was standing at the window overlooking the common, '*Hullo, there goes young Brenda.*' I hopped up from my chair and stood by his side, and now going along the road away from us was a glorious vision with masses of auburn-gold hair hanging down her back.

'*Who is that, do you know her, Sir?*' I asked.

'*That is Brenda, everybody knows Brenda,*' he replied. I said nothing more but thought that there seemed to be one attractive looking girl left here. It was funny that I had not heard of her before, especially if everybody knew her – in which case she is probably spoilt and blasé, though she looked hardly more than a schoolgirl. I resolved to ask Joe Ashley if he knew her.

Joe's explanation was that the Trout was very much exaggerating; one or two in the mess knew her personally, but most only knew her by sight from the mess window as she often passed on the way to school. She lived in Leopold Road. This re-assured me considerably, and I thought I would like to get to know her before too many others did.

Another day I was walking down the High Street and nearly bumped into her. She struck me as most attractive. I saw her again walking along with one of the hospital nurses. I thought, here's an opportunity. One of my officer friends was in hospital with a temporary trouble so I went along to see him and got him to introduce me to that particular nurse. I did not beat about the bush, and asked her, '*Sister, who was that girl with whom you were walking along yesterday?*' I described the girl, the time and the place.

'*Oh yes, that was Brenda Reeve, why?*'

'*Well, I wish you would introduce me to her,*' I replied.

She thought for a minute and said, *'Come down to the gardens on Saturday afternoon. She is coming with me to listen to your Regimental band and I'll introduce you then if you like.'*

Then she added, *'You are not wasting much time are you; why, you have only just been introduced to me.'*

I had to add lamely something about her knowing too many officers to bother about me, and that time was short in these days, not knowing when we might be drafted abroad suddenly.

When Saturday came I was duly introduced to the young lady. She was only sixteen and had just left school – and I was quite smitten. I got to see a good deal more of Brenda from then on. She soon after put her hair up. When I had first seen her I had wanted to get to know her with no clear cut ideas in my head, but by now she had completely bowled me over. After this I kept on seeing Brenda as often as I could, and it was amazing how often it was that henceforth we seemed to meet by chance. She had her sister-in-law staying just then with her parents in Leopold Road with a baby girl in a pram, which Brenda often used to wheel out into Hamilton Gardens on the cliff top. It soon became a regular meeting place for us there and she had a good excuse for exercising the child.

After a while I met Brenda's parents and I was asked to their house. As there was a war hanging over our heads, and as I was very much in love, I began to press my suit very vigorously. I explained to the young lady that I wanted to marry her, but I did not wish to leave her a very young widow, or saddled with a cripple for life. I wanted to be engaged to her but not to marry until immediately after the war.

Brenda seemed to be in love with me and she accepted my ideas, though she was probably too young really to realize what she was taking on. We were both very happy and her parents seemed to accept the situation quite well. It was not long before the matter got to be known in the battalion, and of course when we happened to be together one day we met Joe Ashley and I introduced him to Brenda. Being the sort of chap he was, he said to the embarrassed young lady, *'How do you like him, Mrs Moneybags?'* Moneybags was sometimes my nickname in Felixstowe, very much enhanced after a whole lot of us, Brenda included, happened to go to the local cinema and a film was showing in which a character called 'Moneybags' was included.

It was not long before most of the officers in the regiment did know Brenda. The Trout's statement had been somewhat anticipatory. One day Colonel Crocker the CO came up to me while I was walking along with Brenda. *'Well, Moneybags, when are you going to introduce me to your young lady?'* There was no need for me to do so as he was already introducing himself and it was not long before he was calling her Mrs Moneybags to her face. Poor

Brenda, I hope she did not really mind; it was a big jump from her school days just a few weeks previously.

Of some of the other officers I can still call to mind, there were young Tommy Taylor, Morison, and Gibson, and many others whom I regret to say I have forgotten by name. I had a very happy time there. Then one day I was passed fit for active service, and in this new condition of mind the thought of war appeared more horrible than ever.

CHAPTER THIRTEEN

'Brother Boche has had a bad time all round'

Robin had been doing his military duty since the outbreak of war. His brother Rex, destined for a career in the Foreign Office, would never experience life in uniform. However, as the war continued, Phillips became of age to join up and became an officer with the Royal West Kents. His commission is dated 7 April 1916. Phil had also been a pupil at Bedford School but was withdrawn by his mother, probably for his behavior, and sent to St Helier in Jersey. Later he was returned to Bedford School as a boarder. He was brilliant at games and average in class. It's thought he ended up with a closer relationship to Aunt Ethel than Robin. Like many other young men who didn't know what life was like at the front he was relishing a chance to take part in the fight.

Not everyone felt the same, however. Thanks to mounting casualties and waning enthusiasm, it had become clear that there would not be sufficient volunteers to fill army ranks and, in 1916 for the first time, military service became an obligation rather than a choice.

Until now Britain had always prided itself on having a professional army. Even after 1914 men went to war because they chose to while other armies had reluctant soldiers in the ranks. With no end to the war in sight, this arrangement had to change. The Military Service Act made a spell in the army compulsory for single men aged between 18 and 41. Two months later the net was extended to married men. Before the war had ended the upper age limit was raised to 51.

Conscription wasn't popular, with thousands marching in protest in April 1916. Military Service Tribunals, which heard appeals against a call-up, were kept busy with those who claimed they were already doing important war work, were medically unfit or had moral objections to the fight. Despite a large number permitted to stay at home by tribunals, conscription raised more than one million men in a year.

The row about conscription was one of several black spots that England experienced in 1916. Dublin was for a short while paralysed by the Easter Rising, a rebellion orchestrated by republicans seeking independence from Great Britain – a dream that had nearly been realized prior to the war. Although the incident fizzled out without making any significant gains, the execution of its leaders marshalled enormous support for independence.

On the same day the rebels admitted defeat in Ireland, a British garrison held under siege in Mesopotamia surrendered in what was later described as 'the most abject capitulation in Britain's military history'. After 143 days in dire conditions 13,000 men were taken prisoner by the Turks at Kut. Many died on a forced march to captivity.

At sea, the Battle of Jutland in May 1916 was celebrated as a triumph when in fact there was little to choose between the losses and gains of both sides.

A week later Lord Kitchener, 66, was lost at sea when a German mine sank HMS *Hampshire* as it headed for Russia from Scotland. A hero among working people, he was often derided by politicians and few of the country's powerful elite mourned his death.

On 1 July the Battle of the Somme began, heralded as a major set-piece to throw back the Germans. In reality there were almost no gains made on the first day despite the deaths of more than 19,000 British soldiers.

One bright spot of the year was the introduction of Shrapnel helmets – better known as tin hats – for soldiers in March 1916, replacing a soft cloth cap. At first the weighty helmets were unpopular but they soon showed their worth by protecting men from injury and even death.

The arrival of the tank, an apparently strange innovation of the First World War, also wasn't an instant hit among soldiers. Originally called a 'landship', it was a coming together of armour plating, caterpillar tracks and the internal combustion engine in a bid to resolve static warfare.

When they were first unveiled in 1916, one newspaper described them as 'like toads with no wheels or legs.'

Some of the first models were armed only with machine guns. Others had two six-pounder guns. Both types travelled at the modest rate of four miles per hour and inside the crew of eight suffered grievously from its lack of suspension and ventilation. Yet for the first time it seemed there might be a way of breaching enemy lines without wholesale slaughter.

The name 'tank' was an experimental one, as no one prior to September 1916 knew what one looked like. Initial outings ended in failure as the clumpy vehicles got stuck in Flanders mud.

Even at the Battle of Arras, where Robin was injured, the role of tanks was far from conclusive. However at the Battle of Cambrai in 1917 tanks began to show their potential after 376 were deployed.

For their part the Monypenny brothers had some cause to celebrate.

After Phil had joined his unit at Chatham in the early spring 1916 the two brothers met frequently in London whenever they could get leave. They thus grew much closer to each other than they ever had been as boys and Robin was proud to see what a fine officer Phil had turned out to be.

The Royal West Kents – part of the 5th Division – had been hard hit at the Somme, losing something in the order of 17 officers and 575 men during the course of the campaign. Phil left England at the end of August to help plug the gap. He was joining a body of soldiers that had earned a reputation for its reckless courage, being dubbed 'the mad division'.

Soon after linking up to his battalion Phil was contributing to the legend by launching himself into the thick of the action, as one regimental history records.

'[On 21 September] *two parties of four men each, under 2/lts Monypenny and Noakes, tried to capture a German sniper. They did not actually get one but they did some damage. 2/Lt Monypenny's party crawled through the wire and got into the German trench. The sentry fled screaming with 2/Lt Monypenny after him. Unfortunately however although this officer fired all six chambers of his revolver at the flying German he found he had forgotten to load his pistol and therefore scored a 'wash out'. A few Germans who were encountered were killed with bombs, and our two parties returned without casualty.'*

The following day Phil was slightly wounded but remained on duty. The battalion left the Somme region on 26 September. His progress overseas was charted by some sparse diary entries and some more illuminating letters to Aunt Ethel.

28 August 1916. Left London by 9.30am train – reached Folkestone 11am. Left Folkestone 12 noon and arrived Boulogne 2pm. Had lunch and tea there. Left for Etaples 7pm arrived 10pm and posted to 40 I.B.D. Camp.

30 August 1916. Started at 3pm with 51 men for the Somme. Stopped at Abbeville and a Roman's Camp from 3am to 8am.

30 August 1916
2nd Lt. P. Monypenny
1st att: 3rd Royal W. Kent, 40 I.B.D,
Dear Aunt Ethel,   *A.P.O. S.17, B.E.F., France*
I landed in France about 2pm on Monday 28th. We had lunch and tea there and then we went by train along the coast 10 or 15 miles, arrived there about 8.30pm. We are still here and we have not the slightest idea when and where we are going next. We were told at the beginning of the war reinforcement officers used to train for 14 days before going up to the front line. We are now about 50 miles from the front line. But this afternoon I have to take a draft up to the front line on the Somme, I think. But I have to come back and that will mean about Saturday or Sunday. The worst part of this job is that when I get back I shall probably find all of my officers gone. I shall have to stay till I am wanted.

Yesterday I went to a little town 3 miles from here and had dinner there. We work from 7.45am till 1pm, that is all. We are not allowed to leave camp without a permit. Most times we are only given 15 minutes notice to get ready for the front line.

Yesterday we had a terrific storm. I was sleeping through it when I was rudely awakened by the loudest crash of thunder I have ever heard. I honestly thought aeroplanes were bombing us. Officers who saw the flash of lightning said it was awful and only a second before the crash. Then 15 minutes later a stream of water rushed right across the front of our tent. I am in with Sutherland and Dickinson, both from Darland. We have to go with pack and rifle on the square here, called the Bull Ring – a term of frightfulness.

If you write to me here at once, I shall certainly get it as I have to come back, I think, I am not sure. I might be told to stay there, then they will forward your letter to me at once. When I get to my destination I'll send you my address. Write at once to this address, see?

We censor our own letters & when I get to my next destination I'll let you know where I am now. Send this on to Robin will you & when you get Rex's address let me know it.

Well I am jolly glad I came out but I shall be jolly fed up if I am going to stick here for some time. I must end now. I hope to be under shell fire with my draft by Friday.

Your affectionate nephew,
  Phil

1 September 1916. Had breakfast with CO started back at 3pm on a motor lorry.

2 September 1916. Arrived at Roman's Camp 6.30am, walked to Abancourt where I met Lt Mott of the Essex who knows Robin. Left at 10am arrived back at 6pm and found that Sutherland etc. had left for the front on Thursday last the 31st.

[On 7 September Phil joined his unit which had just come out of the trenches.]

6 September 1916
1st R.W. Kent Regt.,
5th Division, B.E.F.

Dear Aunt Ethel,
A lot has happened since I last wrote to you. After I conducted that draft I did two days training in the bull ring and then I was ordered to go to the 1st Battalion. I left last Tuesday afternoon and arrived here late last night. The Batt. had only just arrived out of the trenches and I found out that I had just missed an awful push. Well, very soon indeed we are going back again for 4 days as a last course before the battalion has a rest way back. Coming along in

the train yesterday we could hear a faint booming and then I got a lift in a motor lorry to a village from where you could hear the guns very loudly and also see the flashes. Later on I got a lift in a ripping big car (I was all by myself) and going along this road you could see these flashes which lit up the whole sky.

Today I went for a ride on a horse to Fricourt Wood and Mametz Wood – with the guns behind. Well I am still glad I came out. I landed at Boulogne and then entrained to Étaples – took that draft to Vauchelles about 8 miles north-west of Mametz and then I am at present quite close to place I must not mention.

I scratched the others out because I forgot, then I found out that they were stale news, having been in the papers some time. As I am writing now the guns are making a thundery noise & the band is playing cheerfully some ragtime just opposite my tent. Well, very soon indeed I'll be knowing what the real stuff is going to be. Our officers have had a bad time. Meakins whom I knew very well is missing and so is his great pal Venner as I told you before. A frightful strafe is going on now and it keeps up till midnight and then it slows down a bit. It generally starts heavily after pm. You might send me 2 pairs of thick socks and 2 pairs of thin of any colour, c'est ne fait rien. *And also some milk chocolate. You must send them as soon as you can get them after this letter. You might send this to Robin afterwards. Do you know there is hardly any trench warfare down here – no trenches mostly fighting in the open and in shell holes.*

Well cheerio with a bit of luck I ought to get through three or four days in trenches!!!

Your affectionate nephew,
Phil

7th. Went for horse ride to Fricourt and Mametz village. Posted to D Coy.

8th. Addressed by Divisional General. Went to Méaulte. Played cricket. Paid Mess 25frs and Kitchen's fund 20frs.

9th. Nothing doing. Packing up.

10th. Left early for trenches. Fine day. Entered Leuze Wood about 9.30pm. Got shelled at Angle Wood about 8.30pm. Had 5 men and 2 NCOs in my platoon. Saw my first dead man on my parados. Plenty of wounded men came back from no man's land. No dug-out of any description. Spent a fairly quiet night with occasional machine gun firing.

10 September 1916
1st R.W. Kent,
5th Division, B.E.F.

Dear Aunt Ethel,
I am writing this in a field just before my last proper meal for some time & in front of the guns. In a few hours we are starting for the front line. I personally am going to be in support I think, but I might possibly have to join the others in

the firing line. We are going into a ticklish bit of the line & I am afraid we are going to have a hot time. Well, never say die. I shall let you know as soon as I get through it. Just received your letter I.B.D. means Infantry Base Depot. My platoon of six men, 1 Lance Corporal & 1 Corporal & myself.

   Your affectionate nephew,
    Phil
   P.S. I shall get through it don't worry.

11th Monday – Trees were being blown to bits, one tree fell right across our trench. A tree was hit by a shell and it was fully lit up by the flash of the explosion. The piece of shell hit me on my steel helmet. Three of my platoon were wounded. In the morning the wood had been fairly populated with trees and by night when we left about 9.30pm there were very few trees left. Capt Bellman was wounded on the nose from a piece of shell which bounded off 2/Lt Jenkinson's steel helmet where it had made a big dent and then it just touched 2/Lt Dando's knee.

11th Monday morning – very fine day. One Boche aeroplane came over. Little M. Gun firing. About 2pm after lunch heavy Boche shells commenced which grew more and more intense. Later on shooting became more accurate on our front line from the end of the wood to the other and our artillery also replied vigorously. Parapet and parados were both hit within 10 feet of me and Sgt and myself were slightly stunned from the shock of the explosion.

About 4pm our artillery ceased for about ½ hr and hostile artillery stopped about 6pm till 6.45pm when it came on again and it was now dark.

Lt Dando got shell shock from 8-inch which burst on parapet in front of him, Lt Dauveney B Coy got wounded on left hand.

Had about 30 casualties in the whole battalion. We left at 9.30pm back to Casement Trench for the night.

Monday [11?] Sept 1916
1ˢᵗ Batt Royal West Kent,
5th Division, B.E.F.

Dear Aunt Ethel,
Last time I wrote to you I was sitting in a field just before having my last proper meal for some time. I gave that letter to one of the officers who were not coming up. I said that I was going into the support trenches. Eventually I had to go into the firing line. We never went near the supports. As for the strength of my platoon it is quite true. I have still got the same number now. We went in on Sunday night and as we were coming along we got nicely shelled. No communication trenches to come up along in you know, out in the open all the way and the star shells were going every minute.

   I am sitting at the present moment in a trench and in a little hole let into the side of the trench with my NCO in charge of the platoon. Not 100 yards away shells are bursting into the trench killing men. I saw my first dead man when I first got settled in our trench. He is at present in front of me on top of the trench. Just at this very moment a shell, whiz-bang, hit the trench behind when my 'little mary' did not half jolt up and down. That is the closest one we have had up to now. There is also a sniper in front of us who puts the wind up us occasionally. I don't want to boast but I am quite happy just now except for the smell. I have a steel helmet and a piece of steel coat pinched up across my knees. Aeroplanes are fighting battles just above. We are coming out soon. I'll let you know more details later on where I have come out of it. Brother Boche has had a bad time all round.

Your affectionate nephew,
Phil

P.S. I went through some dead men's letters and I found a £1 note. I shall return it to the donor.

In a letter written the same week he confessed to his aunt: '*I am jolly happy out here. I have not regretted coming out nor did I when I was under shell fire but I wanted to come out of that of course. Do you know when I was under fire I felt as if I had been out there for a long time.*'

But his next letter reveals how much more difficult trench life was to become.

Not dated
1st R.W. Kent Regt.,
5th Division, B.E.F.

Dear Aunt Ethel,
The letter I have written in pencil I wrote in the front line trenches just before an extremely heavy artillery bombardment. I shall never forget it for the whole of my life unless I have a heavier one. My platoon corporal who has been 18 months out here said that it was the heaviest German artillery bombardment he had had so far. Well, we went in on Sunday night and Monday afternoon about 2pm after I had written the first letter. Well four times I thought I was done for, shells hitting the tops of the trench and they deafened me and also covered us all in mud and earth and pieces fell into the trench making this noise 'hiss – thump' and cutting the bottom of the trench within a foot of my legs. Men came by wounded all over the place and there was one who had two huge holes in his helmet so his head was soon covered in blood streaming like anything.

Well I wanted to come out here very badly and it was a thick test and I got it thick too. I would not have been here if the Boche had attacked as near the end I had 2 men, 2 NCOs and myself to look after 50 yards of trench. We would have put up a good fight of course with M Guns & rifle fire & lucky for us we found plenty of Mills bombs in the trench. You look in the papers of last Monday and see what they say of the Leuze Wood where we were. We get our papers here 3 days late.

My men behaved splendidly, every single one of them. I had 3 casualties wounded cushy fortunately. It was an absolute wonder I & my corporal were not touched. A pack, a canteen and my tin of milk were all ripped open by shrapnel just in front of us on the side of the trench. Well this lasted until 9.15, 7 hrs of it. We were to have been in 4 days but we were suffering rather heavily so we had to be relieved. A jolly good job too. Now we are going right back to the coast I think for two or three weeks rest and then we go up the line north but of course we don't know where yet. Look here, it is getting quite cold here of nights would you send me out a few pants but they must be cotton – thick cotton but not cotton wool. I shan't be able to get leave for another 3 months. I might get a few hrs for Xmas if I am still going strong.

We got relieved Monday night instead of Thursday we were extremely lucky, as another day like that and none of us would have returned.

Your affectionate nephew,
Phil

20th. Went back to Maltz Horne Farm near 15th Brigade Hq. Very fine day. Went over the Juggernaut tank.

21st. Went through Arrow Head Copse, Guillemont, Trônes Wood and just to the right of Ginchy. Slightly shelled. Very fine day. Many dead Boches lying about.

22nd. Left Maltz Horne Farm for support trenches in front of Morval. Going up got hit on helmet with a piece of shell and 15 minutes later a whiz bang exploded 2 Mills bombs 10 feet away and a small piece entered my left arm. Slight confusion among men. About 5 men got wounded. Had to see MO. Told to come back next morning. Nearly lost myself going back. Moderately whiz-banged at night on our parapet. Could not sleep.

23rd. Came back to Hqrs. Half hr after leaving Hqrs it got heavily shelled. Major Fynch while slightly wounded and Sgt Major Hamnan had both his legs broken and his batman was killed. Left B Hqrs 2pm and reached Maltz Horne Farm 4pm. Got inoculated at ambulance, had dinner having lost myself for 3 hrs – slept there also.

Not dated – envelope postmarked 23 Sep 16
Dear Aunt Ethel,   *My Regt., B.E.F., France*
Thanks for parcel which I received night before last when I was in the reserve trenches just before we moved again. Now we are in reserve trenches behind our own Division. I am at the present moment lying out on the ground with my boots off resting my feet. 20 minutes ago a shrapnel shell burst above us 100yds

*away and not a soul moved. Immediately afterwards everybody roared with
laughter.*

*You know these tanks or armoured cars that have been lately such a success,
well there is one ten yards away and I have been all over it. It's a wonderful
invention it will go over all trenches and jolly big shell holes. It knocks trees up
to 8-inch thickness easy as mowing grass.*

My address in future is my Regt & B.E.F. France c'est tout.

*We are going up again soon. We have had only a few days rest really not
what we were going to have. If what is to happen in the next few days does not
happen, we shall go over the top for my first time and then, all being well, we
shall go into rest and then into a different part of the line I think.*

*I got a letter from Robin night before last saying he had just been appointed
adjutant of 3rd Batt, well I hope he does well I am just going to write to him to
congratulate him.*

*I have just had a shave and wash the first time since last Monday and I think
it is Thursday today. No one seems to know the date. It gets awfully cold at
nights nowadays but one cannot carry greatcoats and British warms about as it is
not trench warfare here.*

*By the way my guide when I joined the Batt: has walked off with my British
warm & cap comforter which was in it. He is not in my Regt. So I can't fix
him, so could you send me out a cap comforter as it is extremely useful & I have
not such a thing as a cardigan, which I want badly*

Your affectionate nephew,
Phil

Phil also wrote to his brother, as he promised he would, who was still in
Felixstowe.

Not dated – envelope postmarked 23 Sep 1916*
Dear Robin   My Regt., B.E.F., France
*Thanks awfully for your letter which I received night before last in the Reserve
trenches, we have been moving since then and are in some of the reserve trenches
in reserve to our own division, soon we are going up and if it does happen in the
next few days we shall have to go over the top which will be my first time.*

*Well congratulations for your appointment as adjutant which I hope & guess
will mean 3rd pip. I was jolly glad to hear it & I am quite sure you will be good
at it.*

*Well talking about retreating! When I was in that wood my platoon consisted
of 6 men, 2 NCOs & myself, for the last two hours of that strafe two men,
2 NCOs & myself. What if the Boche had attacked, not much chance for us, but*

* Sent to Robin at Felixstowe

I am sure we would have put up a good fight as there were 2 MGs on my right & one on my left where I was.

It is getting awfully cold at night now & there are no proper trenches, well it isn't trench warfare. Must end now as the ration party is just going back. Just now a shrapnel shell burst 100yds away not a soul moved but everyone roared with laughter.

I have just been all over one of these tanks!

Your affectionate brother,

Phil

Not dated – envelope postmarked 26 September 1916

Dear Aunt Ethel,   *Same address*

I am sorry I could not write this letter before this to tell you about being wounded but I really have not had a chance to. Last Friday night we went up to the trenches & we were going along in the dark all in the open and I was bringing up the rear of the company when I first of all got a piece of shrapnel in my steel helmet, but it did not touch me fortunately. Then a shell burst within 10 yards of me and it exploded a Mills bomb & it was a piece of Mills bomb that hit me in the left arm and the first thing I said was 'Hurray I have got a cushy one.' Two or three other fellows were hit. Both my Coy stretcher bearers were hit – I shan't forget that night again – Mills bomb going off so close to me. When we got into the trenches my Coy commander told me to go & see the doctor at once & get bandaged up & inoculated. I did not want to go but when I saw the doctor he said he would not be able to inoculate me till the next morning, so I went back to my platoon which was isolated from the rest of the coy, at least 200 yards away from any other troops, but we had M guns in between. We were in support & about 300 yards from the Boche.

Next morning I went & saw the doctor & he said I would have to go down the line back to get inoculated. You have to be inoculated for tetanus. My wound is not bad enough to get home to Blighty but I don't mind. I get my gold braid all right & my name will be in the list in the papers. I expect you got a letter from the WO.

Our Batt Hqrs got a very bad time on Sat afternoon – absolutely shelled out.

Your affectionate nephew,

Phil

PTO

I got both your parcels thanks and, that 2nd chocolate was ripping – awfully nice – indeed please send me some more. I am at present with the transport, the Batt has come out of the line.

My dear Aunt Ethel,   *2 October 1916*
I have just received your 4th parcel and your last three letters.
I acknowledged all your parcels so I don't know whether you could have got my letters or not.

I do not know why the WO did not send you that telegram & they should you know.

No, it is not bad enough for me to be sent home, which I don't particularly want yet as I have not done my bit over the top yet. We were not in that last stint capturing Morval, we held the line for the troop who went over and captured it.

I am jolly glad to hear about Rex having got so far safe he must have had some very exciting times. No – my arm is all right. Yes, I think I was lucky having a steel helmet on that time, but never mind it's all in the day's work. I have received the cardigan & comforter, which are very nice indeed.*

I can tell you that we have left the Somme altogether and we are in the north part of the line but I can't tell you where.

Your affectionate nephew,
    Phil

Diary – 4 October 1916 – Into the line

                                                        6 October 1916
Dear Aunt Ethel,   *Same address*
I am just writing to tell you that this is our third day in trench warfare. We left the Somme 28 September. I am just south of the place where Robin went through both its battles & where Robin was Coy Commander during those battles.

I received your last letter dated 27/9/16 and also one from Enid.

Well it is a strange sort of warfare this, having to keep one's head below the parapet all the time. Yesterday I had a most amusing time, I found a dummy, exactly like a man the face was, and I got one of my sergeants to help me, I have two platoons now. I stuck this dummy up and snatched it away quickly. The Boche sniper saw this as quite soon afterwards when I put the dummy up he fired at it. The range was about 300 yards. The sergeant signaled a miss each time. He had about 10 or 12 shots and 3 were hits. I never laughed so much in my life. I saw two of them the other morning and I waved my hand to them but they bobbed down. Last night I was sent out with a wiring party in front. There is an old communication trench from ours to their trench and I had to wire inside the trench which was more like a ditch and ¼ full of mud & water. You

---

* Rex went to Persia via Leningrad and Moscow. (Persia is now Iran and Leningrad has reverted to its original name of St Petersburg.)

would have laughed if you had seen me groping along this trench on my hands & knees with my revolver handy. Every bush became a German & I expected one to come round every corner.

Must end.

Phil

Dear Aunt Ethel,   *9 October 1916*

In haste a few lines as the Q. Sgt has just come up with the rations – he takes letters back. Well life is still cheery here. I have killed ten rats with my revolver. I am getting quite a good shot. Put up a message for the Boche to see but he has not shot at it yet. I have had all your parcels and I have answered all your letters. Just got your last choc which I prefer best. Is that cake coming out? Could you find out my state of accounts from Cox and Co and let me know as I happen to be Coy Mess President & I have to keep the food going regularly. In haste.

Your affectionate nephew,

Phil

Robin has not written to me.

10th (Diary). Gone relieved – measles broke out!

11 October 1916

Dear Aunt Ethel,   *Same address*

We are at rest now for a few days & I don't think I told you that I am Mess President for my Coy. I had to buy a gramophone today & so we want some decent records. You might send mine out, not all of them, but all the new ones and those one-steps. We are going up again soon into a hot part, a lot of raiding & bombing but not on the Somme. Send those at once if you can.

Phil

Dear Aunt Ethel,   *19 October 1916*

I hope you will excuse the paper being so dirty, but one has to be careful with all papers & also it can't be helped especially when one is soaked through & covered from head to foot in mud as I am now. Last Tuesday morning we came into these trenches and that night I was sent into no man's land round some craters that are 50 or 60 feet deep. You feel absolutely lost in one of them. I had to find the Boche where he was exactly. The nearest Boche is 30 yards away. He is a sniper & I got right behind him and I was gaily going to cut through some barbed wire when I heard someone give a loud yawn within 10 yards of me & I didn't go any further, I did not think it necessary.

Last night I had to go out again & I heard them talking quite plainly but I could not make out any words.

*One has to crawl on one's stomach there & back & it is about 130 yards
there. It has been pouring for the last 24 hrs & the trenches are all falling in.
Thanks awfully for letters & apples which I got safely.*

   Your affectionate nephew,
      Phil

Dear Aunt Ethel,   *Tuesday, 24 October 1916*
*Thanks for yours of 18th. Well, lots of things have happened within the last
fortnight. Today week we went up into the trenches for 6 days & I have never
been worked so hard in all my life. The first night I had to go out patrolling.
The next night I had to take out another patrol. The next night another officer
went but I had to go out to show him the way. Well, out of all these my
Company Commander was most pleased with mine the first one. Well, the next
night, Saturday, the captain sent out two patrols to attack a sniper's post and if
possible capture somebody. Well, I and my party went bang in front of the
snipers' loop holes while the other party went round to prevent any retreat. At a
given signal when the MGs were to fire, we were to advance. There were one or
two mistakes here. I should have given 5 secs firing for the MG and the other
party did not get quite to the right place. But a stint like that can never be
carried out perfectly. Well, I charged with my men and was the first to reach the
Boche trench. But as I charged the Boche sentry bolted howling like a tiny kid
which made me loose off with my revolver. I also fired into his shelter which
was pitch dark. I was guarding the next corner when a huge Boche came within
10 yards of me and I let fire with my revolver which only clicked and I even
found time to use bad language. But my sergeant mercifully put a bomb just
behind him which did go off. But we did not find time to investigate what
happened when they returned compliments by bombing back so we had to
evacuate the trench, but I am glad to say that I was the first to get into their
trench and last to leave it. Another mistake the other party made was that they
nearly bombed us.*

   *I apologized to my Captain on not being able to bring back a Boche but he
seemed quite pleased, sent in a long report which got into Brigade orders and it
made the Brigadier quite pleased, who I'm told, told our CO to congratulate us,
but the CO has not had time yet.*

   *Thanks for records and cake which I have got safely (the cake). Thanks for
Cox's trouble and I am glad about casualty list which I have not seen.*
      Phil

11 November. Hunted pheasant. Cold and misty day. Lt Cathy came up and
Lt Anderson killed by sniper.

   12th. Killed rats; worked out a scheme for attack. Cold misty day.
Lt Plumber came up.

Dear Aunt Ethel,   *13th November 1916*
*Glad you got the cheque, but as for saving money out here is a puzzle for me
especially how Robin did. I asked one of my officers here how one would save it
on just the pay and he said he could not and he is an old man and married. You
might ask Cox again for the state of my accounts as our cheques take a month to
get home and money is the only thing that worries me in this world of war. If
I was to get leave today & I found out I was in debt – I would not feel happy till
I was out here again and I would not really mind if I never got leave at all, of
course I don't expect leave for a long time yet. If we do go back to the Somme of
course there won't be any.*

*The records have not come yet. Of course I'll let you know all my adventures
when I do get home as I don't in the least expect to be killed yet.*

Your affectionate nephew
Phil

*The cake was not so good as I expected as Elizabeth's but we all liked it very
much. You might send another.*

Dear Aunt Ethel,   *26 November 1916*
*Thanks very much for your last two letters which I acknowledged by postcard.
I am sorry I have not been able to write much lately but I have been away from
the battalion for 6 or 7 days on a sniping course which did not interest me very
much as it was dull work and miles away from the firing line. If it was not for
a good few officers being sick I would be Battalion Sniping Officer – not much
of a job.*

*Our real CO has just come back from home from dysentery. He left us
immediately after my first stint on the Somme and that stint I shall never forget
in my lifetime. Since I have joined the Bn again I have had rather a trying
time. I have had trouble with my stomach for 10 days and a sergeant got shot
through the head and I myself had been standing there 20 minutes before, and
the poor fellow lived for an hour afterwards, although he was unconscious the
whole time, thank goodness. I never saw such a sight. Two men were wounded
from a ——— which was a grand sight and I was only 100 yards from it. You
will see it in the papers of yesterday 25th – Sun too. Then I nearly got shot
twice last night and all this happened in one day which is a bit trying and today
they have been shelling and so it has altogether been a warm time. There is no
more news for the time being. I have got the records but they took a long time
coming.*

Your affectionate nephew,
Phil

Dear Aunt Ethel,   *2 December 1916*
Sorry I have not written to you so often but I have not felt at all well for the last fortnight and the last 36 hours I have been in bed with the usual touch of flu only a bit worse.

Yes, I got the records but they were a long time coming and I also got your last cake with the bulls eyes. By the way you might send out my greatcoat as it is getting frightfully cold although we have had no snow this winter.

Your affectionate nephew,
  Phil

Dear Aunt Ethel,   *5 December 1916*
Soon after I wrote my last letter saying I had been in bed or the last two days. My fever went up and I had to go back to bed and I have just got up again for the afternoon feeling rather weak so consequently missing the trenches this time a bit.

The doctor is very keen on sending me down the line which I don't want in the least as there is the risk of losing the regiment, & that I don't want to do in the least. The doctor doesn't seem to know what exactly is the matter with me.

We have not had any snow yet but it is extremely cold at times so I want that greatcoat of mine. I feel rather knocked up lately, I don't know why except that one day's bad work up the line I suppose had something to do with it.

Otherwise no news.
Your affectionate nephew,
  Phil

Dear Aunt Ethel,   *8 December 1916*
Thanks for last two letters 30/11/16 and 3/12/16 with the fruit salad which has already been eaten with the help of the mess. I have also received your last cake with bulls eyes which came in very handy as I had a bit of a cold then. I have got seven days rest here with the transport as I have been in bed some time thus feeling rather weak on my legs. I am feeling much better now though except for the want of a bit of exercise which I can easily get here by going out for a lot of rides.

The weather is getting rather rotten and also cold & the two together is decidedly rotten. Glad to hear about Reggie being back in England again, hope he is much better now with that arm of his. If you get to know his address you might let me know and also ask him to write to me.

Ask for leave for Xmas! It is impossible as there are so many officers here, a good many who have been out here over a year without leave.

Now for Xmas I would like another cake, a tin of the best cocoa and a new pair of leather gloves with fingers and with fleece inside and a big chicken. I have

*bought two or three pairs here but they seem to be no good and yet they are so
expensive.*

I'll enclose money for chicken, 10 francs.

Your affectionate nephew,

Phil

P.S. *A big chicken! Phil*

Dear Aunt Ethel,   *25 December 1916*

*Sorry I have not written lately, but I have been feeling miserable, owing to one
of my best friends in this regiment having been horribly wounded by a trench
mortar – something like Robin's only much worse. Robin's trench mortar fell
behind him you can see but this officer's one fell in front. He will be disfigured
for life and a useless right arm & a stiff leg. I have seen him in hospital out
here and there seems to be some hope of him living but poor fellow he will be
useless. I think he was one of the pluckiest fellows I've known and he is liked
very much indeed.*

*I received the greatcoat safely, thanks, and a parcel with a cake and a tin of
Roundtree's cocoa, but no parcel of tinned turkey & chicken with gloves but I will
let you know as soon as I get it.*

How is father getting on – well I hope.

Your affectionate nephew,

Phil

CHAPTER FOURTEEN

'There were several cases of men being missed in the dark by their comrades, and actually drowned in the mud'

Officers like Robin and Phil, with private incomes, were responsible for kitting themselves out for the Western Front. Their uniform consisted of an open collared shirt and jodhpur-style cord breeches, both in khaki, knee-high leather boots, gaiters or puttees and leather gloves. A Sam Browne belt was worn to hold their pistol of choice and a sword scabbard. In the winter they needed trenchcoats and greatcoats to keep out the rain and the cold. As for equipment, they would have in their canvas or leather rucksack, a compass, binoculars, map case and water canteen.

At first bold insignia was used to indicate rank. As the war progressed, and the accuracy of German snipers was proved time and again, the braid became less obvious. Sometimes officers discarded or disguised their 'pips' during battle to make themselves less of a target.

In command of Robin's brigade was Sir Adrian Carton de Wiart, a legendary figure injured seven times after arriving at the Western Front early in 1915, in the face, head, stomach, ankle, leg, hip, and ear. Famously, he is said to have pulled off his withering fingers when a doctor decided against amputation.

In 1916 he won the Victoria Cross in the wake of the Battle of the Somme. His citation reads:

> '*It was owing in a great measure to his dauntless courage and inspiring example that a serious reverse was averted. He displayed the utmost energy and courage in forcing our attack home.*'

Much later, he confessed that he enjoyed the war. No surprise then to know he also served in the Second World War and, on the eve of his 60th birthday, was evacuated from Norway when the campaign there foundered. En route to aid Yugoslavia before German invasion, his plane crashed and he became an Italian prisoner of war. When Italy left the war he was freed and went to China via India and the 1943 Cairo Conference, attended by key Allied leaders.

According to his records, Robin embarked for France on 25 January 1917 and joined the 2nd Battalion on 13 February.

ROBIN

The summons came as a bit of a shock. I pulled myself together; *'What's this,'* I thought as I read my marching orders, *'Proceed to Ex Force and report to the "umpteenth" Fusiliers.'* I dashed off to see the Adjutant, Captain Heppel. *'I say, can't something be done?'* I asked. *'Good heavens, I want to get back to the 2nd Essex; who the deuce are these "umpteenth" Fusiliers? I am not a Fusilier.'*

The Adjutant said he would see if the CO could do anything. The CO kindly wrote to the War Office but only got a sharp rebuke for his pains. I was dreadfully annoyed. I knew Colonel Jones wanted me back. I knew all my own crowd; but to be pitch-forked into some strange new battalion, probably one not long in existence, and perhaps with officers of the type I had met at Milford Camp; and I did not suppose that I, a stranger, would be very welcome. However orders were orders.

Off I went and arrived at Folkestone one evening. In the train on the way there I thought things out a bit and wondered whether I would dare act on my impulses. There was so much red tape that probably it would be lost in the maze of officialdom. At Folkestone there were two boats ready to sail, one for Calais, the other for Boulogne. I made discreet enquiries which elicited the information that to reach the Fusiliers I should have to take the Boulogne boat and for my own battalion the Calais boat. Fate seemed to be playing into my hands.

So finally, making up mind, I stepped up the gangway of the Calais boat.

'Your papers please,' said somebody with red tabs. I pretended to be a bit of a fool and fumbled about looking for them in my haversack. I stood aside doing this while he attended to others.

'I can't find them I must have misplaced them somewhere.'

'Where are you for?' he asked. I told him. *'This is your boat; get aboard and have a look for your papers, and bring them along to me presently.'* Thereupon I slipped along on board and took good care to keep out of sight. I was feeling a bit uncomfortable about it, wondering whether I would get into serious trouble. However the die was cast, I must keep it up.

Arrived at Calais, we marched up to the rest camp. On being asked for my papers there, I told them that the RTO at Folkestone had stuck to them, and I had forgotten them till the boat had sailed. A good deal of cursing followed this, and I suppose they thought either me or the RTO or perhaps both, particular sorts of asses. It seemed to upset the even tenor of events, because others were drafted away a day or two after our arrival, whereas I called day after day at the orderly room and no orders came for me. They seemed at a loss as to what to do and though they wired third echelon, the latter naturally had no particulars of me; my particulars were of course with some other echelon who must have wondered what had happened to me.

Three weeks went by and I got desperate, so I wrote a private letter to Colonel Jones at the front saying that I was on my way to him but had got stuck at Calais for three weeks, and could he do anything to get me up. Urgent orders came very soon after to move up and I was glad to see the last of that dusty, dreary 'Rest Camp'. So a bold initiative in an awkward corner sometimes worked.

This time the battalion was in the Somme sector. This was shortly after the Battle of the Somme and matters were still simmering and sizzling over there. We had a long and weary train journey through the night and part of the next day. Then we mounted a lorry which deposited me at our battalion quartermaster's stores some eight miles behind the front line. This was about 4pm in the afternoon. I was looking forward to a good sleep in one of the bunks of a Nissen hut. Two other officers had come up with me to join the battalion, I presume they were junior to me, I cannot remember, but shortly after our arrival at the stores a message came through that the CO wanted me up that night to take over a company. I heartily cursed my luck, I was tired and weary and longing for a lie down; also l hoped this would not be a repetition of what had happened at Ypres.

I said to the Quartermaster, *'How does one get there; do I get a guide?'*
'Yes, a guide will be here for you, but you will have to foot it all the way.'
'What, foot it eight miles, why?'
'This is all recently torn-up ground, a mass of criss-crossing trenches blown to bits; the whole surface of the ground pock marked with continual shell fire; a tangled mass of barbed wire everywhere; roads smashed to bits till they are hardly traceable. No vehicle can cross it; horses would break their legs; therefore there is as yet no organized means of transit by vehicle or animal. You cannot walk on top of the ground or else you will get lost; therefore some of the old German communication trenches have been cleared, joined up and made just passable. You have to follow them all the way from here to Battalion Headquarters wherever that may be; after that it is a matter of wandering from shell hole to shell hole.'

This must be my purgatory, what had I done to deserve it? Ypres was bad enough but this sounded worse; at Ypres I was 100% fit, I doubted if I was now. However we started an hour before dark my guide and I, and it took us just three hours steady plodding to pick our way to Battalion Headquarters, which was in a little dugout somewhere below ground where Colonel Jones and the Adjutant, Captain Irwin, were sitting by the light of a flickering candle.

They seemed quite pleased to see me. The colonel apologised for dragging me up that night but said that he was very short of officers and that B Company had just lost its only officer, that matters were a bit critical, and he must have someone to take over. I thought, hullo, B Company again, but they would remember not to let me down this time if any of the same men were there, which was probably not so.

There seemed to be a suppressed air of amusement in that headquarters' dug-out which I could not understand till a few minutes later. After explaining various orders to me, they told me that owing to the scattered position of the posts and gaps between them in the line etc, it was necessary now to have a password, and that the password for that night was 'Brenda'. It nearly floored me and I thought at first it was just a strange coincidence, but thinking of it again and seeing the twinkle in their eyes I realized that somebody must have written to them about me from the garrison battalion at Felixstowe, and it was probably Irwin's way of having a little joke. However I said nothing and pretended not to notice, so whether the joke fell flat or not I do not know; I was too tired anyway to savour it.

After giving me a bit of supper I was guided up to B Company. We stumbled over a mass of shell holes in the dark; I wondered how my guide knew the way, and finally we dropped into a miserable sort of ditch where under a bit of sacking a candle was fitfully burning and the sergeant major was waiting for me.

The fact that now I was an old soldier, wearing wound stripes, and had already once commanded this company made a tremendous difference in the way I was accepted compared to the previous time I first saw B Company; also any who had served with me before had realized I would stand no nonsense. After talking things over with the CSM we crawled about looking at our position as much as we could in the dark, and then I rested my weary body on some sand bags.

Towards morning a tremendous gunfire started. I got up and seeking the sergeant major was told that this was our daily morning hymn of hate; our hymn, mind you! The last time I was out I had almost forgotten we had any artillery; it was only the Germans who played this tremendous hymn of hate. This was a treat to hear now; the shells were swishing close overhead in thousands; they seemed to follow each other in a continuous stream. I thought to myself, at last we are getting some of our own back.

The weather turned beastly cold and wet, which added to the general discomfort of things. For the first time I wore a steel helmet; they had come into general use just before my arrival. The numerous dents and grooves in many of them testified to the soundness of the idea and thus to the saving of numerous casualties. I found mine rather heavy at first but soon got used to it;

it gave me some sense of security, if one could think of any security at all in such a spot. The weather seemed to get steadily worse, bringing all active fighting more or less to a standstill. The ground was in a terrible state of quagmire. Quite a lot of time was spent in hauling each other out of the morass, a most unpleasant, stinking and tenacious morass; terrible position to be lost in on a dark night when one could not see the worst spots. There were several cases of men being missed in the dark by their comrades, and actually drowned in the mud, having vanished and perhaps their bodies accidently discovered some days later.

We were at this time in the neighbourhood of Mailly-Maillet, a village but in name, there was hardly a brick left to mark the place; but Mailly-Maillet will always remind me of mud, murderous mud, foul mud. Mailly was just behind us and Thiepval, on our right front, had been captured shortly before my arrival. As soon as the weather improved, fighting broke out again on our left around Beaumont Hamel where, for some weeks, there were continued minor successes, including the capture of Beaucourt.

Again the weather got bad and matters slowed down. When it improved Baillescourt Farm was captured in an assault with a large number of Prussian prisoners. Our artillery seemed to be continually active which was very re-assuring to me, after having heard mainly German guns at Ypres.

We were continually active in sending out patrols whenever possible. These few months of dismal, dark winter of 1916/17 I find the hardest to remember in detail of the whole war. It only comes to me as a horrible night-mare of mud and mist, shell holes and night raids among which I can only remember indistinctly one in which I lost a subaltern, shot through the eye by a chance bullet in the dark somewhere in no man's land and we managed to drag him back to expire on our own parapet, or rather, line of mud holes.

One night about the middle of February, somewhere opposite Serre, I went out as usual stalking the German trenches. We gradually drew nearer and nearer and got to the barbed wire, expecting every moment a blaze of musketry. There was nothing doing. We thought that Jerry must be pre-paring something especially diabolic for us, allowing us to get so near without protest. Would he suddenly let out a flood of fire from numerous flame-throwers and incinerate the lot of us? Unpleasant thought. I'd rather die some other way. We waited breathlessly on our stomachs. Presently I crawled along again, looking for a gap in the wire and having found it, my party with bombs ready crawled through and over the German parapet and into his trench.

'*By Jove,*' I thought, '*we have caught you napping this time.*'

We divided into two lots, one going each way along the trench, senses alert, nerves keyed to a pitch, but somehow I was greatly puzzled and particularly scared, this was uncanny, this was some new and devilish cunning. I could not make it out at all. Having gone some 50 yards in one direction I posted two men and walked back to see how my sergeant had fared in the other direction. I met him about where I had parted from him. His was the same tale, but he could find no enemy.

I gave orders to hold tight and sent a message back to the effect that we had reconnoitered inside 100 yards of enemy front line trench but could find no enemy. I was instructed to hang on and have some more men up to hold the position and if possible to reconnoitre a bit further. I had three of my platoons come up leaving one in reserve in our original front line trench. We spent the rest of the night cautiously nosing around for some distance but were still mystified and unable to contact Jerry. Towards dawn I received a message to say that the enemy had withdrawn his main position some three miles back and the British would that day move up to get in touch with him again. So that day the whole front in this sector moved slowly forward through areas of mud, the outpost patrols now and then coming into contact with snipers or machine-gun units that had been left behind to worry us.

Part of the line passed through Serre without opposition, moving forward a bit each day with slight opposition occasionally elsewhere, carefully reconnoitering beforehand before the main line made a fresh move, keeping in contact with our flanks. The Germans had laid waste everything behind them, blown up buildings, cut down fruit trees, poisoned the wells, left booby traps everywhere for which we had to watch carefully, losing a certain number of men through them, never knowing when one would step on or touch one inadvertently. The village of Puisieux was a complete shambles, even including smashed up furniture.

In and around Puisieux we chivvied some machine gunners and snipers and got held up just beyond by some strong barbed wire and a new line of trenches. Apparently the move forward was general over a considerable front extending from Arras down to the French troops on our right.

Towards the end of March 1917 our division (4th) was sent back for a long rest and special training. Spring was coming now and as we marched away daily for two or three days from the battle areas we came back once more to civilization and green grass, trees and fields amidst the delightful little untouched villages nestling in the hills and valleys in the departments of the Somme and Calais.

We billeted each night in a different village as we moved along. Each day the men's spirits seemed to cheer up as they swung along singing the latest catchy songs, we passed through the town of Doullens, the first French town that seemed untouched by the war that I had been in for a long time, we stopped there for one night. I lived in a real town house for one night. The next day the brigade (12th) moved on and we finally settled ourselves scattered about in various farmhouses round about the villages halfway between Auxi-le-Château and St Pol. The former place seemed to be the centre of several military schools and specialized classes, while the latter was the headquarters of the local RASC. My own company was quartered in and around an old farmhouse, the men in various farm buildings, while I myself was offered a room in the farmhouse itself.

The family consisted of Père and Mère and about seventeen children. No one room seemed to be devoid of inhabitants. I told my batman to fix things up while I went off to fix up the men, report to the HQRS in a village nearby and find out what arrangements there were for messing everybody. When I came back that evening, wishing to change into slacks and have a good scrub, I enquired of my batman where my abode was, he showed me to a room where my valise was spread out on the floor. There were two double beds in the room, so I asked him what was the idea re the beds, he said that he could not quite understand the old farmer and his wife when they had pointed out that spot for me. However I changed and washed and presently tackled Madame. It appeared that the beds were occupied at night by two small boys in one and by two sisters aged seventeen and thirteen in the other (bed). Trying to explain the impropriety of my position there, the mother shrugged her shoulders saying that she had nowhere else to offer me. So I sent for the sergeant major and told him to find me a corner in a hayloft somewhere near the men. Young ladies in my bedroom might be fun but hardly conducive to discipline.

After a day or two's cleaning up and bathing we got down to the serious matter of training, i.e. company drill, bayonet fighting, etc. to pull ourselves together again. Then battalion drill, route marching, general tactical training and finally assault tactics. For the latter, a regular plan was made over the surrounding country of the exact formation of entire positions and defences of the German Army in front of Arras which we were to attack in one grand assault in the near future. The officers studied special maps issued to them. Some of the senior ones and all company commanders were taken up in aeroplanes to view the actual German defences, and on several occasions the whole division worked together in rehearsing its part in the assault to come. A line of drummers in front acted as a moving barrage.

Ours was the 12th Brigade of the 4th Division and our brigadier was Carton-de-Wiart, a famous one-armed and one-eyed general who had been wounded seven times. He used to come up on his horse and question each officer personally. I remember being the target of his questions for nearly an hour one morning, during one of these exercises. I took a great liking to him and had much confidence in him.

We used to ride sometimes when off duty to Auxi-le-Château, a very attractive little town or to St Pol. In the latter place I bought a gold filigree bracelet which I sent home to Brenda. I thought it might help her to remember me, should I be destroyed in the forthcoming holocaust.

We lost our Colonel Jones who was promoted brigadier to take over a brigade in another division. I was truly sorry to see him go although glad for his sake; if he lived he would go far. He was replaced over us by a special reserve major, who of course had not the experience and training of Colonel Jones and so had no easy job to take charge of us just before a big offensive. He had, however, excellent support in Captain Irwin as an adjutant who was a regular and with long experience on this Western Front.

Having been in charge of a company for some months I had been an acting captain. I was soon confirmed in my rank of a regular captain, having now a regular commission, with only three years service, instead of ten years to reach captaincy in peacetime.

I now heard that my young brother Phil had not only got his commission but was already out in France with his battalion, the 1st Royal West Kents whom he had joined some weeks previously, so we both were in the two regiments that our ancestors had commanded many years previously. Though proud of the lad, I was none too happy, I thought him too young to have to go through what I knew he must. After all he was only just nineteen years old that month and he would probably be commanding men old enough to be his father. The extraordinary coincidence was, however, that I received from Phil a letter that my recent Colonel Jones had taken over the brigade that Phil's regiment was in. I was pleased at that. I knew that Jones would get to hear of Phil.

About now I came in contact for the first time with Australian troops. In the past few months the Australians had had some hard and successful fights and had shown themselves excellent and fearless scrappers. They were indeed a fine upstanding lot of men of large frames and their uniform and hats added to their looks. Unfortunately, however, they gave the Military Police a good deal of trouble behind the lines. They were rather inclined to kick at rules and regulations which were essential for the proper conduct of the war, and thereby, if anything, undid some of the good work at the front. They have been greatly extolled as soldiers by some writers in a scrap or free for all, but when good discipline throughout is also a necessity for proper control and maneuvering of an army as a necessity for the successful conduct of a war, one cannot call them first class soldiers. Their mode of life in the open air in the bush at the backblocks on the outback station gave them fearless individual initiative as well as healthy strong bodies.

The war must have been less of a trial to them than to the half-fed under-grown masses who had nothing but the dirt and smoke of the slums of our manufacturing towns and the mass outlook of a dense population, most of whom had probably never had a night away from a warm, snug though possibly poor, bed. It was always a wonder to me how those English lads got down to it, set their teeth to all iron discipline and took to the business in hand with grim determination. Exceptions there are to every rule and no doubt there were amongst the Aussies as well as our own men. But the English or at any rate the English press, are ever over generous to our overseas comrades and belaud them, while inclined to forget their own.

We saw something of the South African troops as well. I was very taken with them; they seemed to have a mixture of our own seriousness and the Australian dash and initiative. I had not at this period, come in contact with any New Zealanders, though we had read of their excellent qualities from time to time in the Army reports.

CHAPTER FIFTEEN

'Nothing daunted we moved on, men dropping faster here and there and the gaps being filled up from those behind'

The Battle of Arras in 1917 was intended to bring the war to a close. Conducted in concert with a French attack to the south, the aim was to punch a hole through German lines. Robin was injured on its first day.

Before they were moved to Arras, there was training to ensure that every man in the regiment could throw bombs, let off rifle grenades, operate a trench mortar and fire a Lewis gun.

On 8 April the battalion was marched to the assembly area, in time for zero hour on the following day. To one side of the Essex Regiment were the Lancashire Fusiliers, to the other side the Somerset Light Infantry.

Action began unfolding early on the following day, Easter Monday, in flurries of light snow. The Essex men got involved in the afternoon with three prisoners being taken before enemy artillery had burst into action. Four 5.9 guns were quickly captured, along with more prisoners within half an hour.

An advance party of wire cutters could see the backs of fleeing Germans. However, three were killed when two machine guns suddenly burst into life. Lewis gunners strode forward, shooting from the hip, to stop the deadly rattle. It was in the responding shell fire that Robin was wounded.

He was among sixty from the battalion who were injured that day. Eleven men were killed and four were missing in action. There were 230 prisoners taken with twenty-four guns, three trench mortars and seven machine guns captured.

Three days later Lieutenant Colonel Mullock was killed and his place as commanding officer was taken by Major Irwin who had saved Robin in the gas attack of 2 May 1915.

Although Robin saw the initial objectives secured and the battle continued with some Allied successes, its main aim of shortening the war was not achieved.

ROBIN

So the pleasant days passed all too quickly and we gradually moved up behind the front of our objective. This was the biggest drive yet of the war. The

Divisional Commander had a parade of all the officers and gave us a final lecture, adding that the concentration of guns and ammunition was the heaviest yet made and to remember that all possible would be done to support us. We were given definite objectives which we ought to be able to take owing to the weight of the attack, but we hoped it would not stop there, that we would break through the German line and keep on moving gradually for the Rhine. How often had I heard similar talk.

As we neared Arras we noticed great activity on all sides, guns and ammunition and reinforcements moving up. The sky was full of aeroplanes, numerous aerial combats occurred above our heads. We watched, in the distance, our airmen continually bringing down German sausage balloons. Gradually we were advancing into the jaws of Moloch.

On 7 April we encamped about four miles west of Arras on the main road. We could hear the guns thundering away; everything was in readiness for this supreme test, everything worked out to the last detail.

The assault was to be made in three distinct phases. The first assault, after the preliminary bombardment, was to be made on the Red Line, those series of trenches about half a mile deep which composed of the enemy's first line of defence. For this purpose the troops were already in position in and around our own front line which was about a mile east of the town proper of Arras. The second wave was to follow the first, then go through them and take the Blue Line, consisting mainly of a line of strongly fortified redoubts and the deep railway cutting of the Arras–Lens Railway. The troops for this were first assembled in the underground caves in and around Arras, and moved up in the morning of the attack.

Our division was to take part in the third wave and capture a Green Line, a double row of strongly fortified trenches a mile beyond the Blue Line. For this purpose we were moved up on the morning of the assault along the Ste Catherine – St Nicolas route via the square or round 'Place' in Arras itself.

Arras was pretty well knocked about, though nothing as bad as Ypres had been when I was there. Shells were still falling as we went through early in the morning of 9 April. A dull miserable wet dawn it was.

As we passed the Faubourg St Nicolas we came below a ridge where the artillery were massed, literally wheel to wheel and pounding away as I had never heard before, we had to put cotton wool in our ears to prevent our ear-drums from bursting. The noise was appalling. There was a terrific artillery fire being poured into the German lines and as our brigade waited en masse behind the guns we could visualise to ourselves that terrible fire that we had so often undergone and which now on our behalf was tearing up the landscape and snuffing nearly every living thing in its path, unless it was well underground.

While here we heard that the Highlanders in front of us had swept over the first line (Red Line) and found no resistance, as everything was obliterated. The second wave had encountered some resistance along the cuttings and embankments of the Lens–Douai railway which had given the enemy a certain amount of shelter.

After about an hour's wait we followed up, at first in artillery formation. The fight was waging away to the front of us and we moved forward over the shell-smashed German lines; barbed wire lying around as it had been churned up, dugouts blown, dead bodies, or rather, bits of dead bodies, with here and there an occasional Jock who had been shot by some solitary survivor.

Presently we passed over the second or Blue Line where our side were consolidating their gains, collecting their wounded and cheering us on.

As we moved past them we moved out into extended order and an artillery barrage came down to cover our advance. I was actually in the front line of this advance and the barrage kept a wonderfully even line, a curtain of continuous fire, about 100 yards just ahead of us, creeping forward at walking pace.

The smoke and fountain of earth helped to conceal our advance as well as tending to diminish any fire from snipers or machine guns or any entrenched infantry ahead of us. A few small tanks waddled along behind us (the first I had seen) to help us in case we got caught by a snag in the way of a redoubt or nest of machine guns. The German artillery up to this point had been fairly effectively silenced, though a few shells kept falling. One such shell actually hit a tank and knocked it out just behind me. It was not long however before all the tanks were out of action and I don't think we thought much of their use at that time.

When we had gone about 500 yards two guns of the German artillery hidden in a dip running across our front opened point blank at us. We took them in one concerted rush after they had bowled over a few of our men, the fact of being in a thin extended order saved further slaughter and saved the rest of us.

A few of the gunners who resisted with small arms, were bayoneted, the rest had their hands up in surrender; they were collected and sent to our rear under escort. There were several deep dug-outs on the uneven slope of the dip. A party specially told off for the purpose and armed with smoke bombs, bombed these dug-outs and drove out a number of gunners like rabbits. Having cleaned this nest out, we moved on. This little affair had delayed us a bit and our barrage had disappeared a way ahead of us, with the result that we now came under considerable rifle and machine-gun fire and the German shelling was beginning to wake up again.

We presently came up to the northern outskirts of the village of Athies and two lines of defence facing us. The wire was fortunately pretty well cut up and defences considerably battered. We found considerable resistance however. It must be understood that our wave consisted of several lines of men in extended order five paces between each man and some ten or twelve lines 50 yards behind each other. As the leading line found resistance those behind, closing up, lent weight to the attack. We rushed the defences in which the few remaining Germans gave only a half-hearted attempt to resist with cold steel. There was some chasing in and out of a few battered buildings in Athies and a cleaning up of the two lines of trenches (dealing with Germans).

So far our casualties had been fairly light and we sent back a further batch of prisoners. Our final objective for the day had yet to be overcome and we set out on another half mile of advance. In the first few hundred yards we were hardly fired at except by artillery and we managed to shake our lines out into parade-like order again. By this time our own artillery had either ceased to function or was so far ahead as to be useless to us. Whoever was responsible for liaison between our part of the attack and our supporting artillery seemed to have fallen down on his job; anyhow from now on we were on our own, without them and with much heavier German shelling against us.

We came across another dip where we expected further resistance, but the place which had been occupied by artillery had been abandoned, our friends to our left had apparently turned their flank and forced them out.

So with renewed optimism we pushed ahead. Then within sight of our last objective, the last of the Green Line, we came under really heavy fire. Nothing daunted we moved on, men dropping faster here and there and the gaps being filled up from those behind. We moved steadily on with the casualties continually increasing. When within charging distance we rushed at the barbed wire, which to our dismay we found utterly untouched by our artillery and at least 30 yards deep; some of it was terrible stuff with barbs an inch long and so close together as to be almost contiguous. We were being blazed at, at point blank range. I could hear the swish of machine-gun bullets as they swept up and down our lines.

Feeling utterly nonplussed for a moment, I dived down to earth, the men following suit. I got them firing through the wire at the German parapet and got my nearest Lewis gun going, sweeping over the Germans in an attempt to check their fire. Under cover of this fire a party to my right had discovered a gap in the wire and dashed in.

On seeing them move we got up and made a dash straight ahead across the wire. I tore my hands and breeches knees, but kept going, the machine gunner right opposite me getting more frantic with his gun as he swung it round to and fro and it is no exaggeration to say that as he swished his gun around, one bullet clipped my right ear and the next my left ear – had anyone ever a narrower shave. The one that clipped my left ear got my sergeant who was just behind me, right through the head and he went limp over the wire.

This was the first and last time I saw red, really saw red. I lunged forward, revolver in hand and blazed at the German gunner and his crew. How they never got me I don't know, I was in a tearing rage and shooting fast, bowling them over. I suppose the man actually on the gun went down first and the others were too dazed to act quickly enough.

The next thing I remember was a score of hands stuck up saying '*Kamerad*'. I would have emptied my revolver into them again if I had had time to reload thinking of the dirty swine who had fired at us when we were under difficulties, at point blank range and now that we were on top of them they surrendered. I never knew till then that I could swear so. In white heat I let loose the most vile vituperation imaginable and only came to my senses when I realised that my men were seeing red too and had started in to cut them to pieces.

Feeling suddenly ashamed, I had the greatest difficulty in restraining them and it was not till my flow of language had turned on them and several Germans had been bayoneted that I succeeded. We cleaned this trench up of the enemy, sent the prisoners back, reformed and went on to the enemy support line 100 yards further on which we found deserted; they had probably come up to support the line we had just taken. So our final objective was reached.

Somebody asked me where I was hit as my face was pouring blood on both sides; I put my hand up and found the tips of the lobes of both ears bleeding, where the machine gun had nicked the edges. I had forgotten about it in the general mêleé.

We called the roll to find who was missing. Our CO had been killed by a shell while attacking this trench and one other officer in this battalion wounded. The casualties were fairly light considering the nature of the final assault, but I think the Germans' rifle fire had been erratic owing to nervousness of seeing lines of bayonets steadily advancing at them and never seeming to falter, and I don't think they were too well supported from the rear, it had been a long day for them. The main body had dropped back to consolidate a better position and these had been a sort of rearguard.

This was now about 2pm and we snatched a meal from our haversacks and prepared to consolidate the position.

Other people across the River Scarpe, not far from us on our right, had advanced somewhat ahead of us, so apparently it was decided by the Staff that we should yet go ahead to keep up with them. To the right front of us was the village of Fampoux and to the left front what was known as the Hyderabad Redoubt.

We were ordered once more to launch our weary selves at these two objectives and the line joining them. So the brigade once more pushed ahead. The evening fire was very heavy now, especially machine-gun fire at long range from Greenland Hill away to our left front over and beyond the Hyderabad Redoubt. Our right flank, after a desperate assault entered and captured Fampoux, but our centre and left got a heavy mauling and were held up till further reinforcements thickened the line and pushed ahead.

The shelling by the Germans had now become very heavy and in our last dash towards the redoubt what felt like a thunderbolt struck me in the region of the heart and I went down in agonizing pain; a piece of shell from a high explosive had struck me in the chest. It was now getting dark and there I lay breathing in great gasps. I never lost consciousness, it would had been better for my agony of mind and body if I had.

I thought, owing to the region of the wound and the awful agony, that I had had it this time and that I was mortally wounded and would be left there in the dark to die. I did not want to die, life was sweet, especially just now as I wanted so much to see my sweetheart again. I kept calling her name in a low moan. No one who has been full of the vitality of life one moment and struck down almost dying the next, knows what the mental agony of it is.

I lay there three hours; it seemed three years. The attack here had failed and our line had fallen back on the last of the Green Line we had taken that afternoon so that I was now in no man's land, and unless men came out into it I should not be found. However, I finally heard somebody moving about. A pair of stretcher bearers were wandering round looking for wounded. They bumped into me, picked me up, put me on their stretcher and started off back. They were 'Derby-ites', men over forty called up under Lord Derby's scheme before conscription was actually in force.

These men were either feeling their age or had just started their baptism of fire, at any rate as they carried me along they panted and puffed and they were very clumsy with the stretcher and jolted it along. Of course it was dark and I suppose easy to stumble. I was surprised later when I had had time to think about it that they had been brave enough to come out into no man's land – of course they had been ordered out to look for wounded, but probably had no idea where they were as far as proximity to the enemy was concerned.

I was in terrible agony with every jolt. They kept tripping over wire, falling into shell holes and every now and then when a salvo of shells came at all near, they would drop me and run for cover. I thought in the dark they would fail to find me again or even desert me. I cursed them heartily and grew desperate. I still had my revolver with me; I told them that if they dropped me like that again I would shoot them both; also unless they pulled themselves together and went more steadily and slowly instead of trying to hurry and trip over everything, I would place them under arrest and report it at the dressing station. This seemed to steady their nerves a bit and after what seemed an eternity I was taken down a deep dugout where a field dressing station had been established.

A doctor bent over and examined me. The exhaustion of the stretcher trip had nearly caused me to swoon. He said something but I could not reply. When he had cut my clothes away and saw my chest I heard him say to someone, I am sure he thought I was unconscious, '*I am afraid he is in a bad way, but he may pull through.*' It did not cheer me up much.

I lay on the stretcher all that night; I suppose I must have shown more life towards morning for I was taken out and put in an ambulance. I remember very little more after that until I found myself in a ward of the Duchess of Westminster's hospital.

It was about midnight when I arrived there and there was a sort of soft, subdued, electric lighting from the ceiling. It was a large, magnificent ward. To me just from the dirt and blood of the battlefield, and not having seen the inside of much more than a hovel for many months, it seemed like a fairy palace, and presently a fairy herself, in the form of a lovely young nurse, appeared. She put her arm under my neck to lift my head to give me a drink and crooned softly to me, or so it seemed. Life was good after all, I thought, only if I could get over this lot of trouble. I shuddered to think that I might have left my carcass in that cold blood-soaked no man's land, and in the flower of my youth have been cut off from so many good things yet to be, and plunged unwillingly into that great mysterious and doubtful beyond.

I slumbered with the aid of a sleeping draught and woke to a spotless whiteness of morning in the ward. I craned my neck round to see what my surroundings were; there must have been forty or fifty officers in that ward. On my right was a cheerful, young, handsome subaltern, half sitting up in bed. He had had two neat little holes drilled through some portion of his chest which had touched neither bone nor vital part, and were fast healing up; but he had also lost one foot which had been smashed by a shell. He was soon chattering away to me, telling me about the hospital, etc. He said that many of the young ladies there acting as sisters were society ladies and even some titled ones, though they had all assumed other names while in that capacity. I asked him about the little nurse who had attended to me; he said that she went by the name of Miss Frazer but he believed her to be the Honourable somebody or other. Later we used to joke and have fun with the said Miss Frazer, and she was very nice to us. I tried hard to draw out of her her real name, but she would not give it away. The Duchess herself used to come round the wards in a white uniform with a little red cross on her bonnet.

On my left behind a screen was a poor Canadian lad who had had his leg badly injured by a shell. He kept having to have bits off as gangrene had set in, and one day he departed this life to the gloom of those around him. His bed was soon filled with another bad case. We used to enquire eagerly of news of the war, as to how the latest offensive was faring. The sisters told us that the casualties were coming in very heavily. I was anxious about my brother Phil, wondering where he was and how he was faring.

To my astonishment in walked Phil one morning, grinning all over. The great lad had heard of me being wounded from Brigadier General Jones who had told him he could have a week's leave to come and see me, so he had hitch-hiked on the first available lorry, and by going from one to another that happened to be travelling in my direction he managed to get four days in Wimereux. By Jove I was pleased to see him and so hale and hearty. He told me he had been in the same battle but further north at Vimy Ridge, that his battalion had been incorporated temporarily with a Canadian brigade and that their day had been fairly successful. After several advances they had been relieved for a week, and that was how he had got leave to come away. He brought me a cheering message from General Jones who was the first to inform Phil that I had been wounded and where I was in hospital. I don't know how he knew, but it showed his interest in those who served under him.

Phil spent many hours at my bedside, as long as the ward matron would allow him. In the afternoon he had a dip in the sea where he met some Canadian nurses who invited him up to tea at the Canadian General Hospital. He told me next day how much more free and easy and with a carefree cama-raderie they seemed to be compared to our rather conventional English nurses.

I asked him where he was putting up. Oh, he said, those Canadian nurses had found him a bed in the hospital and let him feed at their mess.

'*I see what you mean*', I replied, '*I am afraid there is too much red tape in hospitals like this one for that sort of thing to be possible; the English authorities would be horrified at the thought. Thank those Canadians for me too will you, I appreciate them fixing you up like that.*'

I introduced Phil to Miss Frazer, and in his polite gallantry he asked her how his brother had wangled his way to be nursed by one so charming and could he book a bed there should he be wounded.

Phil said to me, '*I suppose, Robin, this wound pretty well prevents you coming out again to the active front?*'

'*Oh,*' I replied, '*not necessarily, I still have all my limbs and though the wound is very near the heart – actually it has cut the pericardium or sack in which the heart rests – yet it has not as far as I am told done any vital damage; but they are waiting to see if they can operate, because it is so close to the heart where the piece of metal is lodged. I have been X-rayed and they now await the specialists' verdict. If they can take it out I should be all right, if not my days are numbered.'*

'In any case,' replied Phil, *'what with three wounds and a gassing I don't think they ought to send you out again.'*

I told him about Carton de Wiart, my brigadier and his seven wounds, loss of eye and one arm, and still on the battlefield. But he argued that de Wiart was a general and not a fighter in the front line, etc. Well, I said that a general certainly has more comforts and is not so often in the front line, otherwise he could not do his job properly but Carton de Wiart was seen up there as often as any general. However the gist of what Phil was getting at was that he wanted to tell me about a circular memorandum which had been sent round his brigade asking for officers to volunteer for the Indian Army; and Phil suggested that I put in for it so that I at least would get a change from the Western Front should I happen to be passed medically fit again.

My first reaction to this was not at all receptive. I did not fancy leaving the British service and I explained to Phil that I was now as much a regular soldier as he was from Sandhurst. He agreed, but said he knew two regulars who had put in for transfer to the regular Indian Army because it was much better paid and would mean a permanent commission as much as the English one; and he pointed out that at least one of us might see something more of our father who must be having a terribly neglected and lonely sort of life. I certainly agreed with this latter point of view.

I thought to myself, I wish Phil would put in for it. A subaltern's life on the average lasted only three weeks in this war on the Western Front and he had already been out considerably longer than that, though he would have said much the same of me.

Finally having thought it over I said to Phil, *'Look here, old chap, how about both of us putting in for it. It would be nice for both of us if we soldiered together in India. I will promise to put in for it if you will do the same, how is that?'*

'Well, I'll think about it, Robin, and let you know.'

'Don't be too long over it, Phil, remember your allowance of three weeks being the average of a subaltern's life is long passed; it seems a callous thing to say to you but I'd like to see you survive this war as much as myself.'

Then the cheerful lad went off again like going to a rollicking football match instead of to the grimmest struggle man had ever undertaken.

CHAPTER SIXTEEN

'I am also beginning to feel the effects of this war especially in the dark, when a gun fires not very far away or a sniper skims the parapet'

There's a gap in his letters at the beginning of 1917 as Phil enjoyed leave. The Royal West Kents had a relatively quiet time consolidating after their losses of the previous year. In addition to training there were games of football, boxing, cross country and tug-of-war competitions as well as travelling entertainers including the 'Whiz Bang' Pierrot troupe, the Royal Engineers Band from Chatham and a mobile cinema.

The tempo was hiked in April when the battalion was involved in the Battle of Vimy Ridge. Phil is now openly admitting that the war has affected his nerves in letters that sidestep the censor, as officers were trusted to censor themselves.

Phil and Robin were separated by a few miles at this point, although the opportunities to pay social calls were inevitably limited.

In October Phil went to the Ypres Salient, where Robin had been gassed two and a half years previously.

21 January 1917
Somewhere in France

Dear Aunt Ethel,

I have burnt my gloves you sent me, that yellow pair and I am awfully angry about it because they were a jolly fine pair. I got them wet coming across* and I put them by the stove in our mess and the stove got red hot and burnt through the gloves. You might send me another pair. I think you can get a brown leather pair but I am not sure & you might also send me another pair of those socks I bought – those bed socks. You can get them in a shop half way up Regents Street. The shop is full of brown woollen clothes. It is colder today and there is plenty of snow hanging about. There was quite a small strafe up the line this morning with guns.

Have you heard from Rex again. I have forgotten his address. How's Dorothy eh?

Your affectionate nephew,
Phil

---

* Rd'AG-M notes 'ie across the channel I expect he means'.

23 January 1917

Dear Aunt Ethel,   *Somewhere in France*

I wonder if you have got my first letter posted on Friday night I think. I have received no letters from anybody yet, it looks a long time I suppose because I had none during leave. It is still freezing & frightfully cold, absolutely agonizing in early morning parade. You can't feel your fingers after a few minutes.

Has Robin come out yet?

By the way you know I enquired about my accounts at Cox's & I was £9-12 in debt with Dec' money still coming, well that was on the 17th. I got a letter from Cox's saying I was £7-14 in debt dated the 16th I shall wait for Dec allowances before replying. When ought my income tax to come in?

Let's have all the news when you can.

Your affectionate nephew,
   Phil

27 January 1917

Dear Aunt Ethel,   *Somewhere in France*

We are now in the line and it is bitterly cold. Every bit of a trench is frozen hard as iron and in some places there is about 4 to 6 inch thick ice and we go sliding and slipping all over the place. I shall be jolly glad when the Spring arrives with the warmer weather because this I loathe & hate although it is very dry indeed.

There is no news here at all. I expect you have got my letters by this time. Could you send me out another cake like the last and also a tin of Rowntrees cocoa, also a small packet of peppermints as I don't like & don't take rum, they will come in handy to keep me warm.

I expect you heard that explosion [at Silvertown]* the other day, it was terrific I expect.

Must end now as I go on duty now.

Your affectionate nephew,
   Phil

29 January 1917

Dear Aunt Ethel,   *Somewhere in France*

We are not in the actual line now but resting in a tumbled down house with a glorious log fire, it is absolutely priceless after a few days of awful cold in the line.

It is still very cold but I believe it is beginning to thaw & so consequently it will be awful & gallons of water all over the place. We are all very happy

---

* An explosion at an ammunition factory in Silvertown, East London, on 19 January 1917 killed 73 people and left 400 with injuries.

though & I can't write this letter properly because the officer next to me keeps on punching and pulling me about, but he is a jolly nice chap.

There is nothing to write about so you must not expect much news except that two or three times it was pretty warm whizzbanging that is a small 18-pounder gun of theirs.

    Your affectionate nephew,
      Phil

                                       8 February 1917
Dear Aunt Ethel,   *Same address*
I hope you got my last letter, I wrote, I think last night. It has not been so cold the last two days but all the same it is cruelly cold. I did not get much sleep last night. At 3.30am this morning we were awakened by a nice strafe by Fritz. We happened to be in rather a strong dugout so we were safe but we could see the flashes through the entrance. There were plenty of whiz-bangs and shrapnel bursting for 1½ hrs right over us. Twice I had to go out and take a message & got back safely both times, but once coming back three shells burst right in front of me but I was not touched. You will see it in the papers I expect. Otherwise there is not much in the way of news here. Let's have all the news you can give.

    Your affectionate nephew,
      Phil

                                      14 February 1917
Dear Aunt Ethel,   *Same address*
I have written thanking you for the gloves & also cake & cocoa. It is starting to thaw here and so there is a great deal of mud & water and it is also cold.

    We were inspected by Sir Douglas Haig yesterday & complimented on a raid we had done a few days ago. You will hardly notice it in the papers as there are only 2 lines about it. It was ripping and I got very warm, we captured a good few prisoners and so I have a good few souvenirs. There is not much news nowadays. I have just been firing with a Boche rifle. I have not heard from Rex yet and only twice from Robin.

    Your affectionate nephew,
      Phil

                           Not dated – envelope postmarked
                                  22 February 1917
Dear Aunt Ethel,   *Same address*
The mail has not come in yet tonight so I write before in order to catch the post.

    I have received the stocking socks, thanks, and also the bulls eyes which everybody took a liking to at once. I have not had another letter from Robin again, I don't know if he has joined his regiment yet.

Yes, that would be best to pay Newcomb's bill with that railway money. There is no news here at all. The weather is awful, simply dreadful. It has started to thaw thoroughly and it has rained the last two days and so there is plenty of water about but not a drop to drink. I have a nasty sore throat & a nasty cough. I am also beginning to feel the effects of this war especially in the dark, when a gun fires not very far away or a sniper skims the parapet & just misses, my heart sinks and I get a peculiar hot air in my mouth, altogether nasty.

Must end now.

Your affectionate nephew,
   Phil

24 February 1917
Dear Aunt Ethel,   *Same address*
I am feeling extremely fed up just now because they have sent me to a school for a few days. They do this occasionally to give officers a rest as they call it. It is no rest from what I hear and it is monotonous. I would much rather be up the line with the rest.

I will let you have more news of it when I get there.

The other day, I don't know if I told you or not, I was working within a foot of a fellow when 'ping', he lay dead at my feet just like Robin's time do you remember? There is an officer attached to us now, a Captain, he was there in the trench about 15 yards away when it happened. He had never been out before & he turned as white as a sheet & had to sit down. Afterwards he got quite annoyed with another officer whom I know very well because this officer calmly put a cigarette in his mouth and asked for a match, & getting no reply he again asked for a match very curtly. Must end now.

   Phil

27 February 1917
Dear Aunt Ethel,   *Same address*
I have gone to school now, I think I gave you a slight hint that I was being sent to school. Well we arrived here I & another fellow, we were told to have certain things but fortunately there was no matron to check the things. Then I was told that tea was at 4pm & dinner at 8pm. I was told I must be in for dinner but need not be in for tea. Then I was allotted a bed in a dormitory where there are 36 little beds. We are taught in the yard to slope arms by numbers & also to form fours by numbers also. We were told to be good little boys and not to break any rules whatever! We have a monitor (i.e. orderly officer) to see that all good little boys are in by 10.30pm & in bed by 11pm. We work from 9.15am to 1pm from 2pm to 6.30pm & the remainder of the time is our own! There is not much news otherwise. I'll try & write you a more interesting letter next time. I have still a bad cold.

   Phil

10 March 1917
Dear Aunt Ethel,   Same address
There's no news here. Yesterday I heard from Rex saying he was very fed up
and was willing to change places with the last tommy in my regiment. He said it
was very dull there except for polo twice a week and that nothing exciting ever
happens. He said the journey out was great especially in a Ford car across the
desert.

I have written him a letter saying that it is not to be his lot to come out here
he should not try to get into the army.

We experimented with a huge explosive this morning to blow up barbed wire
and my word it did make a row & it did tear the wire up (Bangalore torpedo).
By this you can tell I am still at the school. Hoping to get a letter today. By the
way thanks awfully for the 2nd lot of bulls eyes, they were very nice

Robin is sure to get three pips & pay.

Must end now. Yours,
    Phil

14 March 1917
Dear Aunt Ethel,   Same address
Thanks for yours of 7/3/17 which I received day before yesterday. Yes, we are
getting on fairly well at the school. We finish next Friday & I go back to my
battalion then which is out for a rest for a little while. We have had two lots of
exam papers. The first lot I got good paper for it & attention paid to lectures but
rather untidy. Well I have always been untidy & I don't think I shall ever be
tidy. The second lot we have not heard yet. My Coy Commander & one officer
have got the MC now, I don't know if I told you.

If Robin is training hard that means business – always does. And we are
training hard so look out for squalls as they say and my bet is there will be some
storms too. Glad to hear about Rex, I hope he won't be able to get into the army,
two of us is quite enough out here and if both go well there will be Rex & Bert
& later on the other two. Yes, I have heard from Rex and I think I said so in
my last letter to you.

It has turned much warmer, very wet. Glad to hear Robin got his pack back.
By the way soon I shall be sending home most things else they will be lost when
we start work!! Do send the gingerbread & if possible one of Elizabeth's as I call
them.

Yours,
    Phil

5 April 1917

Dear Aunt Ethel,   *Same address*

Thanks for yours of 2nd inst. just received. Yes, I got the gingerbread, bulls eyes & toffee, thanks. I was very sorry to hear of Mr Raven's death, it must be an awful blow to Margaret. This letter is just to let you know that something is going to happen in the next few days, & it is quite possible that I shall never be able to write a letter to you or anybody. I am not writing this to cause anxiety but to let you know at least prepare you in case anything does happen & I get killed. If I come through I'll write at once & let you know as much as I can but I feel sure I shall come through. I am at present in a camp now in tents & up to my neck in work so I can't get much time to write to anybody.

Give my love to Enid, Dorothy etc and please tell Margaret how sorry I am to hear of R's death.

Yours,

Phil

Later. Yes I was very glad to hear that Robin got his Captaincy & I hope he sticks to it. Yesterday was very cold & today is quite warm and we have been out the whole day. My Brigadier asked my Colonel if I had a brother in Robin's Regt. as he used to be Robin's Adjutant. My general is a topping old sport awfully nice looking man & very affable to everybody.

Yes, I have had a platoon all to myself for a long time & I hope to do well with it in the next show.

I am glad to hear Reggie is getting on all right & is well. Sorry I have not written to Enid lately but I have been very busy lately with the Battn. You might show her this letter.

The other day we had a fearful fall of snow just as we came into camp. I am getting slightly fed up with the war now. By the way I got a very sweet and short letter from Dorothy. What's the matter?

12 April 1917

Dear Aunt Ethel,   *Same address*

Sorry I have not written lately but I have been over the top for the first time in a big attack as you see by the papers on Monday 9th & we were right in the middle of the attack but I can't tell you anything. I did not sleep from Sunday morning till Wednesday 7am so you can imagine how tired I was & then I slept from 7am till 3.30pm. My Brigadier told my Colonel that Robin was not far from me and might come over to see me. I must end now as I am very tired.

Yours,

Phil

17 April 1917

Dear Aunt Ethel,   Same address

Thank you for your last letter with chocolate, which I don't think lasted very long as so many people seemed to like it. I got it the night before last at the beginning of mess & it was gone at the end of mess. You might send me some more for my birthday with the cake you promised. You keep on asking to know about where I am at present. Well at present I am behind the most important place where the Canadians had this great victory & we took the highest part of that ridge, but it is not mentioned in the papers about us because it is information for the enemy I suppose.

The weather here is simply awful, it keeps on raining day after day & it is very rotten especially when we are under canvas. You might send me a little pocket writing pad. No other news

Your affectionate nephew,

Phil

P.S. Do you mind giving Enid and Dorothy a photo each of myself as Enid asked?

20 April 1917

Dear Aunt Ethel,   Same address

Thank you for yours of 15th instant. It came as a shock to me because I had been out on a working party all day yesterday and in the evening when I got back I got your letter saying that Robin was wounded severely. Well I had tried to get a few hours leave to go & see him as my Brigadier said he was not very far from here, & I was expecting to be told that I would go when I got your letter. Well yesterday late last night I phoned from Brigade HQ to the hospital to enquire how he was & they told me he was there & that everything was quite satisfactory. I am afraid it will be a great disappointment to him just after getting his 3 pips again for the 2nd time, and also he must have been wounded just before this last big show, and I should also think that he will never come out here again, as his last wound will affect him; it isn't as if it was his first wound.

I hope he will come through it all right, everybody was very sympathetic especially the CO as the Brigadier had told him that Robin was very, very keen out here & that will make it a bigger disappointment, but I hope he won't think of those points too much as it won't be too good for him. He is in the Duchess of Westminster's hospital, I think, & I am trying to get leave to go & see him.

I am at the same place as the last time I wrote to you and quite safe but any moment we might be in for a show so it is very uncertain.

Your affectionate nephew,

Phil

P.S. When writing to Robin you might tell him that Brigadier Jones was very sorry to hear that he was wounded.

CHAPTER SEVENTEEN

'We were a very cheery and happy crowd together and dances were arranged for us about once a week'

In the Spring of 1917 there was new hope among the Allies. Three days before Robin was injured America joined the war. A new global power, it had observed from the sidelines for several years – not least because there was a substantial population of German descent within its borders. Irish Americans were equally lukewarm at the prospect of America entering the European war on the side of the British.

But as Germany persisted with its policy of sinking shipping regardless of the flag it flew, the number of American casualties rose until the government, led by the Europhile Woodrow Wilson, won substantial backing and declared war.

The injection of men and equipment was timely as Russia was about to withdraw from hostilities following a revolution that toppled the Tsarist regime and instituted the first government brandishing a socialist manifesto. Moreover, French troops on the Western Front were heading towards a large-scale mutiny, after three years in the trenches with little to show for the wholesale loss of life. The arrival of the Americans was one of the 'carrots' used to encourage soldiers back to the front line.

Amongst the technology hurried along by the advent of war was the X-ray machine. A German physicist, Wilhelm Roentgen, is credited as being the first to discover the existence of X-rays. It soon became apparent there were hazards when the new science was applied, with human guinea pigs losing their hair or contracting cancer.

Marie Curie did much to improve the safety of the X-ray machine. At the start of the First World War she fitted ambulances with X-ray equipment and drove them herself to the front line where she and other volunteers could operate them.

They were used to detect bullets, shrapnel and broken bones, helping doctors to make swift and accurate diagnoses. The use of an X-ray machine on Robin no doubt facilitated his recovery. He was at a hospital in Le Touquet sponsored by the Duchess of Westminster, who was married to one of the richest men in the world at the time. After the war she divorced the duke and remarried a former aviator whom she met when he had been treated at the hospital.

ROBIN

I was X-rayed again for the second time at this hospital, the surgeon was apparently still doubtful. The duchess herself was in attendance this time; she used to be rather fond of the X-ray rooms.

Shortly after this I was transferred to England. My wound was caused by a jagged piece of shell about 1½ inches long and ½-inch thick that had smashed my breast bone, split the tips of two ribs and cut through the pericardium or covering of the heart. As it had then lodged itself behind the heart, it was felt sufficiently serious to be operated on by an eminent Harley Street surgeon. We crossed the Channel again in much the same fashion as the previous time, but at Charing Cross I noticed that there was none of the eager crowd that had received us on the previous occasion. The public had grown more used to ambulance trains and had settled down to the grim job of war after the early excitement and enthusiasm had worn off.

This time I found myself in the Fishmongers' Hall, which does not sound exactly aristocratic. When I first heard the name, before I had seen the place, I thought what a come down it was from the Duchess of Westminster's hospital in France. It was, however, a magnificent place – even better than the Empire Hospital of my previous experience – and had been loaned to the authorities to be fitted up as a hospital by the Fishmongers' Company, one of the wealthiest concerns in London. It was a wonderful place where we each had a room to ourselves.

I was operated on not long after arriving there and when the great surgeon came to see me, after I had come to, he said, '*Well, we have made a good job of you. You will be quite all right now, but I think your soldiering days are over.*'

This last remark rather disappointed me, for, though I was not in love with the war, I felt then that I would like to have soldiering as my profession. Anyway, I had no other training and if I still happened to be in the land of the living when the war was over I should have loved to carry on in my regiment.

It was not long before my relations and friends were informed of my whereabouts and they came along each and several of them to see me. It was quite soon too when a radiant vision appeared at my door. I thought Brenda very beautiful; prejudiced eyes perhaps, though I would say not. We had a glorious and tender meeting and she and her mother stayed in London several days to be near me.

When I was getting better I was asked as to where I would like to convalesce and I said near Bournemouth if possible. The summer was ahead of us and the south coast seemed attractive. I never thought that red tape would actually accede to my request, but shortly afterwards I found myself in the neighbourhood of Bournemouth, at Highcliffe-on-Sea to be exact.

The wife of a rich Calcutta Englishman was doing her bit by turning two large country houses of hers into convalescent homes for officers. Everything was excellent and half the young ladies of the neighbourhood were doing VAD work in addition to a staff of trained nurses. The houses were in beautiful grounds, quite close to the sea, near a world famous beauty spot. We were a very cheery and happy crowd together and dances were arranged for us about once a week. As the weather grew warmer those of us who were well or on the way to recovery were allowed to bathe. In the summer Brenda and her parents came down to stay nearby, so I had a very happy time.

One day Phil turned up. He had ten days leave home and spent about a week of it with us. I remember several people remarking when he appeared in his bathing suit what a splendid figure of a man he was. He had a powerful build. That week was all too short and I was very glad that Brenda had met Phil. I reminded Phil of our pact and hoped he was doing something about his application to the Indian Army, but as far as I remember he was non-committal. As events turned out it was the last time any of us saw the lad. As explained later, a year afterwards he went to join the 'Glorious' company on the other side and his CO wrote that his transfer would have been shortly through; it had been delayed for reasons not under his control.

In the autumn I was again passed for home service and went to join the depot regiment again at Felixstowe. Of course this meant I was still near my fiancée, it being her home town. Most of the old crowd was still there, as far as the cadre of the regiment was concerned, since they were mostly those so wounded previously as to be unfit for further active service – Joe Ashley with his caustic humour, Colonel Crocker and so on.

Being a captain, and fairly senior one at that, now I was given charge of a company soon after arriving there. Funnily, if there was trouble brewing of any sort and I was about, I generally seemed to get mixed up in it. First of all the officer handing over to me was ordered off to France in a hurry and had to leave next morning. In the ordinary way when taking over a company in semi-peace conditions as this was, a form had to be signed by both to the effect that everything was correct after the books had been inspected and all articles on the strength of the company checked by both the receiving and handing over officers.

Now the company I was to take over consisted of about 900 men (usual company strength was about 200), returned from overseas through hospital and in all states of physical condition from A1, ready to return to France, to C3 or hopeless. They were scattered all over the town in about twenty billets.

They were continually changing, drafts going off and others returning from hospital. There were only one quartermaster sergeant and a couple of orderly room clerks who were permanent. The officers in charge had altered at least once a month. It was impossible to check everything such as rifles, bayonets, blankets, uniforms, equipment and a hundred other things in a week, let alone in one evening. This was not an ordinary company of 15 to 200 men all in one building, and with a full complement of officers and NCOs; even then to do the job properly would take at least a couple of days.

The officer going off the next morning gave me a general résumé of things as he had found them, and then handed me a slip of paper which he had signed and to which I was to pen my signature which would be saying that I had taken over the company complete and all correct. Of course this was a farce. I was in a quandary for a moment, I did not like this way of doing things but I knew it was absolutely impossible to check everything by the next morning.

I took my courage in both hands and refused point blank to sign. The outgoing officer was aghast, but I was adamant. When the orderly room was informed I was sent for by the adjutant who asked for an explanation. I said to him, '*Are you I the habit of signing a blank cheque?*'

He replied no, but asked me what I was getting at. When I told him he took me to the colonel who at first tried to overawe me. But when he saw that I was stubborn he began to listen to me and eventually saw my point of view. I carried on as company commander without having signed the necessary document. As fate would have it, a travelling inspection board came round shortly afterwards to check everything in the battalion. (It may have been that my action caused higher authorities to initiate this board, but that I don't know, it may have been coincidence.) Anyway I thanked my lucky stars that I had refused to sign, although I believe there were some ill feelings carried out to France against me about this matter.

The board checked my company and found six rifles short and 1,100 blankets missing, as well as a number of minor items. I was put on the mat by the board (who so far had not heard my side of the story).

'*Well,*' said the president of the board. '*You are the OC Coy and responsible for it. You know what is missing now, what have you to say for yourself?*'

Inwardly I was furious but I kept calm outwardly and replied, '*I cannot be held responsible for what has been going on for months before I appeared on the scene. I only took over this company a few days ago and as there was no time to check any-thing with the last officer, who left at a day's notice, I refused to sign the handing over documents. I was still in the middle of checking things over for my own satisfaction when the board arrived.*'

The CO and the Adjutant were sent for and they had to admit the truth of my statement. What would have happened if I had signed that document

I shudder to think. A court of enquiry was held and the matter dragged on over months. Certain witnesses who had got scattered into various units all over France had to be found and were brought over to give evidence. I was exonerated from all blame by the board and the losses had to be written off, to be paid for by the taxpayer as it could not be properly cleared up. Some of those who should have known better carried their resentment back with them across the water and did not always say nice things about me. What did they expect me to do, stand the racket for other people's failures? I wasn't quite such a mug.

Owing to this trouble it was decided to have a more permanent company of staff officers who were unfit for further active service, though owing to continuous changes by medical boards it was not entirely possible to effect changes. Anyhow, I was taken on the permanent staff as so far as it was then known I was not fit for further active service.

While in hospital I had had a startled recollection that the last time I had been wounded I had wanted to have a bayonet fighting course, but had some-how forgotten about it and luckily the matter had not worried me unduly during my second period in France. Now however, though I was for the time being unfit I was determined to get in a course in case I was passed fit again. Being in charge of a company there was some difficulty in being spared even for a short time but I managed however to get away for a course to Aldershot for a fortnight. When I came back to the battalion I had to be in charge of bayonet fighting instruction of the whole battalion as well as commanding my company. I began to wonder if it was worth volunteering for anything. But it also started the ball rolling, for during the next few months I was sent off at intervals to three more courses; musketry at Hythe, a Lewis gun course and a drill course with the Grenadier Guards at Chelsea barracks.

All this time I was still responsible for my company. I was sure I had brought it about by being too enthusiastic. At Chelsea the squad of officers I was in had a Welsh Guards Sergeant to drill us and he did put us through it. He thoroughly enjoyed cursing officers and would rap out sarcasms just for the fun of it, even when it was not necessary. However, I enjoyed myself and passed out with distinction. We had two New Zealand officers in our squad and they were surprised at this democratic interlude in our Imperial Army.

On rejoining the battalion I had to take a class of officers in the Guards' drill. I must say regimental drilling seemed much inferior to what we had learnt at the Guards!

During this time I made several new friends in the battalion, two partic-ularly, though this pair were a good deal younger than me and much junior to me. They had lately come from Sandhurst and were really awfully nice boys.

They were about Phil's age, though junior to him in rank as having graduated several months later than him.

They were Cadie and Chawner and I thought to myself life would be nice in the regiment after the war with boys like these to have as one's brother officers. They both were drafted to France shortly afterwards and I had a letter from Cadie saying that most of the fighting then consisted of nightly raids by both sides in endeavours to capture prisoners. He said he was not at all enamoured of these raids as they were very nerve shattering. He said he had heard rumours that I was one of the originators in the battalion of silent raids, why had I thought of such a thing? I think he must have been pulling my leg. Alas, these two really fine young chaps, the benefit of whose company I had had for only a few short months, were killed in these very similar night raiding parties which went out to capture German prisoners for the purpose of identifying German units.

Just about now I had a letter from Phil in which, amongst other news, he said he had sent in his application for the Indian Army and he asked if I was keeping my side of the bargain by applying myself. I had almost forgotten about the matter, chiefly because being so far only fit for home service, I naturally did not think that the Indian Office would accept me. However, it was not long after this that I had another medical board at which I made myself out as fit as possible. After considerable humming and hawing and suggesting I had better have another three months home service, I finally persuaded them to pass me fit for active service, whereon I immediately applied for the Indian Army. I felt I would not let Phil down.

To my surprise I was required to undergo yet another medical examination. I had already been passed fit to go into battle but now, as previously, I was to be examined for possible peace-time service should active service allow me to live that long. But perhaps it was something to do with service in the tropics, though I probably would not have been re-examined had I been posted to a British unit fighting in the tropics. However I was passed fit, and immediately wrote off and told Phil about it. He apparently had heard nothing yet; I suppose paper work was much slowed up out there through the exigencies of battle.

CHAPTER EIGHTEEN

'What an awful night to die on!'

War is an expensive business. Although Britain had the economic benefits of an empire, the conflict on the Western Front and elsewhere was draining the country's coffers. War loans or bonds were issued almost as soon as war was declared, to help finance the lengthy endeavour. The government offered its citizens the chance to purchase bonds that could be redeemed with interest in the Twenties. It was a patriotic gesture for those confined to the home front, to invest in the fighting men at the front. One estimate puts the cost of the First World War to Britain in today's money at £22,368,229,000.

The subject of the row between Phil and his Aunt Nellie isn't clear although it certainly involved money. His frustration at having to ponder financial matters while battling for survival is evident.

With pay standing at a shilling day, the financial reward for serving soldiers was not immense. Consequently, they set great store by the medals they received in recognition of their service.

There were five different campaign medals; the 1914 Star for the earliest men in the field, the 1914/15 Star for those who served in Belgium and France between 23 November 1914 and 31 December 1915 and in other theatres between August 1914 and the end of 1915. The British War Medal was for those who served abroad during the war while the Territorial Force War Medal was for the men of the Territorial Force who joined up before 30 September 1914 and served overseas but were not eligible for the Star medals. There was also a Silver War Badge available from September 1916 for those men retired or discharged from the army through injury or illness.

Gallantry medals were harder to come by. Just 633 individuals won the Victoria Cross, Britain's highest honour, during the First World War.* Officers like Phillips could be awarded the Military Cross, introduced in 1915, and the Distinguished Service Order. Men in the rank and file were eligible for Distinguished Conduct Medal and a Mention in Despatches. From March 1916 the Military Medal could be awarded to warrant officers, NCOs and women.

Robin learned he had missed out on a medal for political reasons. Phil received one to reward several notable acts of valour.

* According to *Victoria Cross Heroes* by Michael Ashcroft.

There was still plenty of opportunity for brave acts as trench warfare was continuing much as before for men in the army. Men who raided German trenches were convinced the enemy soldiers' pleas for friendship, using the term '*Kamerad*', was a ruse for the purposes of distraction.

Meanwhile, the Royal Flying Corps was rapidly expanding before joining forces with the Royal Naval Air Services in April 1918 to form the Royal Air Force.

Until October, Phil was under the command of Captain William Ralph Cobb, also awarded a Military Cross, who was killed on 5 October 1917 aged 21.

26 April 1917

Dear Aunt Ethel,   *Same address*

Just got the Blighty* *and also the cake which I was very glad to get as it is a great change from bread. We also are having splendid weather which is very nice when we are under canvas, as we are now. Let's have any news of Robin you can, by the time you get this you will have seen him. Can you send some of that 'Gold' choc?*

I enclose two photos of myself I had taken whilst I was down at the base to see Robin, which he will have told you about by the time you get this. They were very hastily taken & are not very good.

I might have a piece of very good news for you but don't hope & don't think about it. I'll let you know what it is, if it does come off.

Yours,

Phil

28 April 1917

READ LETTER FIRST WITHOUT STOPPING   *Same address*

Dear Aunt Ethel,

I am out on a working party at the present moment and as I have nothing to do but watch the men, I decided to write a letter. All sorts of guns are right round us firing away as hard as they can, making a fearful noise.

Well, tomorrow I shall be 19, impossible to believe but I don't think I believe I feel it. What I said in my last letter about a good piece of news is that I have been put in for the MC. Not my company commander but another one told me so & sincerely hoped I would as I know all the coy commanders & like them very much. Now I want you not to tell anybody at all until I hear that I have either got it or not got it. If I do get it, it was not only for this show as nobody did anything special, but for past work as I have done a good many night patrols. I shall be of course very pleased as it will help me a lot afterwards as a regular.

---

*A humorous weekly magazine was issued free to First World War troops.

I don't know for absolute certainty that I have been put in for it but the captain who told me swore that I had been & drank to the success of my getting it. If I do, it will be rather good getting it after a big show before my 19th birthday after 8 months out here. When I have made certain that I have been put in for it I'll let you know & then you can tell Robin but nobody else, & ask him to tell nobody. You see my meaning because it might mean a disappointment to people I know, if I don't get it. It won't be very much of a one to me because I personally think I have not done very much to deserve it.

So don't expect too much. I should like some more of the 'Gold' choc & a bigger slab if you can as it is jolly good stuff.

I am keeping very well, hope you like the photo.

Your affectionate nephew,
    Phil

                                                    6 May 1917
Dear Aunt Ethel,   *Same address*
Yours of 1st just arrived. I have heard nothing more about the news and I don't know when it will come out officially; and of course I shall be very pleased if I do get it but you must not hope too much & I am not thinking about it at all. Glad you got the photos, I personally do not think much of them. Yes, send one to Rex & tell him I would like a letter from him occasionally as it is getting pretty wearisome out here, always on the move to go in & out anytime & to be in any fighting. Very glad to hear of Robin's successful operation & that he has got over it well.

Yes, don't say anything till I hear definitely one way or the other.

We are in a lovely German dugout with 43 steps down well away from the Boche.

Must end now,
Your affectionate nephew,
    Phil

                                                    17 May 1917
Dear Aunt Ethel,   *Same address*
Thanks for yours of 13th also the one with the choc. Glad to hear that Robin is getting on much better. Yes, we keep on moving practically every other week. Yes, I won't forget about being wounded & where to ask to go to. Yes, Rex seems much happier now at Ispahan and he seems to be getting his proper pay now. I can't send Bert a photo yet as I have left them down in the transport, but will at first opportunity. As for a piano in the dugout – no such luck. But this is rather good. The candles all go out when a shell bursts anywhere here, or if a big gun goes off here, and we all feel the blast of them but we occasionally sing to ourselves and we even call each other nasty names else we would never be happy.

I am getting fearfully sick of this war & I am getting quite windy nowadays –
nervy – but I suppose it is no good thinking about it but just carry on.
   Your affectionate nephew,
      Phil

7 June 1917
Dear Aunt Ethel,   Same address
It is still very hot and I am dying for a bathe. I have been riding and jumping
lately and am getting on quite nicely. I had a letter from Aunt Nellie which
I enclose because I can't understand what she means about the money & interest?
And I am afraid I wrote a strong letter back on things in general because I think
I am past being called a naughty boy as if I was a kid of 6 with a nurse & bib.
I don't like it & she won't like the letter. For all I care she can take that £100
& I'll give every bit of it back if she treats me with it like that. Last night I was
out working from 8.30pm – 4am on the go the whole time. Had dinner at
7.30pm & then breakfast at 4am without sleep, the same tonight so I must close
as it is too hot to carry on.
   Your affectionate nephew,
      Phil

15 June 1917
Dear Aunt Ethel,   Same address
Thanks for packet of cigarettes which I received safely last night at the bottom of
the dug-out I am in now, so you can imagine where I am at the present
moment. One has to be very careful how one moves about in this trench as the
Boche can easily see us. It is infernally hot so you can imagine what it is like in a
trench with a lot of different things buried about the place.
   I have not been inoculated. I got out of that because it is too hot for that sort
of game. There are a lot of bombs buried in the sides of these trenches. Sgt Major
pulled a string last night and a couple of bombs went bang. It gave me such a
start that I bumped my arm against a sharp piece of wood, so I suddenly saw
visions of Blighty but I found out what I had done afterwards & of course was
very sorry.
   Yes, I'll let you know as soon as I get those 250 cigarettes. I don't know how
Aunt Nellie will take my letter because I was annoyed. I don't care really
because she has been rather too patronising as if I was her own son and she was
my governess. I would rather be left alone in these times. My Colonel told me
that there was no Derby running this year so what about the ticket?
   About re-investing that money, she said she was taking £20 out, one whole
year's, to put into the War Loan. I personally think those people who have plenty
of money & no relations concerned in this war can do that, but by the way,
whose money is that £100? I was in a working party in the early morning of

*the north push, at least just getting into camp but I did not hear because there
was a strafe on.*

What is Robin's address? Glad to hear he is getting on so well.

Your affectionate nephew,
    Phil

                                                                19 June 1917
Dear Aunt Ethel,   *Same address*
*You'll be sorry to hear that I have not got the MC. I did not expect it so I am
not so disappointed as I could have been if I had expected it. Only 3 of us had
been put in for it; the Adjutant, one Coy commander & myself. The former two
got it and they both said they were very sorry I had not got it and drank my
health for a success in the near future, and the Adjutant said it may come yet
because my recommendation had not been sent back yet. Well never mind, it's
good enough for me to have been recommended and have some officers &
especially the CO think I did deserve it, but as it was not for something
absolutely definite I am not disappointed. Please don't tell everybody because it is
not the same, not nearly the same as if I had got it.*

*We have had two pretty severe thunderstorms but nothing else of importance.
At our Divisional Horse Show I met a Major Forester-Walker, a connection of
ours I believe. I think he knows Rex best. He is a major in command of a battery
of howitzers. His rival, also a major, is one of the best, topping chap. Mother
wrote me a rather nice letter re Aunt Nellie's, saying I should not say or write
things like that to them as they are people of importance in India but I don't
care if they are Lords & Ladies or Viceroys. It makes no difference, so by that
I don't know how she will take it. Mother complains of Davie not eating
enough & going to bed very late. I suppose he does not know what punishment is
yet. No cigarettes yet.*

Your affectionate nephew,
    Phil

                                                                12 July 1917
Dear Aunt Ethel,   *Same address*
*We have moved back a little but not very much and we are living in a deep
dug-out built by us and it is awfully badly constructed compared with the Boche
ones. In the trench we have a little shelter where the drinks are kept and we call
that The Bar. The mess is another shelter just behind the trench and we got
about 20 whiz-bangs thrown at us at breakfast which of course was a huge joke
just because we had a few narrow escapes. One officer was awakened for
breakfast by a shell that landed 15 yards away.*

*Could you send me a box of Carter's Crisps as they come in handy in the
trenches.*

Yours,
    Phil

17 July 1917
Dear Aunt Ethel,   *Same address*
I wish I was coming home now to go down to Charmouth with you all. Glad to hear about Robin getting on all well but I hope they don't rush as I think it would be cruel to send him out again. I have given up smoking as my nerves have gone to pieces. I can feel my heart bleed sometimes when a shell comes along. The other night I was standing just on top of the trench talking to an officer of another Coy and he said, 'what an awful night to fight on!' It was pitch dark and raining blueberries and I said, 'What an awful night to die on!' And the next second a 5.9 roared along and dropped 3 yards behind me. We all went flat on our faces except one man who had been standing just behind me and he was blown right over me and I thought he had been hit but he hadn't been and I also thought my last second on this earth had come. The next second I was at the bottom of the dugout and my legs & arms were shaking like leaves and somebody made me drink a glass of port which made me feel better. No other news. Got a very nice letter from Mother, the nicest one I have ever had.
    Your affectionate nephew,
    Phil

18 July 1917
Dear Aunt Ethel,   *Same address*
I got a letter from Reggie yesterday, no news. We have had rotten weather lately and it is raining hard now, but we sit in this tin hut here & listen to the late CO's gramophone all day to try to bring us back to civilization as much as possible. Yesterday was the first day I had my clothes off for the last 11 days & I had a good bath this morning and I feel better. I am afraid I have contracted a heavy cold but I hope it wears off. There is nothing in the way of news.
    Yours,
    Phil

1 August 1917
Dear Aunt Ethel,   *Same address*
Thanks very much for your last two, 18th and the one before that.
    Sorry to hear about Rex being so fed up but I wish I was with him. We are in the line again now but the weather is rotten, it keeps on raining.
    What do you think of the north show we have just had? Please thank Robin for the 2nd lot of illustrated papers. We cut out all the pretty actresses and stick them on the walls of the dugout to make the place look a little more homely. Any Tatlers *or* Sketches *you get, you might send them out because we do this to every dugout we come into. We have been out for 6 days and I had a game of tennis once and dinner with some artillery officers I know well, awfully nice chaps, and there was an ADC to a general there. He is a marvellous fellow at*

the piano, better than Rex, so that's saying something. There were ten of us in the hut & each of us asked him to play any two tunes out of any play there has ever been in a London theatre & he played them with a delightful touch. Just before, he had heard a tune on the gramophone & he sat down & played it off at once on the piano. Must end.

    Yours,

      Phil

27 August 1917
Same address

Dear Aunt Ethel,

Thanks very much for yours of 22nd. Well, tomorrow will be the anniversary of the day when I landed in France so one year's active service without a break, except for a leave is pretty good don't you think? And also 8 months out here under age. I wonder how much longer I shall be able to stick it. There is nothing happening here at all and we have not budged either way. I could do very well with a month's batting, tennis and football away from shells. I am the youngest but one in the battalion & the youngest is married with a baby son – so I think I must be getting quite old. Sometimes I feel it very much.

    We gave our doctor a farewell dinner the other night & I am afraid a good many of us were very merry indeed at the end. The old Doc has left us for good now with a month's leave to begin with. An awfully nice chap & we shall never forget him, I for one will not. I wrote to Robin for his compass & field glasses as we have got to have them & if he can't lend me his I shall have to buy them. Must end.

    Yours,

      Phil

1 September 1917
Same address

Look here, Aunt Ethel, I want to join the Royal Flying Corps for the rest of the war, because I am sick of this life. The battalion has not been the same since our CO, the one and only CO Colonel Dunlop DSO, left us and everybody seems to be leaving. Five have just put in for the RFC, three have already gone and others have put in for it. In my spare time I shall get hold of some mechanic to show me the parts of a motor bike, I've ridden one, & also how to drive a car & learn a bit of morse and that's all you need. Then, if they let you in, you go home for 6 weeks for a course on it all & to learn how to fly. I would be no good as observer so I will have to go as a pilot. The next time I write I might be in quite a different place. It might be near where Robin got first wounded.

    Your affectionate nephew,

      Phil

5 October 1917

Dear Aunt Ethel,   Same address

I expect you will get my last FSPC before this letter. Well, I have had some
exciting times since I last wrote to you. I have been over the top again for the
2nd time in my life and I had a much tougher time. I expect you will have the
news in the papers before you get this letter, and I expect you will get a telegram
saying I have been wounded again. Well, it is very slight. I got a little piece into
the back of my head just under the skin and another piece hit me on my right
wrist bone & glanced off. Luckily it did not hit me a little lower because it might
have broken my wrist & then I would have got home to Blighty. As it is I am
down at the transport recuperating.*

*I don't know whether you will be pleased or not, I had the satisfaction of
sticking four Boches with the bayonet. I quite enjoyed doing it at the time. Two
of them I caught pretending to be asleep, I woke them up with the bayonet &
then stuck them because they did the 'Kamerad' stunt. I don't know whether
I killed them or not. They tried a lot of their dirty tricks again, shooting behind
our backs and throwing bombs after doing the 'Kamerad' stunt. I don't know
when I shall get my next leave. Let Robin know all about it will you.*

Your affectionate nephew,
Phil

7 October 1917

Dear Aunt Ethel,   Same address

*Just received yours of 3/10/17. I have received the watch thanks, and returned
it to its owner. Well by this time you will have had my postcard saying that
I have been slightly wounded again but not bad enough for Blighty and also
about my sticking 4 of the enemy with the bayonet. Well I have some worse news
for you. My Company Commander, Captain W.R. Cobb MC, got very badly
wounded and died of wounds. It is the biggest blow the Battalion has had for a
long time. You can imagine how popular he was when I tell you that many
people including the Commanding Officer himself absolutely broke down about
him. All the men are talking about him as The Captain & say that he deserves
the Victoria Cross and I hope he gets it too. I'll tell you more about him when
I can. I also enclose a photo of him. I would like you to frame it, and also have
the MC printed on or painted on his breast, at least only the ribbon. I think it
can be done. Well. Must end.*

Yours,
Phil

---

* Field Service Post Card.

9 October 1917

Dear Aunt Ethel,   *No 2 Stationary Hospital B.E.F.*

You will be surprised to hear that I am down at the base in hospital suffering from enteritis, I don't know if I have spelt it right or not. If you remember about 9 months ago I was very ill once, well it is the same thing now. I stuck it then but I could not stick it this time. I got wet through during that last big battle on the 4th and the clothes dried on me, and then we had an exceptionally cold night & I at once knew I would be ill but I never expected to be sent down as far as this. Somebody told me on the ambulance train yesterday that I would get home to Blighty if I did not get well quickly because they clear the hospitals out during a push, so you might still see me soon but I don't think so. I am lying in bed writing this & it is simply pouring outside. I have got also a most uncomfortable rash on my chest owing to the inoculation I had for my slight wound, which has nearly healed up by the way. The sisters here are rather nice but I have never been pampered so much in all my life. One would think I was dangerously ill, when a matter of fact I feel perfectly well except for a weak stomach and you bet I am not allowed to eat much solid food, which really I object to strongly.

Lying on my stretcher in the train I heard one of the wounded officers say that The Queen's Own have never failed yet in the war (which by the way is quite true). I, of course, said nothing but later on he heard one of the sisters ask what regiment I belonged to & then he asked me in detail how the show got on.

By the way I don't want to boast & I don't think I said it before, but I & my platoon were the first of the Battalion to reach the objective & I was the only officer left in my company. Lucky for me I got sent down for my light wound because Cobb, my Company Commander, got killed exactly where I had established my platoon Headquarters. Afterwards when the Corps Commander inspected us he also said that the Queen's Own had never failed yet in this war. I never had the wind up so much when he inspected my platoon & the number of questions he asked me & the number of Brasshats that kept on asking me my name & Brigadier Jones stepped up to the General & told him that I had stuck four Boches with the bayonet in the attack.

Well, how's everybody? I assure you I want to get home very much indeed & yet I don't want to leave the good old Battalion.

Must end now.

Your affectionate nephew,
Phil

Not dated – envelope postmarked
19 October 1917
APO S17 FRANCE.
OFFICERS CLUB

Dear Aunt Ethel,

Thanks very much indeed for yours of 14/10/17 which I received the morning I left hospital & I and am now at the base with a certain Coy - Commander Capt Scott MC, who is a very nice chap. I hate this place, simply loathe it, because they put you on the square & treat you as if you were a recruit & that you had just put on khaki for the first time. Some of the instructors here have never been in the line, I hear, & they try to teach you what to do in the line, which is rather ludicrous don't you think? Especially when I left my Battalion only about 10 days ago immediately after a big battle. After doing nearly 14 months continuous active service with a Batt., to be treated like this is about the limit.

However I came here yesterday & I expect to go tomorrow. I also had a row with the gas instructor – he was positively rude to me & he is only a 2 Lt & old enough to be my grandfather. I told him a certain thing never happened at the front that I had just left & he said, 'listen to this chicken trying to teach his grandfather', which made me say that I could be sarcastic too & very rude. I am afraid I used some strong language which shut him up at once. I told him one could only learn by making mistakes, or asking questions. By the way you'll be pleased to hear I got my second pip which has pleased me immensely.

When I was in hospital the officer who was in the bed opposite was the son of old Dimmick the master [at Bedford] rather curious & we had a good talk although he left eleven years ago & I only 2½ but he knew all those XV fellows who were there when I first joined. By the way I have not voiced this opinion before, but he was of the same mind as myself that ever since Mr Carter took over the school the old traditions of the school were gradually dropped & forgotten, although he put a stop to one or two things that were unpleasant.

I have heard unofficially that another little stunt won't do us any harm again soon which means more dirty work. I suppose & I expect I will get my packet this time. I am quite well except for a cold in the head but sometimes I feel positively weary in mind and body, because now I find it a bit of a strain to keep my nerves steady in front of the men although once I get into the battle properly I feel alright because we have too much to think about. When I get home on leave I'll explain to you in detail what my feelings were like in this last show.

Don't say anything again to anybody at all, but I have been put in for the MC again because my 2nd in Command told me, but I don't expect to get it & I shall be fed up this time. I suppose I ought to be satisfied with the two pips, & 2 gold bars & some wounds for those bars, what?

By the way I got to know the Honourable Miss Howard who is a nurse & was in the next ward to the one I was in & she is a jolly pretty girl. I remember having seen her photo in the Sketch *or* Tatler. *Well I must end now.*
    Your affectionate nephew,
        Phil

                                                    10 November 1917
Dear Aunt Ethel,   *Same old address*
I am back again with the old Batt., very much fed up with life so I have promptly written for the Indian Army Papers and I am resolved to join the Indian Army if I can. You will be sorry to hear that the MC has fallen through. I am very annoyed because I told too many people at home about it. I did so because I felt absolutely certain that I would get it after the way the Major spoke to me about it and I am very annoyed with the Major for telling me anything about it at all as it was only likely to disappoint me if I did not get it. Well it is done with & it can't be helped. I am not one of those chaps who would resolve to have a very good try for the next one in the next show, which would probably mean either a VC or a bullet. The latter is more likely. Another thing I hear, please don't repeat this, is that another officer on BHQ staff is going to get one because the Major was annoyed the Batt. did not get more than two and of course he could not put me in again. Another thing is that one of the officers of my company, a 2nd Lt commissioned this year and a ranker, is going to be a captain and I shall be a platoon commander. Well, the sooner I get into the Indian Army the better for me.
    We are quite close to a large lake down at which our aeroplanes dive and fire at a wooden target. Yesterday I saw one of our aeroplanes chase a Boche and bring it down in flames, and the first night I got back we got violently bombed by the Boche not very far from here. I came back just too late to go up the line, rather lucky eh! Well I have no wish for this sort of warfare. I wonder what the Batt. will do to me when they come out, I expect I shall be super-numerary officer to a platoon commander.
    Have you got Ralph Cobb's photo back yet & has the MC been painted on nicely. Rather swanky paper this, I have just borrowed it because I have not any myself at present.
    One officer, a Lieutenant who has come back to us after being on the Brigade Staff for a few months, is not even 2nd in command to a company, when he used to command the company on the Somme. So it is a topsy-turvy life with a vengeance.
    Don't mention anything to anybody about the MC unless you are asked but tell Robin & tell him the same.
    Your affectionate nephew,
        Phil

'It is stifling hot & the mosquitoes are simply awful, millions of them & my arms & neck are puffing out with huge bites'

News that the Royal West Kents were heading for Italy was as big a Christmas present as any serving soldier could have wished for. They were destined to take over a front line on the River Piave, now fighting against the Austrians' front trenches made from wood and shingle rather than Flanders mud.

The Italians had been routed in the Battle of Caporetto in November 1917 and Allies found themselves with a teetering southern front. By the time Phil had arrived in the region the Austrians were happy to stay behind their lines while the battalion could not find a way to ford the fast-flowing river for the purposes of attack. Apart from incursions by enemy aeroplanes there was a three-month period of relative calm.

But Robin's memoir reveals how downhearted Phil had become.

ROBIN

In February I received another letter from Phil on the Italian front. His division had been one of those which had been rushed to help to stem the Austrian tide on the Carso when the Italian front had almost caved in.

Poor Phil, by now he seemed to be thoroughly fed up and tired of it, he had had many months of heavy fighting and he had gained the Military Cross in a particularly sanguinary bayonet encounter.

A month later I had another letter saying that something had upset his stomach very badly and he had been ordered to hospital down on the Italian Riviera; that he was very glad of a rest and was having an enjoyable time at Bordighera, where he too had found the lady of his heart. That was the last letter I ever had from him.

When the big German push at Amiens in 1918 was looking serious, Phil's division was brought back from Italy and he was in the thick of the worst again.

On 1 April 1918 the battalion was dispatched back to France as Germany threatened to overwhelm Allied lines there. They spent three months in preparation for the 6am attack in June in the Forest of Nieppe, when Phil was killed. Although the objectives of the attack were achieved, it cost Phil and two other officers their lives.

A major described Phil's role:

'*The right company ('C' under Lt Monypenny MC) advanced and went straight through the enemy front line to his support line. Little resistance was met except at one point, where the enemy's machine guns were posted.*

Sharp hand-to-hand fighting took place about here, a number of the enemy being bayoneted.

The company pushed rapidly on and took its final objective, driving what was left of the enemy towards the Plate Becque. A heavy Lewis gun and rifle fire was opened on them and many were killed whilst attempting to cross the stream.'

It's not known at which point in this account that Phil died.

25 December 1917
Dear Aunt Ethel,   B.E.F.
Thank you very much for yours of 12/12/17. Yes, you have guessed right my address in future is B.E.F. ITALY. We had a most wonderful journey through the South of France.

Thank you very much for the cake, it was not broken but it was very quickly finished. Of course I can't tell you whereabouts in ITALY I am but the weather is bright but intensely cold & I can't speak a word of the lingo.
Must end now to get ready for Xmas festivities.

Yours,
  Phil

Dear Aunt Ethel,   31 December 1917
We have not had any letters again for some days I wonder why? and we are still working hard. Of course I can't talk a word of this lingo, but somehow I seem to make myself understood. We have a rather nice mess here & the people here are very nice indeed. I have a bed with sheets in a carriage stable. It is extremely cold going to bed and getting up in the morning but it is lovely and warm in bed. We are still in Italy, and I am afraid I am spending too much money. Day before yesterday it snowed very hard and it was a glorious day but it has thawed very quickly. It is very warm in the middle of the day but very cold at night.

My tunics are wearing out gradually, will you please send me my good one out as I must have something decent to wear. I have a supernumerary officer in my platoon and he is nearly old enough to be my father. By the way have you had any news of Father lately? I had a very nice long letter from Rex, although he said he was very bored with life. Have you had my Xmas card yet? I sent about a dozen to different people. They are rather good don't you think?

*Please don't forget about the jacket will you? and could you send me about
200 Goldflake cigarettes as they are absolutely impossible to get out here.*
   Yours,
      Phil

                                             13 January 1918
Dear Aunt Ethel,   *Italian Expeditionary Force*
*Thank you very much for your of 23rd- 26th- & 30th-, they more or less came
together, but all our letters don't seem to be getting home & also we get very
scanty mails. I have just watched a very exciting football match, otherwise there
is not much in the way of news except that you will be glad to hear I have got
the MC in the New Year's Honours & I am wearing it now. The enclosed is
from my Brigade Major.*
   Yours,
      Phil

(Enclosures: Pencilled note congratulating him on award of MC, refers to his
gallant efforts on 4 October, signed R.C. Luke; note 'Heartiest Congratulations from B Coy' signed by eight fellow officers.)

                                             13 January 1918
Dear Aunt Ethel,   *I.E.F.*
*You will get these two letters rather quickly, as leave has opened & one of our
officers is starting tomorrow, so I am giving you more details. We are stationed
on the main Rd between PADUA or PADOVA and CITTADELLA in a little
village called BOLZONELLA. There is a big chateau here where an Italian
Count is living and he has all the gardens and stables under English lines. The
weather here is very cold but it has thawed today. When we travelled from
France to come here, we came through Paris, Lyons, Marseilles, along the south
coast of France through Nice, Cannes, Monte Carlo, Arles etc and it was simply
lovely weather.*
   *In my other letter I mentioned that I had got the MC, I am mentioning it
again in case you don't get that letter. I have been congratulated by many
officers in the Brigade.*
   *We got out at two or three places & had lunch & of course I was quite at
home with the lingo. The smell of lemons & oranges & pine trees was simply
glorious. Many an English family came & spoke to us, so you can imagine the
time we had.*
   *Well I must end now as I am going out to dinner to the Hd Qrtrs of the
2nd Kings Own Scottish Borderers.*
   Yours,
      Phil

Dear Aunt Ethel,   *20 January 1918*
I am writing from a school, to learn something of bombing, just for a change. By the way do you remember the course I did at Chatham, it was rather good, so it comes rather easy for me on the whole.

I feel very tired today because another officer & myself went out yesterday to a big town for a day out. We lost ourselves, so had to stop there the night & we came back this morning with several lifts on trams & cars & lorries. I had my photo taken there about 3 weeks ago so I enclose them. I want you to put the MC on them and give them to anybody who wants one.

By the way, leave having been stopped for a long time, I shall not get mine for another 4 months, that is if leave goes very fast now.

I don't know whether they are going to make me Battalion Bombing officer or not, but I would like to be, as it is a cushy job & one does not have to do much in the fighting line, nowadays. I don't think they will because I have been told I am too valuable as a platoon officer for going over the top. Must end now.
     Yours, Phil

                                                                  21 January 1918
Dear Aunt Ethel,   *IEF*
Thank you very much indeed for yours of the 4th- and 6th- which I have only just received at the school, and with 8 other letters from different people. I expect you have got my letter telling you about my MC by now. Of course I am very pleased myself, but what has pleased me ten times more is the letter I have received from my late Colonel Buchanan-Dunlop. It was very nice of him & I am very pleased he has not forgotten me, as I think he was quite fond of me when he was commanding us in France, & every one of us who ever knew him only wish he was commanding us here in Italy. I would willingly die for that man because he is a white man all through.

I am very glad to hear about Jack Ford, please congratulate Cousin Jessie for me.* He has been a long time away from home now, it is about time he got some leave.

I also got a letter from a Cpl from hospital in Glasgow, but I cannot remember him in the least, sometimes I fear I am slowing getting a very weak memory. Every other week I get into a weak state & yet I seem to be always cheerful.

Yes it is quite correct to put MC on the letters, but I shall not get it till I get home & then I shall get it from the King, but I shall be too nervous for that.
     Must end now.
     Yours, Phil.
P.S. I am enclosing Col Dunlop's letter which I want you to keep for me.

---

* Possibly John (Jack) Meredith Ford (1887–1950), and Jessie could be his mother's sister Jessie Mary G-M.

16 February 1918

Dear Aunt Ethel,   66th General Hospital, ITALY

Just a few lines to say that I am in hospital in case you get notified by the
authorities.

It is the usual thing, change of climate that gives me diarrhea, I've had it for
sometime & it seems to get me very easily.

Not very much news here. Very nice climate down here and very warm except
that it has been bitterly cold today, I don't know why. We are on the coast in the
region of the palm trees & orange & lemon trees, which smell very nice. Of
course I have not had a letter now from anybody for a long time.

How's father, have you heard any news of him lately, why doesn't he write to
me? Surely he can find time to write to one of his sons out on active service, I am
fed up about it.

Yours,
    Phil

(Do you remember in Bert's form C.H.L. Rayner? He is with me.)

7 March 1918

Dear Aunt Ethel,   No address

Thanks very much for yours of the 27/2/18, I have just received. I am sorry if
I don't write very often, you see I get out of the way of letter writing because
I don't get many letters regularly like yours.

Didn't I acknowledge the jacket? I thought I had. Thanks very much for it.
I shall be returning one of my others, as I have too much in my kit, before I go
back to the Batt. I am getting on fairly well, but I get sudden attacks of it,
I don't know why, and they are very frequent too. I shall let you know as soon as
I get discharged. Sorry to hear about Dick's mumps, I suppose all kids must get
them some time or other. I am in a small town not very far from a big French
town, which is of course very well known throughout the whole world.

Can't understand why Mother gave her address to the WO when she does not
want to hear anything of me. She must have a very funny & silly sort of pride.

I want the one or the other & not half. Either the proper feeling between
mother & son or broken off altogether.

Just got Rex's letter.

Yours,
    Phil

5 May 1918

Dear Aunt Ethel,   No address

I have just got back to the Batt: and found several letters from you also your
latest written on the 1st May. Glad to hear news of Jack Ford & I am sorry

I could not be home at the same time because I would like to have met him very much before he goes out to India. Glad to hear also about Robin putting in for the I.A & that he won't be coming out here any more as one of us out here is quite enough. Yes, I met Major Penrose and had quite a long talk with him & he spoke very well of Robin.

I am fed up with this life, matter of fact I have had too much of it for my age. It is not an exciting sort of game and it is much too dangerous, so don't know what I shall do. I am getting no satisfaction in this Batt. at the present moment. I know the CO does not like me because he thinks I am too young for a responsible position, so he puts a fellow who is only a few months older than myself, just because he takes life more seriously, so if I am too young for a more responsible position I have now, I ought not to be in this war at all. I wish we had our old Colonel back. My ink has run out.

> *Yours,*
> *Phil*

12 May 1918
No address

Dear Aunt Ethel,
Thanks very much for your last two letters. I have also some that turn up with half a dozen addresses on them & fairly old.

I am settled down again in the old Batt. So well am I known in this Batt. that they don't take the trouble to put my name in orders when I join them.

Weather here is clearing up & it is very like summer & just as warm. There was a very short, sharp gas barrage put down not very far from me the other night but luckily the wind was blowing the other way, so I did not have to put my gas helmet on.

I have just been handed yours of 8/5/18. Sorry about the writing but I have not felt inclined for some weeks, I don't know why. Please thank Robin for his letter of 6/5/18. Tell him I hope he gets into the I.A. & very soon, as it is better than this. Tell him my Brigadier asked after him today & wanted to know if he had got the I.A as he had put in for it 2½ years ago.

> *Yours,*
> *Phil*

We are in a fairly quiet sector, south of where I got the MC.

16 May 1918
No address

Dear Aunt Ethel,
Please excuse short note, I want to catch runner before he goes back. You will be pleased to hear that I have been made 2nd in Command to C Company and I am taking the Company up the line next time. In fact I am in command now as my Captain is away on a course. All of a sudden the CO has turned out very nice to

me so I might get on now. But it is an awful responsibility as I don't know a man in the Company.

Had a long letter from Cyril Appleton who is getting on very well.

10.30 pm.

Yours, Phil

O.C. C Coy

                                                                          17 May 1918

Dear Aunt Ethel,   *No address*

I sent you a little note late last night to catch the post, but I will repeat what I wrote in case you don't get it. When I came back to the old Batt. I found that an officer junior to me & a great friend of mine had been put 2nd in command of my late Coy A. The question was raised by my late Coy Capt. & he told me that the CO would have this fellow instead. Then just before we started up for the line, the Adjutant told me that I would take command of C Coy & take it up the line. Of course I was very surprised & pleased in a way as it will give me a chance of knowing the work of a Coy Commander for a future reference. I am really 2nd in command to the Coy, but I have to take the Coy up the line this time because my skipper is away on a course for a short while. It is rather strenuous for me, because I don't know a soul in the Coy, which is rather dangerous when going in the line, as the NCOs or men won't have any confidence in me to speak of as they don't know me & vice versa, but I am quite cheerful about it & I shall do my best.

We are living in a large wood at the present moment, it is stifling hot & the mosquitoes are simply awful, millions of them & my arms & neck are puffing out with huge bites.

Sorry to hear about Dick's Chicken pox but I suppose most kids get it.

Well, no news here will write again soon.

Yours,

  Phil

                                                                          5 June 1918

Dear Aunt Ethel,   *No address*

Life is so-so out here still. Weather has been excellent, (touch wood) for quite a long time now & I hope it keeps so.

Leave has opened again but it will be some time yet before I get mine. It is over 7 months now, a long time for me that. Well one can't grumble because it is no use. My Coy Commander will be going on leave soon, so I shall command the Coy for about 3 weeks, I expect.

I have not received my Mother's birthday book but I got Father's letter alright. I was never so surprised in all my life, considering it was the first letter

*I had ever received personally written to me by Father and I am over 20 years
now I wonder what people would think if they knew that.*

*Look here if people want to know what I want for my birthday, better collect
the money & buy me a decent pair of silk pyjamas. They must be silk, & either
white or pink, pink preferably. There is nothing finer than to come out of the
line, have a bath & get into silk pajamas & then into my flea-bag.*

*A great pal of mine has just brought down two more Huns in Italy. That's
3 altogether. The last two he brought them down within 15 minutes of each
other.*

Excuse paper, sitting on bottom of trench writing this.

Yours,

  Phil

                                                9 June 1918

Dear Aunt Ethel,   *No address*

*Thanks very much indeed for your letters. I have not had much time for writing
letters because we have been very busy when out of the line as you will see by the
letter I have written to Robin.*

Look here my QMS showed me the enclosed from the paper called Blighty.
I can't find it just now but I'll look for it & enclose it.

*Do you know of a Private H. Monypenny in the 14th King's Liverpools?
I wonder who it can be. Extraordinary thing, seeing that in the trenches.*

*We have had splendid weather lately but it is beginning to get cloudy & we
had a few drops of rain today for quite a long time touch wood.*

*Don't forget my pink silk pyjamas will you? & I'll pay you the money by
cheque or when I come home on leave. What 'opes! as Tommy says! Not for some
time yet I am sorry to say.*

*No, we are not in the big battle but I cannot tell you more than that of where
we are.*

*My Canadian boy in Italy has brought down 3 Huns now. He is getting on
very well because they are very scarce in Italy. But here, I fire a Lewis Gun
practically every day at them & it is great fun, because it is awfully difficult for
him to spot us firing.*

*We are in the middle of a big cornfield & there is one Bosche M. Gun that
cuts the corn occasionally so we have to look slippy.*

Yours,

  Phil

(A cutting from *Blighty* enclosed showing a humorous cartoon by Private H.
Monypenny, 14th King's Liverpools, plus an indication that he had won a
guinea prize that week.)

15/6/18

Dear Aunt Ethel,   No address

It is rather late & although I am rather tired, I have just found time for a letter or two.

You see, I have been very busy lately, because my Company Commander has gone away on leave & consequently I have the responsibility of the whole Company on my shoulders. And this being a new Company to me, I have to get to know the Officers & NCOs as soon as possible because of certain events in the near future. I cannot tell you more but you might know them before or just after you get this letter.

Of course the old Batt. has practically totally changed since I first joined them, but some of the officers are very nice fellows. I have made a lot of friends, very nice friends indeed, in this Division, especially in the Artillery. The Infantry is not half as good as it used to be about 6 months after I had joined, although it is bucking up tremendously.

I don't know if you remember seeing a Major Knox's photo in the Sketch, getting his bar from the King. He had lost his left foot on the 4th Oct show when I got my MC. He was a fine fellow & his senior officer, Major Morgan MC is another fine fellow & he & I are the greatest of pals. Long time ago I used to fire his guns for him.

Another great pal of mine is Lt C.E. Lloyd, an extraordinary brave fellow. He was, in the great battle of April 9th 1917, caught firing his guns in gumboots, silk pyjamas & soft hat. That is a silly incident I know but he is a brave fellow though.

Don't be anxious as I shall come out alright, but I don't want to put the wind up, as the saying is.

If anybody rings up Aunt Dora's place & asks for me ask them to put him on to you & you ask him about me. If you are out, ask them to ask him for details. It ought to be Lt Molony RAF. He used to be in this Regiment.

Must end now. Will write when possible. Goodnight.

Yours,
   Phil

The following is Phil's last letter home:

23 June 1918

Dear Aunt Ethel,   No address

Thanks very much for your last letter. Never mind about the pyjamas, I shall be able to get a pair out here. We are in a sector that is mentioned several times a week in the papers, but beyond that I can't tell you more. It is fairly quiet here, but as there is a bit of a war on, you cannot tell what might happen any day in these hard times. I am still in command of my company and I have got on very

*well, as the CO has been away on leave, but he is expected back tomorrow,
I believe. But I shall not be afraid of him & I shall have my say when necessary.*

*If I get on his wrong side, I don't think I shall get on my General's wrong
side.*

Has Robin gone yet and have you any news of Rex yet?

I must end now as I must work.

Yours,

  Phil

LETTERS OF CONDOLENCE FROM THE BATTALION

1. The CO:

Dear Miss Moneypenny   *30 June 1918*

*It is with very great regret that I have to write this letter. It is to tell you that
your nephew Lieut. Gybbon Monepenny MC, of the Bn under my command was
killed in action on the night of June 28th – 29th. The Bn had taken part in
operations which were very successful on the 28th June and your nephew had led
his company magnificently on this occasion as on others. The line had been well
established when during the night, the enemy opened very heavy fire on the
captured positions & it was in the course of this barrage, that your nephew was
killed. It may be some consolation to you and to his parents that Death came to
their boy instantaneously & that he could not have known anything of it. Brave
to a fault, and unconscious of danger, he was adored by his own men & was the
best of comrades to all in the Battn, and would shortly have been promoted to
Captain, pending his transfer to the Indian Army, for which transfer his
application had already gone forward.*

*Will you please accept my most heartfelt condolences with his parents and
yourself on the loss which they have suffered. His death is much felt in the Battn
but our loss is as of nothing compared to that of his own people. May God rest his
soul & console you all in the loss of one who was I am sure as good a son &
nephew as he was an officer. Although so young, he gave promise of developing
with age into an even more efficient leader of men, & for his present age, was as
good or better a leader than I have seen. With deepest sympathy believe me to be*

  Yours very sincerely,

    B. Johnstone Lt Col

    RW Kent Regt

2. The Chaplain:

Dear Miss Monypenny,   *3 July 1918*

*I do not know whether you will already have heard the sad news of your
nephew, Lt. P.B.S.G Monypenny of the 1st RW Kent Regt. I am sorry to say*

that he was killed in action on Friday last, June 28th. He had led his men in an attack that morning which had been completely successful. Several of his men who passed through the Dressing Station where I was spoke most highly of his leadership. In the evening there was a good deal of shelling, and in one of the bursts a shell fell near to your nephew, killing him practically outright, he died before he could say anything. I buried him last Sunday afternoon in a British Cemetery well behind the line. The CO and all the other officers who were able to be there were present to show their respect for a brother officer.

We have lost few officers, since I have been with this battalion, who will leave such a gap behind them. Your nephew was so full of life and good spirits, that he was quite the best known and most popular among our officers. I knew him very well, and I always had a deep respect for his character, I feel that I have lost a real friend.

It is hardly for me to speak of him as an officer, but I know what a high opinion of him those who were competent to know had. I do not think he knew what fear was and he was the kind of man whom soldiers would follow anywhere.

It is hard to lose a friend such as he was, but one cannot believe that such a life is wasted. He must be still living in the service of our common Master. Death is still a mystery to us, but at least for us Christians it has lost its hardest sting. May God give you comfort and courage to bear the loss of your nephew bravely – as bravely as he lived and died.

I am afraid I am not allowed to tell you where he is buried.* You can however find this out, if after a while you write to the Director of Graves Registration and Enquiries, War Office, Winchester House, St James Sq., London S.W.1.

I have written already to Mr Monypenny in India. I am sorry I was not able to write to you earlier but I could not find out what your address was.

Yours in true sympathy,

G.A. Chase

C.F. Att 1st RW Kent Regt, BEF

3. A fellow officer (attached to the Battalion):

Miss Gybbon-Monypenny: France July 1918
At this hour of your great bereavement because of the loss of your nephew and my 1/Lieut P.H.G. Gybbon-Monypenny of 1/R.W.Kent Regt., I wish to express my sympathy.

I have been with the battalion only a short time, but we were, after only a few days, becoming the best of friends.

*Phil is buried in Thiennes British Cemetery, 9km south-west of Hazebrouck.

I can truthfully say that he was a very brave man, had the best of control of his men under the heaviest of shell fire, and further he was admired and liked by every officer and man in our battalion.

Greater love has no man than to give his life for his friends.

May his people be cherished and comforted is my wish.

Yours very sincerely,
   Chas. E. Fallet
   1/Lieut. M.O.R.C. USA

4. The same:

Dear Friend: *France July 1918*
Your letter of thanks received a few days ago.

I know nothing of particular interest regarding your nephew except that given before. It might be interesting to know that I personally prepared the body for burial and know him to be properly buried and that there was the greatest possible attendance under the circumstances.

I expect to be in London sometime in the near future on leave, and may look you up as requested in your letter.

Yours very sincerely,
   Chas. E. Fallet
   1/Lt M.O.R.C.
   US Army

Conclusion

When they met together, Robin and Phil plotted to escape the cheerless trenches by joining the Indian Army. As it happened, only Robin would fulfill the dream. Phil was dead before the ponderously slow red tape that governed the transfer was completed.

At the end of May 1918 Robin was posted to India, departing from Southampton for the Northern Punjab. In doing so he missed the worst effects of the 1918 flu pandemic that killed more than 50 million people worldwide after the war. Unusually for flu, it felled young, healthy adults rather than the elderly or the sick. Finally eradicated by 1920, its effects were exacerbated by troop movements and close-quarter living conditions.

Initially, life in India did not fulfill its promise. Confined to a desk job, Robin eventually requested a return to the Essex Regiment. Instead he was posted to the 64th Pioneers who were building a military railway in Mesopotamia, in the region of modern-day Iraq. When the railway was completed, he was ordered to march to Persia – Iran – where there were still a significant number of skirmishes, despite the Armistice.

In 1920 he enjoyed four months home leave, when he married Brenda and took a honeymoon on the Isle of Wight.

After returning to the Middle East he was kept occupied with the Arab Rebellion, sparked by a cavalier approach among French and British colonialists in the area. It also fell to him to rescue a group of 'White' or Royalist, Russian women fleeing 'Red' or Bolshevik, forces now in charge there.

When the British evacuated Persia he returned to England and remained in the Indian Army until 1922.

Afterwards, he moved to New Zealand, which was both under populated and under developed, sidestepping the worst effects of the Depression at home. He experienced a new set of adventures but emigrated back to Britain within a few years.

During the Second World War, as a father of three, he re-enlisted, serving on the Home Front. When the war ended he was 53.

It was during retirement that Robin set down his memories in exercise books, poring over the letters he had by then inherited from Aunt Ethel. He had hand-written his life story before his death in 1991, aged 99.

His fluent thoughts and eloquent phrases were later transcribed by his grandson, Tim, and other members of the family, eager that the experiences of one man – reflecting the aspects of the conflict known to many – were not lost.

Research for this book included the regimental diaries of both the 2nd Essex and the 1st Royal West Kents, *The Essex Regiment 2nd Battalion* by John Burrows and *Invicta*, the 1st Battalion Royal West Kents' history by Major C.V. Molony, who was mentioned by Phil in one of his letters.

There were also passages written by Robin that could not be pinned to a particular date as well as letters sent to Phil. The following is a selection that shed further light on the war as experienced by the Monypenny brothers.

* * *

Letter mentioned by Phil from a former 1st Battalion Royal West Kents' commander who has been credited with initiating the truce that marked the first Christmas in the trenches. By some accounts, he walked into no man's land singing then organized the football match which marked the occasion.

In a letter to his wife written on 27 December, he said:

'*Such a curious situation has arisen on our left. The Germans all today have been out of their trenches and had tea with our men halfway between the trenches. They only fired four shots a day. Our men were rather non-plussed (owing to the friendly relations between the two parties) and they couldn't very well take them prisoner. Two of their officers and seventy men even came into our trenches, refusing to return to their own trenches. They insist on staying.*'

From Lieutenant Colonel Henry Donald Buchanan-Dunlop enclosed in No. 95 (21 January 1918):

George Hotel, Grantham

Dear Monypenny 4 Jan 1918

Many thanks for your letter. I also always had a great respect for poor old Cobb.

To get to a more cheerful subject however, I am writing to congratulate you on getting a MC as I saw your name in today's paper. I am delighted that you have got one especially as it was not the first time that you had been recommended for it. Better late than never, however.

I am still at this place trying to camouflage myself as a tactical instructor. I don't care very much for school mastering I must say.

Would you be so good as to thank the following for sending me Xmas cards:
   S/M. Reynolds
   Scott
   ? Thorne

I was very glad to get them as it meant I had not been forgotten. I was also glad to know that the battalion had received the cards as I ordered them late in a hurry and was afraid they would not arrive in time for Xmas. It was for that reason I chose a very simple one.

I have been very busy this month as I have had 2 classes each over 90 strong going at the same time.

Col. Whitty is here going through a course before getting one of the new MG battalions. He may come to the 5th Division.

With love to all I know & best wishes for the New Year,
Yours sincerely,
 H.D. Buchanan-Dunlop

✳ ✳ ✳

'An interesting incident occurred on 8th Dec. Two French soldiers on leave from the Somme received permission to search for valuables which they had buried near our present support line in the Autumn of 1914. The ground had changed shape considerably in the interval from shell fire and the many trenches dug in this neighbourhood.

They were about to give up this search when, to their huge delight, but to the intense disappointment of some of our men, they found a box. The feelings of our men who were hoping to continue the search later on and who had been living, as it subsequently proved, almost on top of the box, can be imagined when the finders informed them that the box contained (according to them) money and jewellry to the value of 15,000 francs. The spot had been in constant occupation for over two years – German, French and British had occupied it and dug trenches in turns, so they were very lucky to recover their treasure.'

(*Invictus*)

✳ ✳ ✳

'Firm ground simply did not exist within three to four miles of the front line trenches. The whole area was reduced to a sea of more or less liquid mud as a result of artillery fire and the weather conditions. Movement was calculated at a rate of one mile per hour and even that rate was looked on as a maximum rate of progression (for it could not be termed marching).'

(*Invictus*)

✳ ✳ ✳

'The greatest difficulty was experienced in communicating with Brigade HQ. About 300 to 400 yds in rear of our Batt. HQ was a large pillbox housing a few brigade signallers. To this pillbox a very large number of messages were sent by lamp, each message being repeated three times. In spite of this of about fifteen messages sent only one or two were received by brigade HQ. Experience showed that the most rapid and reliable means of communication was by carrier pigeon of which we were given a good supply and which did extraordinarily good work.'

(RWK Diary)

*   *   *

(Words written by Robin, although it is not clear to which incident he refers.)

'About ten o'clock the German counter-attack came, and they came in masses. We could not help hitting something by aiming into the blue-grey. I had snatched up a wounded man's rifle and we were all hard into it, the rifles getting hotter and hotter in our hands, the machine guns keeping up a continuous sweeping chatter, men almost getting up on the parapet in their eagerness to pour in the fire. The Germans were mown down in lanes and it was amazing the way they kept coming on. It appeared as if their dense proximity to each other in close formation gave them courage, but what a waste of military strength. How many waves of men in extended order would they have formed and we would have been swamped. But as it was, the nearest to reach us were left hanging on our wire and there must have been a thousand dead in front of us, and thus the attack gradually faded away.

When the excitement had died down and I was pondering over the attack, I thought that surely they don't always attack like that? They would need an inexhaustible supply of men to wear us down that way. But I presumed they would try many kinds of attack. However, I thought, supposing the enemy had managed to burst through our wire and overrun our trench? We would be at a considerable disadvantage in trying to bayonet fight from down there as he arrived on top of us. I discussed this point with my NCOs and they agreed with me that in future we would get up on the parapet to meet them, just before they arrived there and meet them with cold steel.'

*   *   *

Order on 22 November 1917 by Major W.T. Monckton (RWK)

'Feet inspection every Saturday morning and on the day before the battalion goes into the line in accordance with the timetable below. The MO and the battalion chiropodist will attend.

The following points are to receive attention:
   a) boot must be dubbined and soft and fit loosely
   b) laces and spar laces must be in good condition
   c) socks, at the rate of three pairs per man, must be clean, dry and have no holes (and fit loosely).

2. Foot rubbing will take place daily. Men will work in pairs rubbing each other's feet. On no account will any man in the battalion miss this foot rubbing on any day.

3. On the day before going into the line feet will be washed and socks powdered under the direction of the MO. The batt chiropodist will be present.

In the line feet will be rubbed daily with whale oil which will be taken up in water bottles, carried under coy arrangements.

Socks will be changed daily. Clean socks, before being put on, will be powdered, 4 pepperpots of powder will be issued per coy for the tour.

Puttees and boots must not be worn rightly laced or rolled.

When sitting still every opportunity should be taken to raise feet above level of hip if ever so slightly.

* * *

Essex Regimental Diary:

1/3/1917 – Practised March past. War Office cinematograph operator had instructions to photograph the battalion.
2/3/1917 – Cinematograph operator failed to appear.
27/3/1917 – Owing to an outbreak of mumps, D Company put into quarantine.

* * *

An account by someone in the ranks of the day that Robin was injured for a second time:

'We moved off early on the Monday morning to our assembly place just out of the northern suburbs of Arras, passing en route through the artillery area. We seemed to be surrounded by guns when the barrage opened and we had been provided with cotton wool as protection for our ears.

Our humourists called out chaffingly to the gunners, *"don't do that, you'll wake Jerry up"*. The noise was simply deafening and, with the further handicap of the cotton wool, it was most difficult to carry on any sort of conversation. It was a little quieter in the assembly field.

Here we had a good meal and the encouragement of an almost continuous procession of prisoners passing to the rear. I was much struck at the time by the readiness with which our men threw cigarettes to them. They gave them plenty of chaff, too, and the replies were often made in fluent English.

It was after midday when we moved off on what I can only call a leisurely stroll forward ...

The enemy was so conspicuous by his absence that one of our wits surmised that *"being bank holiday, Jerry had gone home to take the missus and kids out".'*

*   *   *

2nd Essex Diary

The 62nd Regiment of French infantry (regulars) are in the trenches on our right. The commandant of this regiment came into our trenches today and one of the officers told him that the eagle we wear was captured from them at Salamanca [in 1812 during the Peninsular War]. He was much interested as they had never known by what regiment it had been taken. He at once pulled out his pocket knife and cut a button off the officer's coat and said that he would keep it as a souvenir.

Feb 27 – One of our aeroplanes drifted very low over the German lines and had great difficulty in getting back owing to a high wind. Our field guns put some shrapnel over the German trenches while they were firing at it, it is thought, with good effect.

*   *   *

An undated order to all platoon commanders from Robin, after he was made a captain:

'Please see that all your men's helmets are folded properly or else they will crack. They are not to carry them on them when they are working or sleeping, as they get broken. They are to be placed in their packs or somewhere handy while the respirators themselves must be carried on the person. Please investigate as to how many helmets are broken.'

To the Adjutant, when he was in charge of B Company:

'Re: Your message concerning the training of young officers sent out recently. On the whole the training seems satisfactory. But there is one point I may mention. The young officers don't seem to have been taught the necessity of strictly enforcing the minor details of discipline. As regards the recent drafts I think the same applies to them, in that they don't seem to realise the importance of strictly adhering to such details.'

* * *

When he was newly made captain there was an issue arising from missing machine-gun ammunition. In response, Robin wrote curtly to army investigators: 'I know nothing of this affair myself, not having taken over the company until after this affair had happened. Your message to me last night was my first knowledge of it.'

After interviewing men in his company about what happened he called it 'a big mix up'.

Index